Power to the Plants

get cookin'

Charl

PRAISE FOR
crazy *sexy* KITCHEN

"I can't think of a better team than Kris Carr and Chad Sarno. Kris is a wellness trailblazer. She has inspired countless people to take charge of their health and vastly improve their lives. Chad is a culinary master who has been an integral part of the healthy eating program at Whole Foods Market. His recipes are simple and totally delicious. I hope you enjoy this book and all its powerful wisdom as much as I do." — JOHN MACKEY, co-founder and CEO of Whole Foods Market

"*Crazy Sexy Kitchen* is a brilliant book. I think one of Kris's best sentiments is that your future is being written with every meal. For me that really sums up how what we choose to eat determines how we choose to live and age. Kris is helping us make those choices delicious." — LOUISE HAY, author of *Empowering Women* and *You Can Heal Your Life*

"Let me in the Crazy Sexy Kitchen right now! It is filled with yummy, healing, tummy-satisfying, taste-bursting joy disguised as recipes. If you want to delight your senses and heal your body with every bite, this book is your guide. Kris Carr has done it again with her crazy sexy recipe for fun, food, and fulfillment." — MARK HYMAN, M.D., author of the #1 *New York Times* bestseller *The Blood Sugar Solution*

"By now you'd have to be living under a rock to miss the message that eating mainly plants is good for all of us. What most don't realize is that this way of eating has come a *long* way in the last decade. Eating your vegetables has never been more delightful and delicious. This book will open your eyes and your palate to a whole new way of life." — CHRISTIANE NORTHRUP, M.D., ob/gyn physician and author of the *New York Times* bestsellers *Women's Bodies, Women's Wisdom* and *The Wisdom of Menopause*

"Kris and Chad make eating healthy a blast! Upon reading this book and trying out a few recipes, you realize that you actually *can* change your life for the better. You can rev up your body with loads of energy, inspire the healer within, and entertain with the coolest, tastiest food *ever!* Get ready for some miracles, because this food is going to lift you to higher ground!" — KATHY FRESTON, *New York Times* best-selling author of *The Lean: A Revolutionary (and Simple!) 30-Day Plan for Healthy, Lasting Weight Loss; Quantum Wellness;* and *Veganist*

"*Crazy Sexy Kitchen* is a must-have for anyone seeking a powerful health and wellness boost. It will revitalize and restore you from the inside out." — FRANK LIPMAN, M.D., founder and director of Eleven Eleven Wellness Center and author of *Revive: Stop Feeling Spent and Start Living Again*

crazy
sexy
KITCHEN

also by **KRIS CARR**

Crazy Sexy Cancer Tips

Crazy Sexy Cancer Survivor: More Rebellion and Fire for Your Healing Journey

Crazy Sexy Diet: Eat Your Veggies, Ignite Your Spark, and Live Like You Mean It!

crazy sexy KITCHEN

150 PLANT-EMPOWERED recipes to ignite a *mouthwatering* revolution

KRIS CARR

with CHEF CHAD SARNO

HAY HOUSE, INC.
Carlsbad, California • New York City
London • Sydney • Johannesburg
Vancouver • Hong Kong • New Delhi

Copyright © 2012 by Crazy Sexy Wellness, LLC

Published and distributed in the United States by: Hay House, Inc.: www.hayhouse.com® • Published and distributed in Australia by: Hay House Australia Pty. Ltd.: www.hayhouse.com.au • Published and distributed in the United Kingdom by: Hay House UK, Ltd.: www.hayhouse .co.uk • Published and distributed in the Republic of South Africa by: Hay House SA (Pty), Ltd.: www.hayhouse.co.za • Distributed in Canada by: Raincoast: www.raincoast .com • Published in India by: Hay House Publishers India: www.hayhouse.co.in

INDEXER: Jay Kreider/Index It Now

COVER/INTERIOR DESIGN: Karla Baker/karlabaker.com

COVER PHOTOGRAPHER: Bill Miles/billmiles.com

INTERIOR PHOTOS (UNLESS OTHERWISE NOTED WITHIN): Andrew Scrivani, with food and prop stylist Soo-Jeong Kang (farm and food photos) and Bill Miles/billmiles.com (Kris and Chad in the kitchen)

INTERIOR ILLUSTRATIONS: Karla Baker, shutterstock/©Allison, shutterstock/©notkoo, shutterstock/©Bojanovic, shutterstock/©GDM

Library of Congress Cataloging-in-Publication Data
Carr, Kris.
Crazy sexy kitchen : 150 plant-empowered recipes to ignite a mouthwatering revolution / Kris Carr with chef Chad Sarno.
     p. cm.
Includes index.
ISBN 978-1-4019-4104-8 (hardcover : alk. paper)
1. Vegetarianism. 2. Cooking (Vegetables) 3. Vegetables in human nutrition. 4. Vegetarian cooking. 5. Nutritionally induced diseases. I. Sarno, Chad. II. Title.
TX392.C2966 2012
641.5'636--dc23

2012022887

Hardcover ISBN: 978-1-4019-4104-8

Digital ISBN: 978-1-4019-4106-2

15 14 13 12   4 3 2 1

1st edition, October 2012

Printed in the United States of America

from KRIS

For my Grandma (Abuelita) Aura. Thank you for inspiring me to use food as medicine. You helped me turn my kitchen into a loving sanctuary and a powerful pharmacy. This gorgeous and delicious (your two favorite words) book is dedicated to you.

from CHAD

To my dear Nana, who passed on while I was writing this book. You were the original superwoman, the rock of the family, my inspiration, and my greatest teacher in the kitchen. Your recipes and love will forever be engraved on my heart.

TABLE *of* CONTENTS

WELCOME TO THE **WELLNESS REVOLUTION,**
a marvelous soireé!

You're invited to a marvelous soirée, a wellness revolution, to be exact. And the sooner you RSVP the better because wide-sweeping change is happening in every home, from Tallahassee to Timbuktu. More people than ever before are embracing the transformative power of a plant-based diet. And it isn't just hippies in hemp and patchouli or Prius-driving latte-guzzlers. From truckers to the First Lady, professional athletes to soccer moms, veg-centered consciousness is skyrocketing.

Some people flock to plant-empowered living for better health; others for spiritual beliefs, animal welfare, respect for the environment, or, best of all, because it tastes great. The simple, fresh flavors in plant-based meals create layers of taste, while the smells intoxicate and satisfy our senses. This food has style and rhythm, texture and glamour.

Plant-strong cuisine is taking the culinary world by storm, igniting the Internet, and permeating the media and pop culture. I am extremely proud to be a voice in an ever-growing movement that will change the course of our health-care system, and thus, our history.

Dang, that's a mighty opener for a recipe book. But scooch in and listen close . . . this isn't your average cookbook. It's a Veggie Manifesto for gourmands and novices alike, and it's filled with nonviolent rabble-rousing and brainiac learning, along with delicious meals. My goal is quite simple. I want to redefine today's kitchen and I want you to feel comfy and cozy in it. The kitchen has heart, soul, and powerful medicine. It's not only fun to get to know this sacred space, it's truly liberating. The goodness born in the kitchen will reach deep into the rest of your life—enriching your health, your home, and the planet.

I hope you're lip-smacking hungry because we plan on surprising your taste buds while transforming your health. They may sound like mutually exclusive ideas since so many of us equate healthy food with boredom, isolation, and deprivation. Not on my watch, mon chéri. Food is ooh la la passionate and utterly creative. Food nurtures our bodies and fuels our ever-dreaming brains. It brings us together. Throughout human history, we've engaged in emotional jamborees, spiritual raves, political debates, cosmic musings, romances, beginnings, endings, and everything in between—all over a good plate of hearty food.

A TASTE OF WHAT'S TO COME

From juicing to planning a happening dinner party, *Crazy Sexy Kitchen* gives you the chops to make your kitchen sing with health, happiness, family, friends, and good times. You'll discover cooking tips; kitchen skills; time and money savers; tools of the trade; produce charts; the tenets of the Crazy Sexy Diet philosophy; and of course, more than 150 nutrient-dense, heavenly recipes.

Like a long luxurious meal, *Crazy Sexy Kitchen* is laid out in courses. The first course gives you an overview of the Crazy Sexy Diet. I'll fill your noggin with sexy science, the answers to many frequently asked questions, and a host of other fabulous factual goodies. The second and third courses are your personal mini–cooking school, designed to help you prepare our recipes with ease and confidence. You'll learn how to shop, stock, and cook! The fourth course is where the muse and the magic lives—the recipes. And last but not least, we've included sample menus, a helpful reading list (for your self-designed syllabus) and lots of resources.

Because raw foods play a powerful role in the Crazy Sexy Diet philosophy, you'll find lovely raw recipes sprinkled throughout the book. For those with food sensitivities or dietary restrictions, our handy symbols give you a heads-up on which recipes are gluten- or soy-free. But don't despair! We also provide some creative food substitution tips that'll help you tweak recipes if needed. Rest assured that your personal palate calls the shots in the Crazy Sexy Kitchen. If a recipe tastes too sweet or salty, alter it. When I cook at home I rarely measure. *Crazy Sexy Kitchen*'s very own Chef Chad Sarno (you'll meet this hot honcho in a dash!) doesn't bother with measuring cups and spoons either. Recipes are more like guidelines than rules. Get grabby. Toss and pinch. And keep in mind that your tastes will change as your palate develops and gets clean. But also, be brave. Try new ingredients and make them your own based on our guidance.

Not sure how to put a meal together? We've got that covered too. Behold, menus to fit every occasion! So tie on that cheeky, cheery apron and unleash your inner plant-based porn star. You know you want to.

my INSPIRATION

Flavorful homemade food holds a dear place in my heart.

Back in the early '70s, my grandma was a chef and my mother was a bartender. Together they ran my grandma's restaurant business and raised me. Grandma's food was loaded with love, buckets of butter, and flames. You read that correctly, flames. She regularly poured 100-proof brandy over her creations and lit them on fire. The result: a dramatic presentation and the occasional curtain casualty. One could say she was Julia Child meets *Where the Wild Things Are*.

Grandma opened her first diner in a renovated trolley car, complete with flower boxes and geraniums. She sewed all the tablecloths and built the counter and booths. Yes, she was a seamstress and carpenter, too. Grandma would often say that her "brains were in her hands." To me, she was a resourceful visionary. Truckers and townspeople alike adored her. While stirring a deep pot in her kitchen you might catch a story about King George's coronation, which she attended, thank you very much. Or you might've been lucky enough to hear her gripping account of escaping from Bogotá, Colombia, on a U.S. military cargo plane to marry her second of possibly three or four husbands (we're not sure).

Next came the Village Gourmet, her French-inspired bistro. That's where my memory kicks in. On Saturday nights, music poured from the piano by the bar where I would sing and dance. Upon completing my

performance I'd skitter around to the patrons with a glimmering eye and open hand. (Please note: I was not allowed to solicit. In fact, I got swatted when caught with the quarters, but I went for it anyway. The moxie started early—five to be exact.) I adored the place. I loved watching the colorful cast of customers laugh and talk and fight and love and most of all . . . eat!

The Village Gourmet was my first classroom. I learned early that food is more than just fuel—it's community. And today, as I work with people to improve their lifestyles, I'm sensitive to the important role food plays in social life and family heritage. But as we're finding out more and more, these traditions often come at a cost. I will always admire the love and art my grandma put into her cooking. At the same time, I can't forget that, despite a long and full life, she suffered chronic health problems that really put a crimp in her effervescent style. Like many Americans, she was overweight, and she developed a list of preventable ailments including high blood pressure, cholesterol, osteoporosis, diverticulitis, and arthritis.

I was headed toward a list of health challenges as well. After I struck out on my own and life got busy, I cut my time in the kitchen short. I lived on processed, fake, and fast food. My fridge was empty while my nuker (a.k.a. microwave) got more play than my boyfriends. After a while, I began to feel as lousy as the garbage I was

putting in my body. The stress (both physical and emotional) didn't help either, and I was mainlining it.

On Valentine's Day 2003, I hit a tipping point in the form of a cancer diagnosis, a rare and incurable stage IV sarcoma to be exact. I was 31 years old, with no medical options and a supposed expiration date— at least that's what one oncologist told me. Another suggested I remove and transplant all three affected organs. Bye-bye liver and both lungs? Silly rabbit, tricks are for kids! No, thank you. Luckily my disease is slow-growing (at least for now; that could change). However, to say that I was in shock, mad, sad, and terrified is an understatement. But I pulled up my high-heeled bootstraps and made a plan posthaste.

I knew in my gut that I needed to fully participate in my well-being. That's when I went back to my roots—food. I discovered I loved being an artist in the kitchen, just like Grandma. Except I added a revolutionary twist to her culinary foundation: cooking consciously and compassionately for the health and happiness of my body and the world around me.

Since that time I've not only been surviving, I've been thriving—*with* cancer. In fact, thanks in part to a healthy and active lifestyle, I actually feel better with the disease than I did without it. If I can feel healthy and happy while living with a life-threatening condition, just imagine how great you can feel! It's been nearly ten years since I first heard those words, "you have cancer." And though I may never be in remission, my disease continues to be stable. Considering what so many fellow cancer patients face, I am incredibly blessed. As one of my cherished cancer buddies used to say, "You don't need to win, a tie works, too!"

When my documentary film about my journey, *Crazy Sexy Cancer,* aired on TLC and then on the Oprah Winfrey Network, the e-mails poured in by the thousands. My story struck a chord beyond cancer. People were ready for big change, whether they were struggling with depression, diabetes, heart disease, or fill-in-the-blank. This was the beginning of my Crazy Sexy movement, and I continue to be wildly motivated and grateful to share what I had to learn the hard way.

crazy = FORWARD THINKING
sexy = EMPOWERED
KITCHEN = PHARMACY

My previous book, *Crazy Sexy Diet*, is the "why" of healthy eating. It digs deep into the philosophy and science of my diet and lifestyle, with a sample recipe chapter near the end. *Crazy Sexy Kitchen* is the perfect sequel. What you're holding in your hands is the "how." These recipes will teach you how to turn your newfound knowledge, commitment, and desires into a beautiful (and healthy) reality on your plate, meal after meal.

In the following section, I'll walk you through the main principles of my diet and lifestyle. Think of it as Crazy Sexy 101. But for a full-on education, covering the ins and outs of eating and living this way, I strongly encourage you to add *Crazy Sexy Diet* to your reading list. Remember, information is power and freedom. The more you understand why you're eating healthy, the better able you'll be to become your own mentor and advocate. It also helps to know what you're talking about when trying to explain and justify your choices to folks who have never been exposed to these ideas or to skeptical loved ones.

Such skepticism should not intimidate you; it should inspire. You have a delicious opportunity to teach and share. Once you begin using the tools in this book, you'll be a glowing example that tradition, fun, freedom, and flavor don't have to be traded in exchange for conscious eating and better health. And besides, some traditions deserve to rest in peace. Sadly, all too often the food we've been laughing and loving over makes us sick. A teacher of mine said it best: "Do heart disease, diabetes, and cancer run in your family? Or is it kielbasa, fried chicken, and Philly cheesesteaks?"

Want to know the sexiest word in the galaxy? Epigenetics. Ooh, tiger! Epigenetics teaches us that our genes are not our destiny. That's right; our genes aren't fixed as previously thought. They're fluid, flexible, and highly influenced by both our inner and outer environment. And get this, just because you may have a genetic predisposition for a chronic disease doesn't mean that the gene will express itself. The truth is we have more control over our health than we think. Over the years of studying a plant-based diet, I've seen that the choices we make truly matter in a concrete—often life or death—way.

Thankfully, many chronic diseases are preventable (and even reversible) with a nutrient-dense, varied, plant-based diet and healthy lifestyle practices. Now that's something to chew on. Sure there are some medical life lemons that get passed down and some that are unavoidable. But more often than we're led to believe, our genes are modified by our food and lifestyle choices, environment, stress, and nutrition. These nongenetic factors can literally switch health issues on and off. Once altered, your genes either support health or open the door to disease. There's a high probability that you have some say in the matter.

There's a bigger picture, too, beyond us as individuals. It's no surprise that the food system today is as broken as our health-care system, since in many ways they're two sides of the same coin. Big agribusiness wins, the small farmer loses, while the environment gets polluted and destroyed, and the average citizen is caught in the crossfire. It doesn't have to be this way. Grab your spatula 'cause we're going to shake shit up and get this wellness party started!

Although I'm a cook and a foodie, that's not the same as being a chef. So when I decided to put my money where my loud mouth was by creating a cookbook, I knew I'd need help—especially with the fancier fare. I wanted to wow you with a treasure trove of recipes for every occasion and for every skill level. Enter my partner in the revolution, Chef Chad Sarno.

I first met Chad through our mutual friend at The Humane Society, the smashing Chris Kerr. Chad and I clicked from the get-go. We both have a wicked (and raunchy) sense of humor and the deep desire to create monumental disturbances in the world (the good kind). Though I'd heard about his culinary genius, I hadn't tasted his food. The day I did was the day this book took shape in my mind. He was my guy. And let me tell you, you're going to be really happy that our worlds collided. Chad is a conscious creator, a teacher, and a plant-based leader. In fact, I consider myself to be one of his students. You can't imagine how thrilled I am to learn along with you! As a consultant and restaurateur, Chad has been spreading his unique approach to healthy, veg-inspired cuisine to restaurants, resorts, film sets, and healing centers globally for many years. Chad is currently a superstar at Whole Foods Market where he's a lead culinary educator for their healthy eating program. Whole Foods Market has a very special place in my heart. It was there that my health journey began. After diagnosis, I left the oncologist's office and went straight to Whole Foods. I've never looked back. A decade later, I am so tickled to see the journey come full circle with Chef Chad.

HITTING THE RESET BUTTON: Chef Chad's Personal Journey

I've always been fascinated by food. As a child, I adored being my mom's sous-chef, manning my station on a stool pulled up to the stove. Like Kris, I was influenced by a long line of strong women. My mom and my Italian grandma, Nana, loved to create elaborate meals highlighting the freshest ingredients. When I recall my fondest memories of Nana, I remember family gatherings filled with delicious, rustic, real food. These meals shaped the foodie I am today. Just like most kids though, despite the fresh food put on the table at home, I had a dirty romance with processed dairy and sugar.

During my childhood, I was asthmatic. I was the kid who had severe asthma attacks at school and on the sports field. Slightly traumatizing? Ah, yeah, definitely. Little did I know that my diet was the culprit. After years of paralyzing attacks and pockets full of inhalers, I finally connected the dots between health and diet. In my late teens, I started hearing about the tie between asthma and dairy products. How could an entire food group, whose supposed goodness had been drilled into us in health classes and school cafeterias, be the root of my childhood challenges? Determined to kick asthma out of my life, I broke off the romance and eliminated dairy products from my diet. Within six months, my asthma disappeared. This was my wake-up call, my aha! moment, the reset button that made me hungry for more answers and led me to a diet that revolved around plant foods.

As a young adult, I started exploring the world, traveling far and wide to work, study, and seek the guidance of leaders in plant-based medicine and culinary arts. My vagabond tour of duty took me zigzagging across the country and to different parts of the globe. From the mystical redwood forests of California to the rural villages of the Philippines, I experienced life and culture through food. As a result of my extensive travel, life-schooling, cooking, and now teaching, I have learned that you don't need to sacrifice outstanding taste for health.

By eating animal-free, whole foods, I've experienced a level of vitality, energy, and health that continues to humble me today. I've seen firsthand the remarkable results that my friends, family, and clients have experienced with this diet. As you will discover throughout this book, our forks are our greatest tool for activism, and there's no better way to take a stand than to learn how to triumph in the kitchen.

It's truly an honor to be working with my dear friend Kris. When we met years ago, we knew that the time would come to share our obsession and passion for food and health. Plants have been the greatest teacher and medicine for Kris and me in such different yet parallel ways. Our shared goal with *Crazy Sexy Kitchen* is to showcase plants in a delicious, sexy, and health-promoting light. It is with great joy that we humbly share these recipes from our kitchens to yours. Join us in celebrating whole, nourishing food while changing the world one bite at a time!

MEET OUR crazy sexy GUEST CHEFS

In addition to our Crazy Sexy Chef Chad, you'll also meet some of our wonderful chef friends. These folks are the innovators. And quite simply, their food gives me orgasmic goose bumps. Pssst . . . many of them have their own restaurants that you sooo must visit. Perhaps you'll see me and Chad there.

Elizabeth Simonson

chef **PAM BROWN** has been a passionate vegan for more than 40 years. Pam began her culinary education in the 1970s, focusing on macrobiotic cooking. Through her travels in Europe, America, and South America, she expanded her talents as a vegan chef. Today, she owns and runs The Garden Cafe in Woodstock, NY, where everyone is welcome to learn, dine, and enjoy plant-based cuisine. www.woodstockgardencafe.com

chef **PETER A. CERVONI** is a professional chef, restaurant consultant, and educator. Currently, Peter is Executive Chef at Organic Avenue, one of NYC's favorite spots for juice and raw foods. Over the years, Peter's recipes have appeared in *Pilates Style* magazine, *Vegetarian Times*, and Frances Moore Lappé and Anna Lappé's *Hope's Edge*.

James Kriegsmann Photographer

Michael Spain-Smith

Erica Michelson

chef **FRAN COSTIGAN** is a professional chef, consultant, and author, internationally renowned as the "Queen of Vegan Desserts." Fran's second cookbook, *More Great Good Dairy-Free Desserts Naturally*, will satisfy vegans and omnivores alike. In Fall 2013, *Chocolate Vegan Desserts for Everyone* will hit the shelves. She teaches in New York City (classes include her unique Vegan Baking Boot Camp Intensive®), and at conferences throughout North America and Europe. www.francostigan.com

chef **RICHARD LANDAU** has been at the forefront of vegetarian dining since he opened Horizons Café in Philadelphia in 1994. His mission has been to translate the carnivore palate in vegetarian cuisine, making it more accessible to a broader audience. In 2009, he was invited to serve the very first vegan dinner at the prestigious James Beard House in Manhattan. In 2012, Richard and his wife, Kate Jacoby, opened Vedge, a "vegetable restaurant" in Center City Philadelphia. www.vedgerestaurant.com

chef **SARMA MELNGAILIS** is the proprietor and co-founder of NYC's premier raw and vegan restaurant, Pure Food and Wine. She is also the founder and CEO of One Lucky Duck Holdings, LLC, which operates the One Lucky Duck brand. Sarma is the co-author of *Raw Food/Real World* (HarperCollins, 2005) and the author of *Living Raw Food* (HarperCollins, 2009). www.oneluckyduck.com and www.purefoodandwine.com

Eric Marseglia

nutritionist **JOY PIERSON** is a nutritional consultant, co-author of _The Candle Café Cookbook_, and co-owner of Candle Café, Candle 79, and Candle's catering and wholesale business. _chef_ **ANGEL RAMOS** is the executive chef at Candle 79. He has been with the Candle group since 1995 and is one of the country's foremost vegan chefs. _chef_ **JORGE PINEDA** is the pastry chef and restaurant manager who helped open Candle 79. www.candle79.com

Jan Ison, The Creative Network Studios

chef **TAL RONNEN** became known nationwide as the chef who prepared vegan meals for Oprah Winfrey's 21-day vegan cleanse in 2008. He is also known for catering Ellen DeGeneres and Portia de Rossi's vegan wedding, Arianna Huffington's party at the Democratic National Convention, and the first vegan dinner at the U.S. Senate. Currently, Tal is the consulting chef of LYFE Kitchen in Palo Alto, CA, and collaborating chef at The Wynn and Encore hotels in Las Vegas. His cookbook, _The Conscious Cook_, was published in 2009. www.talronnen.com

chef **DEREK SARNO'S** experience encompasses many years as a chef, restaurateur, food designer, and educator about plant-based cuisines. Derek currently serves as the Global Healthy Eating Chef and Educator for Whole Foods Market, supporting the company's healthy-eating revolution and inspiring both team members and customers with healthier cooking options. www.wickedhealthyfood.com

Ha Lam

RSVP

Before we begin, I have one rule for you: don't be intimidated. *Crazy Sexy Kitchen* is for the novice and expert chef alike. All you'll need to succeed is a sense of adventure, fresh ingredients, and your five senses.

Cook your way through this book in any order that grabs you. Learn from your successes and your failures. Happy accidents can lead to brilliant inventions. Invite friends over. This food tastes best when shared. Create a cooking posse, a culinary salon where your guests can learn and grow and taste with you.

I wish Grandma were here to witness the birth of this book. If only I could teach her what I know now. She would love this food. It would definitely pass the tough grandma test. I imagine us cooking together in festive aprons, sharing tips and playfully gossiping about so-and-so. My mom would set the table with her creative flair, and the three of us would sit and connect over our healthy masterpiece.

Let this book inspire and motivate you to RSVP to the biggest event of your life. The new Crazy Sexy healthy you starts in the kitchen, and the wellness revolution awaits. Allow me to be your hostess and Chad to be your guide in making your kitchen the true healthy heart of your radiant home.

You have the chance to experience the amazing benefits of clean eating just as we have. It's time to be adventurous, so stock your fridge, sharpen those knives, and roll up your sleeves as we explore the delicious and abundant world of plants. *Bon appétit!*

the FIRST COURSE

CRAZY SEXY DIET & LIFESTYLE PHILOSOPHY

THE 411

Okay, revolutionaries, pull up a stool while the sauce is simmering and let's pass the time with a little health lesson. To do so, I'd like to review some of the core principles from our fabulous textbook, *Crazy Sexy Diet*. Got a notebook and your favorite pen? Go get them. I'll wait.

Crazy Sexy Diet (CSD) is a nutrient-dense, plant-happy approach to eating and living that harmonizes your beautiful body at the cellular level. Tasty beans, whole grains, nuts, seeds, leafy greens, veggies, fruits, fresh juices and smoothies, plus other culinary delights (that you make yourself) are your new BFFs. As you learned in the introduction, this way of living is beyond a diet. It's a celebratory lifestyle that's healthy, awake, and engaged. Now that's SEXY!

CSD is based on a few guidelines that will help you create a stellar self-care game plan.

These guidelines aren't rigid; rather, they're meant to give you a basic structure that will allow you to flourish. But if/when you fall off the wagon or take a scenic side road into a vat of cookie dough, enjoy it! Then get back on track and blaze on.

To help you understand how to shape your plan, I'll break the dietary guidelines into two categories—what creates health and what robs it. And the determining factor of whether a particular food is friend or foe is inflammation. Inflammation drastically reduces the quality and quantity of your life. It saps your energy, weakens your immunity, darkens your mood, and steals your beauty (gasp!). Long story short, foods and lifestyle practices that ignite an inflammatory response just plain suck.

A great tool to help you attain your anti-inflammatory lifestyle goal is the pH scale or acid/alkaline balance. I'll touch on this in a jiffy. For now, just roll with me. Highly acidic foods drain your energy bank account while alkaline foods boost it. When you understand why eating this way works at a cellular level, your enthusiasm and commitment will have you busting into spontaneous cartwheels.

BURN, BABY, BURN:
INFLAMMATION NATION

Inflammation is the root cause of many, if not all, chronic diseases. Cancer, heart disease, arthritis, allergies, asthma, Alzheimer's, digestive disorders, autoimmune diseases, even obesity and diabetes each have major inflammatory components.

We've all felt the swelling and burning associated with a twisted ankle or scraped knee. Ouch! How about the hard-to-swallow pain that accompanies a sore throat? Moan. That's inflammation at play, doing its job by defending us from invaders and injury. Immune system cells swoop in to either attack the culprit causing the commotion and/or fix the situation. It's all good in the 'hood as long as this response is kept in check.

But there's a silent (yet violent) kind of inflammation that can take place without you even knowing it. What you eat, drink, and think (stress!), environmental toxins, smokin', boozin', and even a couch-potato lifestyle can create a fiery cascade of inflammation in your body. When your body hits an inflammatory overload, your defense system gets so overwhelmed and confused that it literally doesn't know the difference between the invader and you. As a result, your well-meaning immune system turns on itself, destroying healthy cells, tissue, and everything else in its wake. It's like when Al Pacino played Tony Montana in *Scarface*. He mows down everything in sight, yelling, "Say hello to my little friend!" In a word: shit.

As part of your anti-inflammatory wellness

plan, I encourage you to reduce or eliminate all icky foods that irritate your body. Like what? Well, most of the vittles commonly found in the acidic Standard American Diet (SAD)—meat and dairy; refined carbohydrates; wheat; processed foods made with high-fructose corn syrup, artificial sweeteners, and trans fats; and let's not forget the chemicals, drugs, and anything you can't sound out phonetically—even if it's vegan. Processed is processed. Nothing compares to Mother Nature's bountiful garden. Therefore, the more complete and intact your foods, the better they are for you.

By decreasing the amount of acidic inflammatory foods while increasing the amount of healthy and alkaline plant foods, you flood your body with vitamins, minerals, cancer-fighting phytochemicals, antioxidants, fiber, and so on. This allows your body to recover from the barrage of bull crap, oxidative stress (created by free radicals), and poisons that pillage your inner terrain. Once your body repairs, it can renew. Pinpointing and addressing the source is beyond revolutionary. That's big healer medicine. You might as well get a business card that reads: Self-care Shaman. Did you have any idea that that sort of power was in you? I did.

Here's a deeper look at a few of inflammation's enablers . . .

MILK AND DAIRY MUMBO JUMBO

Whoa, Kris, don't take my cheese and burgers away! Believe me, I get it. I was a meat and dairy lover myself. In fact, I grew up across the street from a small family-run dairy farm. But when I got sick and wise, I realized that some foods have the power to heal, while others have the power to harm.

Here's the real deal: excess meat and dairy are the poster children for inflammation and health complications. It's no wonder that as the consumption of animal products increases, so do the rates of chronic disease. What was once a better-quality product, eaten on occasion and in small portions, is now the cheap and super-sized centerpiece of every meal. But contrary to popular belief, animal products aren't like lip gloss—you don't need them in order to survive. And you certainly shouldn't eat much of the stuff if you want to thrive (especially if it comes from a factory farm). "But where will I get my protein, calcium, iron, etc.?" Have no fear. My pal Jen Reilly (a.k.a. the Bitchin' Dietician) will answer all your questions in the FAQ at the end of this section. For now, stick with me as we touch on the bigger issues.

Whether or not a particular food is healthy for us doesn't solely stem from its nutritional value. It's also about how your dinner got to your plate. When evaluating the health consequences of eating mass-produced animal

products we must also consider the way the critters were raised and treated. Compassion aside, this is about your well-being. How an animal is cared for from birth to slaughter truly, madly, deeply affects your body.

On factory farms, where 99 percent of our meat and dairy products originate, thousands of animals are often kept in tight holding facilities and squalor, fed unnatural diets (including the excrement and body fluids of other animals) that create serious health complications, and are dosed with antibiotics and growth hormones. These concentrated animal feeding operations (or CAFOs) are a very dangerous way to live. Injury is quite common, as is disease. Unhealthy animals create unhealthy food. These practices threaten our food supply. Would you knowingly drink from a polluted well? We must remember that we humans are at the tippy top of the food chain. This means that we eat everything that the critter below us ate and below them ate and so on.

In addition to animal-welfare concerns, problems with food safety are abundant. Today the meat and dairy industries are run by a handful of corporations that have gobbled up small farms and dominate the market. It's a big business that moves very fast and comes with big risks. Food-borne illnesses arise from the bacteria found in spilled fecal matter that make their way onto our plate. In the case of contaminated veggies, it's not the produce that's devious; it's the poop on the produce that creates the problem. This can happen as a result of contaminated water systems. Ever hear of pink slime, a.k.a. "lean finely textured beef"?

Yet another reason to steer clear of factory-farm products. It's an ingredient in ground beef that's made from leftover meat trimmings sprayed with ammonia to kill pathogens like E. coli and salmonella. These trimmings used to be made into pet food, now they're abundant at your grocery store, in fast food, and even school lunches. While proponents of pink slime firmly believe that the substance doesn't contain safety issues, many consumers don't know that the yucky stuff even exists! Why? Because pink slime isn't labeled. What else is in our food?

What if you want to include meat and dairy in your diet? That's your choice and I totally honor it (and you!). My advice: keep it to a minimum (two or three times per week), as a garnish or side dish, and make the best selections. According to the American Dietetic Association, a portion of meat shouldn't be larger than a deck of cards. Also, do your best to say "no way" to factory-farm products. Instead, look for the Certified Humane Seal (certifiedhumane.org), which is the gold standard in farming. As for seafood, Food and Water Watch (foodandwaterwatch.org) is a terrific resource to learn what seafood products are safest and, therefore, healthiest. Unfortunately, farm-raised fish often experience similar confinement and health issues. As for wild fish, our oceans aren't what they used to be and as a result, high levels of mercury (especially in deep-sea fish) and other heavy metals are abundant.

It will take some extra effort to understand and locate healthier, more humane animal products. But you and your family are worth it. And keep in mind that cutting back or eliminating animal products is super easy to do when you know how to be a Crazy Sexy cook! More love. Less suffering. Everyone wins.

THE BOGUS BAKERY

Dinner rolls, bagels, pasta. Yum. But did you know that there could be a hidden enemy lurking in your floury noshes? Gluten is the protein found in wheat and all its siblings (spelt, kamut, rye, barley). It's the staple of the American diet. But those with gluten sensitivities or wheat allergies deal with lots of uncomfortable symptoms, stuff like bloating, gas, cramps, the scoots (a.k.a. diarrhea), fatigue, achy joints, depression, skin rashes, etc. Folks who are really sensitive experience those symptoms multiplied by a gazillion. They have celiac disease, an autoimmune disorder that causes systemic inflammation; severe damage to the small intestine; and nutrition deficiencies that result in conditions like anemia, malnourishment, osteopenia, osteoporosis, and other chronic diseases.

While not everyone has gluten sensitivities or full-blown celiac, these issues are more prevalent than you might think. Agricultural changes in how we grow our wheat are some of the likely culprits. If you've been feeling like crud for a while and this list of unwanted health issues sounds all too familiar, experiment with a gluten-free diet. Go without gluten for a few weeks and see how you feel. No one knows your magnificent body better than you. Keeping a food journal will help you track your progress. There are blood tests you can take, but unfortunately, they're not always accurate. Therefore, the only way to really know is to abstain. I've received oodles of e-mails from folks who've told me that since following the Crazy Sexy Diet and eliminating gluten, they feel utterly fantastic. Dumping gluten was the missing link. You'll find many gluten-free recipes in *Crazy Sexy Kitchen*, and any recipe that isn't gluten-free can easily be modified.

GIMME SOME SUGAR

Sugar, a.k.a. the legal drug, is another common inflammatory disco that can make us fat, sick, and unhappy (yup, it messes with your brain). You've read the articles and you know how you feel when you dope up on too much of the stuff. Isn't it one of life's cruel ironies that something so addictive is also the thing we're hardwired to crave? And so, unless you're on a strict healing plan or cutting it for Lent or bikini season, you'll probably include some sweet treats in your diet. Indulgence isn't frowned upon or forbidden. We just want to embrace la dolce vita with common sense and moderation. With that in mind, we thought it was important to include dessert recipes in this book. Some are more wholesome than others, but all were designed with your health in mind. We typically use better sugar alternatives and in lower amounts. And when compared to the standard American fructose-fest, these are leaps and bounds better for you.

To monitor my sugar intake, I use the Glycemic Index (GI), a helpful tool that shows how much a carbohydrate affects blood-sugar levels. This is represented by a numerical value, from 1 to 100. The bigger the number, the quicker and higher the carb raises the blood-sugar level. Because they are nearly pure carbs, the simple sugars, like white, brown, maple syrup, and honey, spike your blood sugar the most. The

higher the spike, the more insulin is pumped out by your pancreas. This creates sugar rushes, crashes, and cravings. Over the long term, this insulin roller coaster leads directly to obesity, diabetes, even cancer. On the other hand, complex carbs, like most veggies, whole grains, and beans, are lower on the GI scale. One of the

main reasons they score lower is because they also contain other nutrients and fiber. Fiber slows down and evens out the digestion of sugars—thus keeping you from ripping off your clothes and running naked through the mall. Any food that has a GI rank below 60 is a good choice, especially if you need to watch your blood sugar. The GI list is for whole foods only. So when you're buying packaged and processed foods, you'll have to read the labels and look up the individual ingredients on the list. I'm sure you can guess that the more processed, the naughtier the GI number.

Just for kicks, start checking out the GI value of your favorite foods. You'll find numerous charts online. Where do your meals, snacks, drinks, and treats fall on the scale? Are they below 60 most of the time? Add more low-GI foods to your diet on a daily basis (which is easy with your new arsenal of CSK recipes) so that your occasional higher-GI choices truly are a special treat!

THE pHABULOUS LIFE

Everything from healthy cells to cancer cells to soil quality and ocean life is affected by pH. Understanding the acid/alkaline balance (pH) will help you increase your energy, immunity, and longevity. The term pH stands for "potential hydrogen" which is the measure of hydrogen ions in a particular solution. The pH scale measures how acidic or alkaline a substance is and ranges from 0 to 14. Seven is neutral. Below 7 is increasingly acidic, above 7 grows more and more alkaline. As with most health-related barometers, balance is everything.

Your body is designed to operate within a narrow pH range. For optimal cellular health and happiness, your blood pH must be slightly alkaline (a pH between 7.365 and 7.4). Your body will do anything to maintain proper balance. When there's even the slightest chance that you could become overly acidic (due to food and lifestyle choices, environment, etc.) your remarkable body will mine minerals like calcium, magnesium, and potassium from your bones, teeth, and organs to neutralize the acids. It's sorta like having a supply of inner Tums. This is fine every now and then. But pillaging your reserves over the long term can lead to osteoporosis and other health challenges. You can probably guess where the Standard American Diet falls on the pH scale. It's an acid bath! Excess acidity also sets the stage for bad bacteria

(like yeast and fungus) and even viruses that wreak havoc on our health. Tilting the pH scale in the alkaline direction is easy with a diet filled with mineral-rich plant foods.

Pretty much all veggies, some fruits, wheatgrass, dark leafies, sprouts, green juices, green smoothies, and certain unprocessed grains, beans, and nuts help to make your blood and tissues more alkaline. On the other hand, meats, dairy, eggs, sugary goods, highly processed foods, coffee, and alcohol make your blood and tissues more acidic. Load up on the alkaline foods the majority of the time, and your body will thank you! Plus, eating these treasures floods our bodies with chlorophyll, enzymes, vitamins, minerals, antioxidants, and oxygen.

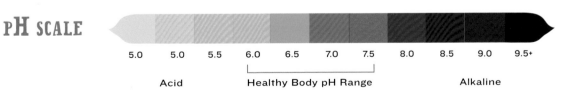

pH SCALE

| 5.0 | 5.0 | 5.5 | 6.0 | 6.5 | 7.0 | 7.5 | 8.0 | 8.5 | 9.0 | 9.5+ |

Acid   Healthy Body pH Range   Alkaline

In addition to choosing whole foods, I love encouraging people to up their intake of raw foods. Many raw dishes are wonderful alkaline boosters.

That doesn't mean you need to eat them exclusively. It just means that we could benefit from including more of them in our daily diet. Why? There are several reasons. Raw foods contain more water-soluble vitamins and enzymes (the spark of all life). Plus, studies show that a diet rich in raw foods promotes a faster resting metabolism. Cooking foods definitely has some advantages, including adding variety to your plant-heavy diet and increasing the availability of some antioxidants. A combo of mostly raw and some cooked foods is ideal over the long term.

DRINK YOUR PRODUCE, CHANGE YOUR LIFE

Green juice = the instant medicine (that takes little energy to digest).
Green smoothie = fiber-licious broom (that cleans out your system).

I can't say enough about alkaline liquid love, especially when you keep the fruit content to a minimum. In fact, drinking your produce will literally change your life. Green juices and smoothies are the most important part of my personal daily practice. If you do nothing else consistently, do this: blend or juice your produce. You'll find many zippy recipes in the fourth course of *Crazy Sexy Kitchen*. What's the difference between the two? Great question, smarty slacks! Juicing separates the pulp from the juice of your veggies, sprouts, and fruits, using a (you guessed it!) juicer. Since your body doesn't have to digest the fiber, it can easily absorb vitamins, minerals, etc., directly into the bloodstream—instant alkalinity and oxygen for your cells. Juicing also gives your body an energetic break, allowing it to focus on repair and renewal.

Smoothies are made in a blender, which means that the fiber stays in your drink (score for your colon!). In addition to fruits and vegetables, you can add protein powders, nut milks, healthy fats (which keep your energy humming), a variety of superfoods, and other ingredients to your smoothies. Each method

has unique benefits, but their biggest strength is shared—filling your body with a large amount of fresh, raw produce. To learn everything you'd ever want to know about juicing and blending, visit Crazysexyjuice.com. Cheers!

REAPING THE REWARDS

As you can probably tell by now, an anti-inflammatory plant-based diet and lifestyle has the power to rejuvenate your body like no other. No need to fast or abstain. Eat, drink, and be merry!

Just let nature be your guide. Your blood, bones, tissues, and organs will thank you. Your eyes will shine and so will your sexy thighs. Say farewell to that drippy nose and itchy skin. Zits? Later, tater. Need more energy? Done, hon. Better sleep? Check.

How about problems with the pooper? Shhh . . . Okay, I know that conversation makes you blush. But we gotta talk turds, toots! Consti-pation creates stagnation and lots of health issues. If you're not "going" once or twice per day, then something's up down there. Get this: your gut is ground zero for your immune system. When bad bacteria take over they diminish your pow-pow-power. Keep the good guys (healthy flora) strong with ample fiber and purified water (to keep ya moving), green juices, and smoothies. Probiotics are a great idea, too.

crazy sexy BENEFITS

Glowing skin

Sparkling eyes

Strong, shiny hair & nails

A kickin' immune system

Regular poops

Happy organs

Clear sinuses

Fighting weight

Sassy sex drive

Restful sleep

Sweet breath

Strong bones

Healthy joints

Lower cholesterol (sans pills)

Lower blood pressure (sans pills)

Balanced blood sugar

Consistent energy

Fewer blues

DO I HAVE TO GO
ALL THE WAY?

Nope. Any step toward a plant-passionate diet is a positive one.

However, the further you go, the better you'll feel and the healthier you'll become. Some people are like turtles. They do best taking it slooow. Others prefer to bungee-jump off the cliff and go "cold Tofurkey." Either way, this veg-tastic approach is full of flexibility and freedom. And Chef Chad + moi (along with our awesome chef posse) are here to help make your transition simple and delicious.

PREVENTION ROCKS!

This book is more than just a collection of recipes. What you hold in your hands is your passport to prevention. I know what you're thinking: *I'm sorry; you've mistaken me for somebody else. I'm young(ish), I'm vibrant. Prevention is for old, creaky people. It's sooo un-chic!* Well, I'm here to tell ya, we can run from our past, but not from our future.

It's being written with every meal. Yes, some physical decline is inevitable as we age. But, like a Mob interrogator says, we can make this easy or we can make this hard. Prevention means the difference between a lot of problems or a little, and facing them sooner versus much later. And it means the difference between an attitude of misery and victimization or of grace and empowerment. Now prevention is starting to sound pretty en vogue, no? You might even say it's the new black.

Speaking of fashion forward, 2,000 years ago the toga-bedazzled Greek philosopher Hippocrates penned the famous Hippocratic Oath. Doctors through the millennia have taken this vow to "do no harm." Good so far. And today's version also includes a sentence that just takes my breath away: "I will prevent disease whenever I can, for prevention is preferable to cure." Whoa! And to understand how to make this happen, we look back to another timeless quote from the ever-hip H-crats: "let food be thy medicine and medicine be thy food." Now that's a thought-provoking connection!

As a cancer patient, I believe with every juicy fiber of my being that prevention is the only lasting cure for what ails us. But while some doctors are beginning to get the memo, the U.S. medical system in general is still heading in the wrong direction. Absurdly, insurance companies would rather treat the symptom with a temporary Band-Aid than fix the actual cause. As a result, expensive medications and invasive surgeries have become the go-to norm. The rising costs associated with this kind of industrial medicine are unsustainable. So it's no mystery why the medical system is in deep crisis. According to a 2006 study by Indiana and Purdue universities, a whopping 87.5 percent of our health-care claims costs are chewed up by people's lifestyle choices. To truly reap the rewards of vibrant, long-term health, we must have a holistic game plan that honors the complex needs of our minds, our bodies, and our effervescent spirits. Change your plate. Change your fate. Empowerment explosion!

crazy *sexy* PLANET

Last, but definitely not least, good ol' Mother Earth will be so grateful when you start eating better. When you take care of you, you take care of her. Health, ecology, spirituality, activism, and love—it's all interconnected. Illness woke me up to this profound concept and allowed me to better understand the issues that threaten us today. What's happening in our bodies is a microcosm of what's happening to the world around us.

We have oceans and streams flowing within us. We are mountains and valleys of delicate terrain thriving with creatures, each with a role and purpose. And like the planet, our ecosystem relies on a clean environment, proper nourishment, and balance. Chemicals poison our rivers and veins; pollution chokes our air and lungs; overacidity plunders minerals from our gardens and our tissues. Destroying our forests devastates our carbon sinks. And just imagine the vast and beautiful array of plants and animals we'll never get to meet if we obtusely ravage their habitats (in order to grow endless food for cattle), rendering them and their wisdom extinct. Are you picking up what I'm laying down? Our global challenges can be solved if we become active dot connectors that take responsibility for our choices.

There are many online organizations that will help you understand the issues. The Environmental Working Group, Humane Society, Farm Sanctuary, Sustainable Table, Sierra Club, and Physician's Committee for Responsible Medicine (PCRM) are just a few. You can start a revolution right at your kitchen table. Invite me over, I'm happy to lick envelopes and get the word out.

BITCHIN' FAQ

||||||||||||||||||||||||||||||||||||||||||||||||||||||||||||||||||

Jennifer K. Reilly, R.D.,
BitchinDietitian.com

Pete Duvall

OUR ANCESTORS ATE ANIMAL PRODUCTS AND THEY THRIVED, SO WHY SHOULD I SKIP MEAT AND DAIRY?

Current research points us toward avoiding (or at the very least, greatly reducing) animal products for optimal health. Why? For starters, the saturated fats in animal products increase heart-disease risk. Animal products also contain carcinogens and are devoid of cancer-fighting antioxidants, phytochemicals, and fiber.

Our lives are far different from when our ancestors chilled in caves and on the farm. Activity levels are much less vigorous and the environment is far more polluted. The way meat is produced has also greatly evolved. Most of our meat today is factory-farmed; plugged with loads of chemicals, hormones, and other toxins; and much higher in fat than it used to be. Plus, we tend to eat much larger portions, so it's no surprise that obesity and environmental illnesses are at an all-time high.

I THOUGHT I NEEDED MEAT TO THRIVE.

Even though meat is a rich source of protein, it is also loaded with artery-clogging saturated fat and dietary cholesterol. In addition, meat is devoid of healthy fiber, antioxidants, and phytochemicals; makes your blood more acidic (which hinders your immune system and compromises bone health); and taxes the digestion system, wreaking havoc on the health of your intestines and kidneys.

Heterocyclic amines (HCAs), which are DNA-damaging carcinogenic compounds, are produced as meat is cooked. The longer and hotter the meat is cooked, the more of these compounds form. In some studies, grilled chicken formed higher concentrations of HCAs than other types of cooked meat.[1] All types of meat, however, can contain some level of these carcinogens. Consumption of well-done meat (which is often necessary for food safety) has been associated with increased risk of breast cancer and colon cancer. No, thank you. Pass the lentil tacos please!

WHERE WILL I GET MY PROTEIN? HOW MUCH PROTEIN DO I NEED? HOW DO I CALCULATE IT?

Can you believe that elephants, horses, and many other powerful animals rely solely on plant foods for protein and complete nutrition? If they can do it, so can we! Protein is abundant in plant foods—the best sources being beans,

||||||||||||||||||||||||||||||||||||||||||||||||||||||||||||||||||||||||||||||||||||||||||||||
[1] Sinha et al. "High concentrations of the carcinogen 2-amino-1-methyl-6-phenylimidazo- [4,5-b]pyridine (PhIP) occur in chicken but are dependent on the cooking method." *Cancer Research* 55 no. 20 (Oct. 15, 1995):4516–19.

lentils, nuts, seeds, quinoa, vegetables, and whole grains. Humans actually need a lot less protein than most people think. A moderately active person can easily figure out their daily protein needs in grams by multiplying 0.36 by their body weight in pounds. For example, a 160-pound person needs about 58 grams of protein each day (160 x 0.36 = 57.6 grams). For strenuous activity, muscle building, or extra stress, 0.45 to 0.54 should be used as the protein multiplication factors since protein needs are higher during these times.

A day of plant protein may look something like this:

Breakfast: 1 cup cooked quinoa with 1 tablespoon raw nuts = 13 grams protein

Snack: Apple with 2 tablespoons raw almond butter = 8 grams protein

Lunch: Large green salad with ½ cup black beans and ¼ cup raw sunflower seeds = 15 grams protein

Snack: Raw veggies dipped in ½ cup hummus = 12 grams protein

Dinner: Broccoli stir-fry with 4 ounces tempeh served over ½ cup brown rice = 28 grams protein

TOTAL: 76 grams protein

WHAT'S A COMPLETE PROTEIN?

First of all, keep in mind that eating a variety of plant foods will give you all the protein you need—you don't need to carry a microscope, calculator, or book of food stats with you to every meal. A complete protein contains all eight essential amino acids (nine for children) in the correct proportions. These particular amino acids are considered essential because our bodies do not produce them; therefore we have to

eat them! Amino acids help our bodies create and repair tissue, and break down food in our digestive system. Animal foods, soy foods, and quinoa have complete protein. Other plant proteins are considered incomplete because they are missing one or more amino acids.

It's still quite easy to consume all the amino acids you need for complete protein with a plant-based diet if you consume a variety of plant foods. As long as legumes, grains, greens, veggies (yes, there's protein in plants!), nuts, and seeds are a regular part of your daily diet, complete protein is easily made in your body. Don't worry; you don't have to eat them all at once. For example, lentils are low in the essential amino acid tryptophan. However, grains, nuts, and seeds are high in tryptophan. So if lentils and rice or almonds are consumed throughout the day (or even over the course of a few days), a complete protein will be made.

WHAT ABOUT DAIRY? I THOUGHT IT WAS GOOD FOR ME.

Dairy products are rich sources of calcium and vitamin D (which is fortified into dairy foods). However, it's easy and much healthier to get all the calcium you need from the plant kingdom, and your vitamin D from sunshine and fortified plant foods that don't pose the potential health risks associated with dairy products.

Recent research has suggested that dairy foods may be linked to an increase in prostate cancer, testicular cancer, and even ovarian and breast cancers. The consumption of dairy products (even organic and low-fat) increases blood levels of insulin-like growth factor I (IGF-I), which is a potent stimulus for prostate and breast cancer cell growth. In addition, the large calcium load in dairy products down-regulates the body's synthesis of vitamin D, which is protective for prostate and breast cells. Also, lactose (milk sugar) breaks down into galactose, which has been studied as a culprit in ovarian cancer risk.

Dairy products are also highly inflammatory and increase mucus production in the body, which exacerbates many chronic issues including acne, arthritis, asthma, Crohn's disease, constipation, ear infections in children, eczema, and joint pain, among others. Wondering what to put on your cereal in the morning? Read on!

CAN I GET ENOUGH CALCIUM FROM PLANTS? HOW MUCH CALCIUM DO I NEED? WHAT ABOUT VITAMIN D?

Nature's best calcium sources are dark leafy greens such as kale, collards, mustard greens, and turnip greens. The calcium in these foods is absorbed at double the rate of dairy calcium. About 30 percent of dairy calcium is absorbed whereas about 60 percent of calcium from dark leafy greens is absorbed (not including spinach and a few other greens which contain calcium but have oxalates which block calcium absorption). Other rich plant sources of calcium

include beans, almonds, figs, and fortified non-dairy milks such as unsweetened almond milk, soy milk, oat milk, hemp milk, and rice milk.

When it comes to bone health, calcium isn't the only factor. Overall diet and activity levels determine bone health and even calcium needs. Countries with the highest calcium intake have the most osteoporosis, so there's obviously more to the bone-health story than calcium alone. Vitamin D—which is necessary for calcium absorption and is best obtained from 20 minutes of sunshine 3 times a week during summer months and fortified, nondairy foods or supplements during winter months—is now being considered the most important nutrient in bone health. In addition, exercise and fruit and veggie intake are crucial for keeping calcium in your bones. On the other hand, a diet high in animal protein, sodium, and caffeine—which make your blood more acidic—cause calcium to be pulled from your bones and excreted in your urine as your body reacts to neutralize the acid in your blood.

The U.S. government–recommended intake of calcium (where animal protein and sodium intake are high) ranges from 800 to 1,300 milligrams a day depending on age. The World Health Organization recommends 400 to 500 milligrams a day. Calcium needs are lower for a person who consumes little or no animal protein, gets plenty of vitamin D from the sun, consumes fortified foods or supplements, eats lots of fruits and veggies, and gets regular exercise, than they are for a sedentary person eating the Standard American Diet. Did you know that 1 cup of boiled collard greens contains 358

milligrams of highly absorbable calcium, and 10 medium dried figs contain 269 milligrams of calcium? Bottom line, a diet rich in plant foods easily meets calcium needs.

HOW COME I CAN'T SEEM TO GIVE UP CHEESE?

Have you noticed that people generally have an easier time giving up potato chips and dessert than cheese? Well, there's a reason! In 1981, researchers found trace amounts of morphine—a highly addictive opiate—in cow's milk and human milk, which is perhaps the reason why breastfed babies get so sleepy after nursing and are so well bonded with their moms[2]. No wonder people have such a hard time giving up cheese. Except, while cheese and other dairy may bring on warm and fuzzy feelings, it's still loaded with unhealthy saturated fat, cholesterol, growth hormones, and perhaps other toxins (especially from factory-farm animals), which will make your insides very unhappy.

[2] Hazum E, et al. "Morphine in cow and human milk: Could dietary morphine constitute a ligand for specific morphine (μ) receptors?" *Science* 213 (1981):1010–12.

Since very few cheese lovers are able to limit themselves to one serving (the size of your thumb), it's best to substitute healthy and tasty plant-based foods when you'd usually reach for the cheese. Try snacking on hummus, veggies, and crackers instead of diving into a plate of cheddar. Sprinkle nutritional yeast on pasta dishes, salads, soups, and stews for a cheesy alternative. Like any addiction, after about three weeks cheese-free, you won't even miss it.

WILL I GET ENOUGH IRON FROM A PLANT-BASED DIET?

Absolutely! Iron is abundant in dark leafy greens, beans, lentils, tempeh, and fortified grains. Plus, vitamin C, which is found in citrus fruits, bell peppers, and dark leafy greens, increases iron absorption. Eating all those healthy foods will guarantee sufficient iron without overdoing it. Consuming too much iron actually increases heart-disease risk.

WHAT'S THE STORY ON SOY PRODUCTS? WHAT IF I HAVE AN ESTROGEN-SENSITIVE DISEASE? WHAT ABOUT SOY ALLERGIES?

Soy products, including soy milk, tofu, tempeh, and edamame, are rich in soy protein, essential omega-3 fatty acids, and phytoestrogens. Soy protein and omega-3s are important for heart health, while phytoestrogens help reduce breast-cancer risk among premenopausal women. Less processed soy foods such as edamame, miso, and tempeh are richer in nutrients and antioxidants, more digestible, and often taste better than the more processed soy foods. Many

meatlike products such as veggie burgers and veggie dogs are made from soy and are highly processed. Although these products often contain food additives, and may not provide as many health benefits of the lesser-processed soy foods, they are still great transition foods when moving from a meat-heavy diet to a plant-based diet. Just make sure that any soy product you buy is not genetically modified. It's always best to keep things natural.

For estrogen-sensitive diseases, such as estrogen-receptor-positive breast cancer, the jury is still out on how much soy is safe. Some oncologists suspect the phytoestrogens (literally meaning "plant estrogens") in soy may encourage cancer-cell growth, and recommend that women who have had estrogen-receptor-positive breast cancer play it safe by avoiding soy completely. However, it's important to keep in mind that in Asian countries where soy products are part of the traditional diet (including during puberty and breast tissue development, which may be a key factor for soy's protective role), not only are cancer rates lower than in the U.S., but the rates of cancer recurrence are lower despite soy consumption. There is also better overall breast cancer prognosis among women who consume the most soy in Asian countries.[3]

You may also want to consider that many of the same doctors who tell patients to avoid soy never mention the abundant amounts of estrogen and other growth hormones found in dairy products. If you're avoiding soy as a result of a cancer diagnosis, please strongly consider dumping the dairy as well. And if an allergy exists or soy needs to be avoided for other reasons, keep in mind that soy is not an essential part of a plant-based diet and can be eliminated without compromising health. There are many soy-free meat-substitute foods that are widely available (and delicious!).

WHY ARE OMEGA FATTY ACIDS IMPORTANT?

Essential fatty acids (EFAs) include omega-3 fatty acids (linolenic acid) and omega-6 fatty acids (linoleic acid). They're necessary in the functioning of the nervous, immune, reproductive, and cardiovascular systems. They also play a key role in cell-membrane formation and function, allowing nutrients and oxygen to be absorbed into cells and waste excreted. In addition, these essential fats need to be consumed in the proper balance in order for optimal overall health. An ideal ratio of omega-3s to omega-6s is 1:3.

Many individuals are low on omega-3s as they are not as easily obtained in the diet as omega-6s, which can make it difficult to get the right balance of omega-3s to omega-6s. While it's possible to get enough omega-3s in your plant-based diet, especially if your overall (and omega-6) fat intake is low, it's not a bad idea to supplement daily with about 1,000 milligrams of omega-3s (from algae) to be absolutely sure you're getting enough.

[3] "Soy food intake and breast cancer survival," *The Journal of the American Medical Association* 302, no. 22 (December 9, 2009): 2437-43; "Soy isoflavones and risk of cancer recurrence in a cohort of breast cancer survivors: the Life After Cancer Epidemiology Study," *Breast Cancer Research Treatment* 118 no. 2 (November 2009): 395–405; "A vegetable-fruit soy dietary pattern protects against breast cancer among postmenopausal Singapore Chinese women," *American Journal of Clinical Nutrition* 91 (2010): 1013–19; "Adolescent and Adult soy food intake and breast cancer risk: results from the Shanghai Women's Health Study," *American Journal of Clinical Nutrition* 89 no. 6 (2009): 1920–26.

WHAT SUPPLEMENTS DO YOU RECOMMEND WHEN ADOPTING A PLANT-BASED DIET?

You don't necessarily need to supplement a plant-based diet full of fruits, veggies (especially calcium-rich dark leafy greens), whole grains, legumes, nuts, seeds, and some foods fortified with vitamins B12 and D (such as fortified nondairy milks). In fact, a plant-based diet is often much higher in nutrients than a meat-heavy one. However, I still recommend taking a common multivitamin that guarantees adequate vitamin D (600 IUs for children and adults[4]) and vitamin B12 intake (2.4 mcg for adults[5]), and 1,000 milligrams of algae-derived omega-3 fatty acids. There's no harm in a little extra, and it's good to be absolutely certain you're getting enough.

[4] http://ods.od.nih.gov/factsheets/VitaminD-HealthProfessional/
[5] http://ods.od.nih.gov/factsheets/vitaminb12/

IF A PLANT-BASED DIET IS SUPERIOR THEN WHY DOESN'T IT INCLUDE ENOUGH B12?

Vitamin B12 is made by bacteria and needed in tiny amounts in the diet. However, a deficiency can cause irreversible nerve damage. Traditionally, there was plenty of vitamin B12 in the bacteria in soil and, presumably, on farm-fresh produce. However, modern hygiene and washing produce has eliminated this source, and it's probably not wise to add dirt back into the diet just to meet your B12 needs. This is why vitamin B12 needs to be supplemented in a plant-based plan. It is plentiful in many commercial cereals, fortified nondairy milks, veggie burgers, and certain brands of nutritional yeast. Vitamin B12 is also present in any common multivitamin. Check the labels for the words "cyanocobalamin" or "vitamin B12."

IS A PLANT-BASED DIET SAFE FOR PREGNANT WOMEN AND CHILDREN?

All the nutrients a growing baby and child need can be found in a well-rounded plant-based diet. As with any diet, pregnant and nursing women should supplement with a prenatal vitamin that also includes the omega-3 essential fatty acid DHA (from algae). Protein needs are slightly higher for pregnant women in the third trimester of pregnancy (about 70 to 80 grams of protein per day), but these can easily be met with a variety of plant foods. Nursing women have higher calcium needs than pregnant or other women, but they can increase their calcium intake with dark leafy greens such as kale and collards as well as fortified nondairy milks.

Babies who are not breastfed need to be given a plant-based infant formula that includes DHA for brain development.

CAN ATHLETES THRIVE ON A PLANT-BASED DIET?

Ever heard of Olympian (nine gold medals!) Carl Lewis, who also happens to be a vegan? More and more triathletes and marathoners are turning to a plant-based regimen for improved athletic performance and overall health. Plant foods are easier to digest, and therefore don't slow athletes down the way highly processed and animal-based foods do.

Athletes performing routine, strenuous exercise have higher protein needs than non-athletes, but those protein needs can be met with plant foods (see previous protein questions). Approximately 20 grams of protein should be consumed within 30 minutes of completing a workout to support muscle growth and prevent muscle soreness. Four ounces of tempeh or a green smoothie with unsweetened soy milk and hemp protein powder are just a couple easy ways to get 20 grams of healthy plant protein following a workout. In addition, calorie needs are higher among athletes. Nuts, seeds, avocados, dried fruit, and tempeh are rich sources of healthy calories.

HOW DO I TRANSITION FROM THE STANDARD AMERICAN DIET TO A PLANT-BASED DIET?

Start by figuring out which plant-based meals you already enjoy and eat them more often: curried lentil stew, vegetable salads, pasta with marinara sauce, and burritos filled with beans, veggies, and rice are perfect examples. Next, take your favorite Standard American Diet meals and have fun "veganizing" them. Replace dairy products with nondairy alternatives. Substitute meat with beans, lentils, and meatless alternatives. Try tofu instead of eggs, and flaxseed meal in baked goods. And finally, try new plant-based recipes (like the ones in this awesome book!) at a pace you can handle, which might be one new recipe per week or per day. You may not love everything you try, but keep at it. You'll notice increased energy, better digestion, clearer skin, and countless other health benefits as you embrace your new plant-based ways!

the SECOND COURSE

PREPARATION

crazy Sexy
STAPLES

Last-minute shopping will likely end in huffing, puffing, exasperation, and takeout! Take heart instead. Starting today, you can begin transforming your pantry and fridge into bountiful pharmacies, filled with wholesome products that will feed your cells with everlasting love.

Keep them well stocked for maximum culinary ass-kicking and rest assured that you don't have to buy everything at once. Some of these items can be pricey. But many staples will last a long time. After your initial investment, your weekly grocery bills will definitely decrease. Upgrade with a spice here and an oil there when possible, and know in your bones that your investment will have long-term health benefits.

note The following list doesn't include every item in our recipes. Rather, it's an overall guide for common, everyday items used in the Crazy Sexy Kitchen. Some of these ingredients may be new to you. Try them! Comfort zones are made for pushing. And don't fret; most of our ingredients can be found in your local supermarket, health-food store, ethnic market, or online (where the deals live!). If for some reason you can't find an ingredient, you can always substitute (be an artist with your spices!) or just skip it depending on the recipe.

FRUITS & VEGGIES: This gorgeous list is endless! You know the basics (broccoli, carrots, kale, apples, berries, pears, etc.), but as part of your wing-spreading we challenge you to get friendly with mysterious produce like bok choy, tatsoi, and watercress. Local rocks. It's often more affordable, so why not support the little guy? Plus, your produce is more likely going to be in season when you buy local, which means it'll be at the peak of sweetness. Organic rules. No need for icky pesticides, chemicals, or genetically modified nonsense. But if buying organic isn't always doable (due to cost and availability), our fabulous friends at the Environmental Working Group (EWG) have your back. They created a terrific chart that will educate you on the produce grown with the most and least amount of chemicals. Chemicals (a.k.a. poisons) love to hang around in your body and wreak havoc on your tissues and cells. They're definitely not welcome at the Crazy Sexy party! Go to page 54 or ewg.org for more information and to download a pocket-sized version for your wallet.

BEANS (DRIED OR CANNED): We buy our beans in bulk and store them in mason jars. But it's always good to have a few cans around for those times when you haven't soaked your beans and are in a rush. When buying canned beans look for products without preservatives, such as calcium disodium EDTA. Also, try to use low-sodium varieties and make sure to rinse them well (no need to pickle yourself!). Commonly used beans include black, navy, white, lentil, lima, pinto, and chickpeas.

GRAINS: Buying in bulk whenever possible will save you tons of do-re-mi. Store your grain in mason jars and remember to wash thoroughly before cooking. Commonly used grains include quinoa, brown rice, millet, and oats. See page 70 for the 411 on prepping methods, cooking times, and flavors. For pasta, we always choose whole grain, sprouted grain, or gluten-free varieties (Tinkyada is the best gluten-free brown-rice pasta line). For Asian-inspired dishes, nothing beats buckwheat soba noodles. Like it raw? We do, too. Raw noodles made from yummy veggies = heaven.

SEEDS, NUTS & NUT BUTTERS: These lil' suckers are packed with protein and energy. You'll find them in many raw meals, as a garnish for salads, as a creamy base for sauces, or a richy-richness for desserts. Commonly used seeds, nuts, and nut butters include hemp seeds, sesame seeds, flaxseeds, sunflower

seeds, pine nuts, raw almonds, raw cashews, walnuts, raw almond butter, raw peanut butter, and tahini.

TOFU: Tofu is a blank slate, ready to take on the flavors of any spice, sauce, or condiment it meets. This soybean wonder comes in a wide array of textures, from soft to extra-firm. Tofu is created by coagulating soybean milk and pressing the curds into a block. Regular tofu is packed in water and stored in the refrigerated section. Silken tofu is packaged in a box and doesn't need to be refrigerated. It crumbles more easily than regular tofu and is used most often in sauces and dressings because of its creamy texture (although you can use it for any tofu recipe if needed).

TEMPEH: Tempeh is less processed than tofu, which makes it a smarter choice on a regular basis. While tofu has practically no flavor on its own and is very soft, tempeh has a nutty taste and a firm texture. Tempeh is produced by cooking and fermenting whole soybeans and then pressing them into a dense patty. You'll find it in the refrigerated section. Brands such as Lightlife offer many different varieties, including garden vegetable, flax, three grain, and smoky strips (great for Tempeh-Lettuce-Tomato sandwiches!).

SEITAN: Seitan's meatlike texture makes it a no-duh for those who are transitioning to a plant-powered diet and want to re-create dishes that traditionally include animal products (seitan brisket, anyone?). It's primarily

made of wheat gluten. You can prepare it from scratch with flour and water (lots of kneading and cooking), but it's speedier to use a mix like Arrowhead Mills's Seitan Quick Mix or buy it ready-made in the refrigerated section.

NONDAIRY MILKS: Dairy = yuck and snot. These alternatives = ah-mazing and healthy! Condensed canned coconut milk is perfect for thickening soups or for making sauces and decadent desserts. Almond milk, hemp milk, soy milk, coconut milk, and rice milk (found in cartons) are all wise choices for smoothies, cereal/granola, or as a substitution for dairy

milk while baking and cooking. If a recipe calls for soy milk and you prefer rice or nut milk, etc., feel free to swap it out or make your own. (See page 93.)

CHEESE: Cheese is often the hardest animal product to give up. But these days there are many healthy alternatives. You'll notice several recipes that call for meltable cheese. Our favorite brand is Daiya. It's soy-, gluten-, and nut-free and comes in several varieties, including cheddar and mozzarella. For a spreadable cheese try our Cashew Cream Cheese (page 237) or check out Dr. Cow's Tree Nut Cheese— their products are out of this world (and the price tag reflects it). Perfect for a fancy cheese platter alternative. Don't forget the olives! How about grated Parmesan? We've got some awesome recipe solutions for the sprinkly stuff, but for a terrific store-bought brand try Parma by Eat in the Raw.

OILS, BUTTER & MAYONNAISE: A little goes a long way, but a good organic oil (especially the ones that are high in omega-3s), is great for your joints and cells, reducing inflammation, and so on. Just remember to tame the flame and don't burn your oils. Free radicals and carcinogens spoil the wellness party! Commonly used oils include: organic cold-pressed olive oil, coconut oil (a.k.a. coconut butter), toasted sesame oil, flax oil, and hemp oil. Though we don't include many high-heat dishes in CSK, when using high-heat cooking oils we prefer organic grapeseed or coconut oil. For neutral-tasting oil that can take high heat, canola can

be used in small amounts. But make sure it's organic, non-GMO, and expeller pressed. We generally use olive oil as our go-to neutral oil. Flax oil and hemp oil should never be heated. Those delicate babies are far too sensitive. You'll notice we include a few specialty oils; if you can't find them you can always substitute with olive oil, but trust us, these food-lubes are like rock 'n' roll royalty. Specialty oils include truffle oil (OMG!) and pumpkin-seed oil. For butter, we love Earth Balance. This creamy alternative comes in several tasty varieties, including a soy-free option, and can be found in the refrigerated section of your health-food store and many conventional grocery stores. For mayonnaise, we love Vegenaise by Follow Your Heart.

EGG REPLACERS: Eggs are typically used in baking as a binding agent. There are a variety of vegan options available, which vary depending on the dish. If you're modifying your own recipes, experiment with bananas, egg replacer (Ener-G is one brand), or ground flaxseeds (for each egg, substitute 1 tablespoon flax and 3 tablespoons water). In savory dishes that mimic an egg texture, such as a breakfast scramble or an eggless salad, tofu is a go-to substitute.

SEAWEED: Minerals, minerals, minerals. We worship minerals! Seaweed is rich in potassium, magnesium, calcium, iron, and iodine. It contains vitamins A and C and even vitamin B12. The fiber in seaweed helps to regulate blood sugar, and if you need to reduce or improve your salt consumption, seaweed flakes

THE **DIRTY** DOZEN

Foods grown with the most pesticides—ranked from really bad to just plain sucky. As much as possible, try buying the organic version.

1. Peaches
2. Apples
3. Bell peppers
4. Celery
5. Nectarines
6. Strawberries
7. Cherries
8. Kale
9. Lettuce
10. Grapes (Imported)
11. Carrots
12. Pears

THE **CLEAN** FIFTEEN

Foods grown with the least amount of pesticides, ranked from best to not-so-good (you could do better).

1. Onions
2. Avocados
3. Sweet corn
4. Pineapple
5. Mangos
6. Asparagus
7. Sweet peas
8. Kiwi
9. Cabbage
10. Eggplant
11. Papayas
12. Watermelon
13. Broccoli
14. Tomatoes
15. Sweet potatoes

Go to Foodnews.org to learn more about the Dirty Dozen and the Clean Fifteen and download your free pocket-size copy of the least- and most-sprayed fruits and veggies.

are a healthy upgrade. Commonly used sea veggies include: nori, dulse, arame, and hijiki.

HERBS & SPICES: Fresh is always best. However, like an eclectic sticker or stamp collection, a dried spice stockpile will become your pride and joy. Go organic as much as possible. Commonly used herbs and spices include: sea salt, black pepper, red pepper flakes, basil, cilantro, mint, dill, rosemary, thyme, tarragon, oregano, coriander, cumin, fennel seeds, ginger, curry, turmeric, onion powder, chili powder, cayenne, vanilla beans, and so on. If you can't find a particular spice in your local store, go online, use a substitute, or just skip it. Did you know that herbs and spices are also available in bulk? Yup, more savings. Dried spices last for about six months or so; after that they get a little musty. Definitely toss the really old stuff. It's kaput. To get the most from your spices, buy them whole and grind them yourself (use a spice grinder or a clean coffee grinder reserved for spices only).

CONDIMENTS: These stunning seasonings will liven up your kitchen big time! Commonly used condiments include: tamari soy sauce (available in gluten-free varieties), Dijon mustard, capers, miso (fermented bean or grain paste), organic tomato paste, veggie broth (broths and bouillons are also available in low-salt varieties), Worcestershire sauce (choose the vegan variety sans anchovies), nutritional yeast (nutty, cheesy, savory flavor and a great source of B12), organic ketchup, hot sauce (meow!), and sauerkraut (great for your digestion).

SWEETS: For added sweetness, commonly used sweeteners include: yacón syrup (low GI), stevia (low GI), Lakanto (low GI), agave, brown rice syrup, maple syrup, and dates. Depending on your health concerns, feel free to experiment by substituting high-GI sweeteners with low-GI options. Just keep in mind that you may need to play around. Not all consistencies are equal, especially when baking. Ooh, and don't forget the raw cacao for a chocolatey delight! Dried fruits and dried coconut are welcome sweet toppings on oatmeal, granola, soy or almond yogurt, and anything else you want to turn into a smart treat. They're also a great snack on-the-go when mixed with nuts and seeds.

WINES & VINEGARS: Cooking wines add swank and savoir faire to any dish. But listen up lushes: don't drink the cooking wine. It's for the food, plus cooking wines usually contain added salt. Commonly used cooking wines include white, red, and sherry. Commonly used vinegars include brown rice vinegar, white wine vinegar, sherry vinegar, apple cider vinegar, and balsamic vinegar.

FLOURS: Baking, sauces, pancakes, oh my! The range and flavor is vast, especially when the flour grain isn't processed (which strips nutrients, taste, and color). To keep your whole-grain or gluten-free flours from going stale or rancid, store them in a ziplock bag in the freezer. Commonly used flours include spelt, chickpea, whole wheat, all-purpose, and almond.

RIPENESS
ROCKS

Ripe produce contains peak nutrition, sweetness, and flavor. Unfortunately, the majority of our fruits and veggies are plucked before they're ready. Early harvesting is common in mass production and transit—yet another reason to try to shop local.

Steer away from limp or slimy greens, super mushy avocados (the meat should be green, not bruised), and brown/spotted bananas (leave those to the banana-bread bakers). There are many handy charts online that break down the physical characteristics you should be looking for when choosing fruit. Make a date with Google!

OH, ONE LAST *tip* Plan to go to the store or farmers' market twice per week. You'll want your produce to be as fresh as possible. Two trips make that dream a reality. Make a list, check it twice, and get in and out as fast as possible. You'll save time and money!

THE
TOOLS

Here's a list of our most coveted culinary helpers. Some are must-haves. Others are optional. And don't forget the additional doodads.

COOKWARE: Say sayonara to regular Teflon, aluminum, and other nonstick cookware. Their lining can break off at high temperatures, adding carcinogenic chemicals to your otherwise healthy meal. Although there are nontoxic, nonstick options out there such as Greenpan, which is made of 95 percent silica, the best  choice is cast iron if you take the time to give it a little TLC and season it properly. Stainless steel, copper, or any heavy-bottom pans are all great picks as well.

FOOD PROCESSORS: Food processors have a million different uses, plus you'll save tons of time in the chopping, mincing, shredding, and mixing department. They're also perfect for making thick creams and sauces, nondairy cheeses, ice creams, nut/seed butters, relishes and condiments, chunky sauces, nut- or seed-based pâtés . . . the list goes on. Here's a cute tip: For a fast and eye-pleasing salad, chop up a bunch of veggies du jour in your food processor. Place them on a bed of greens and dress. Smart! Favorite brand: Cuisinart.

BLENDER: A powerful blender will change your life. It's one of the most important tools in the kitchen. We use our beloved Vitamix daily. While it's on the pricey side, it'll last forever. Use it to make healthy smoothies, sauces, desserts, dressings, batters, and dips. Go to kriscarr.com/resources for more information.

JUICER: Picking a juicer is like picking a mate! With so many on the market it can be hard to commit. In the Crazy Sexy Kitchen there are two types of juicers that will be useful—centrifugal force and twin gear. Centrifugal-force juicers are easier to clean and use, take up less counter space, and are perfect for making your daily health elixir. Twin gears make juice that will stay fresh longer, but they take more time to clean and cost more. However, they're more versatile, since they also make wheat-grass juices, nut butters, ice cream, and veggie pâtés. You don't need both types of juicers to get these jobs done. If it were up to me, I'd start with a centrifugal (the Breville Ikon is a solid choice) and use other kitchen tools to make up for the lack of bells and whistles. Go to kriscarr.com/resources for more information.

PEELER: Ya gotta have one. When shopping around, look for a sharp blade with a substantial handle—easier to hold and use.

SHARP KNIVES: High-quality knives separate the amateurs from the ninjas! You'll learn everything you ever wanted to know about knives on pages 74–77. You don't have to get super fancy or buy an entire set of new knives. Just make sure your knives are high quality, the right weight, and comfortable in your hand.

SLICING TOOLS:

Spiralizers turn honking zucchinis (and other veggies) into raw spaghetti strands in no time flat. Mandoline slicers come in handy when churning out raw lasagna noodles. The Joyce Chen mandoline will run you about 40 bucks, compared to the $100 Frenchy kind. The razor-sharp blades come with various attachments, which are great for shaving, shredding, julienning, fine dicing, and making paper-thin strips

and batons. Warning: friends, please watch your fingers. I'd tell you a gross story but I don't want you to lose your lunch. Let's just say, they bite often. Be sure to use the guard.

CUTTING BOARD:

If you already have this kitchen item—

terrific. If not or if you're in need of an upgrade, try bamboo. For wooden and bamboo boards, you want to make sure to hand-dry them after washing to avoid drying out and cracking. Solid wood boards may need to be seasoned with neutral oil (food-grade mineral oil, or walnut, almond, or coconut oil) every now and then. They're easier to clean and more eco-friendly than plastic. Also, if you're using a plastic cutting board, keep in mind that tiny pieces can break off and make their way into your cuisine. Yuck.

STRAINER & SALAD SPINNER:

Need we say more? They're kinda essential for all things Crazy Sexy.

STEAMER BASKET & SUSHI MAT:

Multiple-layer bamboo steamer baskets are great for steaming veggies and dumplings. A steamer pot set or collapsible steamer work well, too. Sushi mats allow you to make your own rolls at home. Another helpful tip: Use a sushi mat to cover your grains and beans when soaking overnight.

NUT MILK BAG: Excuse me? Oh, you dirty birdie. Keep it clean. Homemade nut milks are simple (and cheap) to make. Check out the Basic Nut/Seed Milk recipe on page 93. You can also grow sprouts in these bags, culture "cheeses," and strain fancy infused oils.

MASON JARS: Perfect for storing smoothies and juices, just fill to brim and screw on top. You want as little oxygen inside as possible, since O_2 oxidizes your glorious drink. Mason jars are also great for storing your grains and beans. They come in a variety of shapes and sizes. You'll find them at craft and hardware stores.

MICROPLANE ZESTER: Need a citrus, garlic, or ginger zest? Mighty Microplane to the rescue!

COFFEE GRINDER: Lay off the java, but save that grinder. It's wonderful for grinding spices, breadcrumbs, nuts, and seeds.

DEHYDRATOR: (optional) Food dehydrators are a helpful addition to a raw-friendly kitchen. Think Easy Bake Oven for raw foodists. You'll also need teflex sheets (sold separately). These reusable, nonstick sheets are needed for wet mixtures (batters) or smaller items that can slide through the cracks or stick to the racks. Some of our recipes call for using teflex sheets; others recommend just using the screens. The screens come with the dehydrator and the small holes allow for air circulation. What can you make with a dehydrator? We're so glad you asked! Raw crackers, breads, cookies, all dried snacks, tortillas, wraps, dried fruits and vegetables, flavored sugars, flavored salts, and so much more! FYI: Excalibur makes the best one.

CANNING FUNNEL: (optional) Get frugal! After your produce goes through the juicer once, send it through for a second trip. Pop a funnel into the juicer mouth and dump in the pulp. You'll get at least 2 to 4 more ounces, which equals extra goodness for your body and pocketbook.

SPRAY BOTTLE: (optional) A spray bottle is a great way to cut down on the amount of oil used for sautéing and low-heat cooking. You can find them at any kitchen or housewares store. We like the stainless-steel variety that uses a pump handle rather than aerosol.

IMMERSION BLENDER: (optional) This magical and convenient electric blending wand allows you to purée a soup or sauce directly in your pot. This way you don't have to haul out your big blender. The whisk attachment is handy for whipping. Giddyup!

DOODADS: Other tools for the Crazy Sexy kitchen include: measuring cups and spoons, tongs, ladles, garlic press, spatulas, kitchen timer, large salad bowls, and a citrus reamer.

HOW TO BE A
BARGAINISTA

Now that you're dedicated to valuing your food more, let's learn how to spend and plan wisely for our Crazy Sexy Kitchen culinary masterpieces. Without further ado, here are the Bargainista basics.

TIGHTEN YOUR BELT IN OTHER AREAS.

Small choices add up. Could you endure one less trip to Starbucks, bypass the cookie aisle in the grocery store, or avoid Amazon.com for a week? I'm not talking about deprivation; I'm talking about pulling back on nonessential purchases so that you can reallocate funds to your Crazy Sexy Kitchen. Once you've reaped the benefits of a plant-strong diet, many things that seemed vital to your happiness turn into total buzzkills. How freeing!

BASK IN THE BOUNTIFUL FRUITS AND VEGGIES AT YOUR LOCAL FARMERS' MARKETS.

There's something magical about buying your produce directly from your neighborhood farmers. Plus, it tastes better and is cheaper. Of course prices will vary by region, but recent studies have shown that across the board, organic produce is less expensive at farmers' markets when compared with nearby grocery stores. If you're like me and get a natural high via haggling, farmers' markets are the premier place to get a deal on your fruits and veggies.

CREATE WEEKLY MEAL PLANS.

It sounds like a drag, but once you get into the habit, meal planning is (dare I say it?) fun. You know the drill. It's 6 P.M., you're thinking about dinner for the first time, the fridge is bare, and you reach for the takeout menus. No more, dear friend. Get the majority of the work over with on a Saturday or Sunday and you're set for the week. Here's how I get my planning on:

- Put on some soul-stirring tunes.

- Take a quick inventory of what's hanging out in my fridge and cupboards. These items will guide my recipe choices.

- Browse the pages of my favorite cookbooks (like this one!) and recipe websites while keeping my current food stock in mind.

- Choose four to five recipes and print them out (I have a binder where I keep the taste-tested all-stars) or tag the pages in my cookbooks with colorful Post-its.

- Make a shopping list with everything I'll need for the recipes. Usually, I already have half the ingredients in my trusty pantry and fridge.

When Monday rolls around, I'm ready to start cooking and there's no excuse for speed-dialing the nearest joint that'll deliver. Good-bye mystery ingredients, wasteful food containers, and the same old menu items. Sometimes I'm in the mood for a basic salad with a zesty dressing alongside a delicious soup. When I feel more ambitious, I roll up my sleeves and cook a main dish with a couple sides. A big honkin' bowl of greens is always on the table. Variety is paramount while planning. The only downside to taking charge of my kitchen? The dishes.

GET CREATIVE WITH LEFTOVERS. Leftovers can be transformed into new meals and snacks in a snap. Last night's Curried Nada-Egg Wraps can become today's topping for a bowl of greens at lunchtime. Have some leftover beans? It only takes ten minutes to whip 'em up refried-style for taco night.

GET SMART WITH BATCH COOKING.

Is rice pasta on sale this week? Perhaps your supermarket is running a special on organic kale or tempeh. Take advantage of grocery-store deals by doubling or tripling your recipes that include these thrifty finds and freezing the leftovers. Grains, beans, roasted or grilled veggies, salad dressings, sauces, soups, stews, and even "meat" balls can be prepared ahead of time and enjoyed in the coming weeks or months. For example, you could cook a big pot of beans in the beginning of the week, and in the coming days, you could integrate those beauties into salads, soups, veggie burgers, and dips.

REVIEW THE DIRTY DOZEN AND CLEAN

FIFTEEN. If 100 percent organic produce isn't in the cards right now, be smart about which conventional fruits and veggies you choose. Certain produce is more susceptible to nasty pesticides. Check out the Environmental Working Group's website to determine your priorities for organic purchases. Choose organic for produce on the Dirty Dozen list and conventional (when needed) for the Clean Fifteen. EWG even created an iPhone app for easy access while cruising the market and grocery store.

GROW GREENS INDOORS. Salads are a main event in the Crazy Sexy Kitchen. By growing your own greens, you'll save noticeable moolah. Lettuce is one of the simplest and cheapest veggies to grow. A two-dollar packet of mixed lettuce seeds will support your salad habit for months. Check out the Resources section

for books and websites that'll kick-start your crops. If you want to start sprouting right away, check out sproutpeople.org or sproutman.com for education and supplies.

MAKE THE MOST OF YOUR FRESH PRODUCE. I feel like a "bad mother" when I let my produce wilt away in the fridge. Don't let this happen to you! When you arrive home from the market or grocery store, wash and store your fruits and veggies so that they're organized and super accessible (Debbie Meyer's Green Bags extend life expectancy). If you find that your produce is about to go south, pop it in the freezer, make a soup or stew, or use it in a scrumptious juice or smoothie. The compost pile is a last resort when you have so many creative ways to make the most of your fresh food. Also when you have leftover produce that is still fresh but you don't have time to eat it right away, cut it up, toss it in a bag, and freeze.

SKIP THE BELLS AND WHISTLES. Superfoods, packaged goodies, and raw-food treats are alluring and tasty, but not necessary. If your budget is tight, make these more expensive items an exception to the rule.

*For more time- and money-saving tips go to kriscarr.com/resources.

the THIRD COURSE

KITCHEN KNOW-HOW

COOKING & PREPPING LINGO

If you're new to cooking or are unfamiliar with any of our culinary terms, check out this dapper lingo list.

BAKE: Baking uses an oven to cook food with dry heat, often allowing you to skip or reduce the butter or oil that you would use to cook in a skillet or deep fryer. Typically, baking is used to cook breads, root vegetables, and dishes such as CSK's Sweet Potato Hash.

BLANCH: Blanching is the brief dunking of vegetables, fruits, or herbs in a pot of boiling water, followed by submersion in ice water (called an ice bath). This method slightly cooks the food, but preserves its bright color and crisp texture.

BLEND: Blending is the combining of ingredients by stirring them together in a bowl with gusto, or by using a blender for a smoother, creamy consistency.

BRAISE: Braising is the slow cooking of food in a lidded pot on the stovetop or in the oven until tender. First, the food is lightly seared to brown the outside. Then, a small amount of veggie stock, wine, lemon juice, or vinegar is poured over the food, and the pot is covered to lock in the steam. This method is used to cook denser items, such as CSK's Seitan Brisket on page 200.

CARAMELIZE: Caramelizing is the sautéing of food over medium heat until the sugars in the food cause the surface to turn a golden brown color. This cooking method enhances the rich and sweet flavors of the food, and is most common with onions. Fennel and carrots also caramelize well.

DEGLAZE: Deglazing is the adding of water, veggie stock, or wine to a pan after a food, such as onions or veggies, have been cooked. The liquid lifts the sugars stuck to the bottom of the pan so that you don't lose these flavors as you proceed with the dish.

DEHYDRATE: Also known as the raw oven, a dehydrator is essential in the raw/living-foods kitchen. Dehydrating dries your food, usually at a temperature not exceeding 118°F. Once dehydrated, your snacks or creative raw dishes take on a baked or cooked texture. This process preserves enzymes and nutrients that would be destroyed at higher heat. Dehydrating is used to make raw crackers and breads, kale chips, fruit leathers, and more.

DREDGE: Dredging is the coating of food, for example a seitan cutlet, with flour, bread-crumbs, or cornmeal and then pan-frying or searing it to create a crunchy outer texture.

EMULSIFY: Emulsifying is the mixing of two or more liquids (that typically separate) by whisking them together and then slowly mixing in an additional liquid to prevent separation.

FOLD: Folding is a mixing technique used to combine a light and airy mixture with a heavier one, while preserving the overall texture. The heavier mixture is placed in the bowl first and the lighter mixture is added on top. Then, a large spoon or spatula is used to lift the heavier mixture over the lighter one, repeatedly. This will gradually and gently mix them together.

GERMINATE: The soaking of nuts or seeds in water, usually overnight, to trigger germination—the point at which the seed or nut begins to sprout. Once germination has taken place, the nut or seed is more easily digested and its vitamins and minerals are better absorbed by the body.

GRILL: Grilling is the cooking of food over an open flame, usually on a grill or griddle. It is easy to exclude oils while grilling by marinating your food in a sauce before cooking. This cook-ing method gives your food a tender yet crispy texture and a smoky taste.

JUICE: Juicing is the extraction of liquid from fruits or veggies by separating the juice from the fiber (pulp) using a juicer. You can choose from centrifugal, hydraulic-press, or twin-gear juicer models, depending on your budget and personal preferences. Check out page 35 for more on juicing.

MARINATE: Marinating is the soaking or coating of foods such as fruits, veggies, tofu, or tempeh, with a marinade (a.k.a. sauce) before cooking. This process allows the food to absorb the marinade's flavors and softens the food's texture. Typically a marinade consists of a salt, sugar, acid, and fat.

POACH: Poaching is the gentle boiling of fruits or veggies in water or broth that's mixed with a combination of alcohol and/or juices, spices, and a sweetener. This method infuses the food with the flavors of the cooking liquid.

PRESS: Pressing eliminates some of a food's water content, which opens up its "pores." Once the food is pressed, it acts like a sponge, allowing more flavors from sauces, marinades, herbs, and spices to be absorbed. In CSK, pressing is primarily used when working with tofu or before marinating mushrooms.

PURÉE: Puréeing is the prolonged blending of one or more ingredients with a blender or food processor, which creates a smooth texture.

REDUCE: Reducing is the simmering of a liquid to lessen its volume and intensify the flavor via evaporation. This method is typically used to richen sauces.

SAUTÉ: Sautéing is the speedy frying of food in a skillet or pot over high heat with a small amount of liquid (water, broth, or oil).

Sautéing lightly browns the food. Stir frequently to prevent sticking or burning and make sure to leave room in the pan (no overcrowding) so that the food cooks evenly.

SEAR: Searing is the cooking of food at high heat on the stovetop, in an oven, or in the broiler to quickly brown it. This creates a crust on the outside layer and seals in moisture.

SLOW-COOK: Slow-cooking is just like it sounds—cooking for a long period of time at a low temperature (175° to 200°F). This method helps to prevent sticking and burning, distribute flavors throughout the dish, and give certain foods a tender texture. The slow-cooking process allows the flavors to intensify and marry (happily ever after).

SLURRY: A mixture of flour (or arrowroot, or cornstarch) and water used to thicken a sauce or soup. After the slurry is added, the sauce is stirred and heated on the stovetop. See the Roasted Chanterelle Gravy on page 235.

STEAM: Steaming is the cooking of food (usually veggies) in a mesh basket or rack, suspended over a small amount of boiling water. A lid covers the pot, locking in the steam, which cooks the food. This cooking technique preserves more nutrients than simply boiling the food. Just don't overdo it!

STIR-FRY: Stir-frying is the cooking of food in a wok over high heat using a small amount of oil or water. Once cooked, food is crispy on the outside and tender inside.

TOAST: Toasting is the cooking of nuts, seeds, or spices on a baking sheet in the oven or in a pan on the stovetop until golden. This process releases natural oils and aromas, enhances flavors, and reduces bitterness. Toasting time and temperature varies.

COOKING
GRAINS & BEANS

Grains and beans are an essential component to a vegan diet. They're loaded with protein and fiber and add heft and heartiness to any meal. Did you know that there are 19 ancient whole grains in the world and more than 800 varieties of beans? Holy abundance!

PREP

First, let's learn about enzyme inhibitors and phytic acid. Grains, beans, seeds, and legumes contain enzyme inhibitors, which delay germination (when a plant emerges from its seed and sings, "Hello, world!"). In nature, rain triggers germination. If we eat these foods before soaking, then it hasn't "rained" yet and the enzyme inhibitors and phytic acid are still intact. Who cares? Your belly!

Enzyme inhibitors block and bind with our digestive and metabolic enzymes. What are they? Digestive enzymes help to break down our food, while metabolic enzymes support every amazing function in our bodies. Bottom line, we don't want to mess with them. Soaking grains, beans, and seeds triggers germination, which neutralizes enzyme inhibitors.

Phytic acid in the body decreases our ability to absorb key minerals, such as calcium, iron, magnesium, and zinc. These minerals are crucial for peppy health. Soaking our grains, beans, and seeds until they germinate activates the chemical phytase, which is an enzyme that neutralizes phytic acid. *Voilà!*

BEAN & GRAIN TLC

ALWAYS GIVE YOUR GRAINS AND BEANS A BATH AND A SORT-THROUGH.

Place them into a bowl filled with water. Swish the little suckers around, strain, and repeat until the water is clear. This helps to remove dusty residue and the occasional dead bug (ew!), not to mention stones. Yup, from time to time you might find a little rock in your batch. Protect your choppers with a quick sift.

SOAK YOUR BEANS AND GRAINS.

As previously mentioned, soaking your beans and grains overnight will greatly reduce enzyme inhibitors and phytic acid, making them easier to digest (less toots!). Just be sure to use fresh water for cooking. Even if you can only

TO SALT OR NOT TO SALT?

Salt pulls moisture from beans, so wait until they're almost tender then add salt to the cooking water. You'll avoid adding too much sodium, which would just get lost during the cooking process.

soak them for a few hours, it helps and your body will thank you. And get this: soaking beans for around 18 hours can reduce phytic acid by 50 to 70 percent. Dang! Plus, soaking your beans and grains first will reduce cooking time.

BEAN *tip* Adding a piece of kombu (seaweed) increases the effectiveness of this process.

COOKING METHODS

The following beans and grains are most commonly used in our Crazy Sexy Kitchen. Each is unique in flavor and texture. If you haven't already, get adventurous and start enjoying these hearty, inexpensive, and healthful additions to your meals. Here's an introduction to our faves—why we love 'em and how to cook 'em!

GRAINS

MILLET

This soft, fluffy, and slightly sweet grain is an excellent alternative to brown rice when you're in the mood for something off the beaten path. It's also one of the only alkaline grains!

Ratio: 1 cup millet to 2 cups water

Cooking time: 25 to 30 minutes

Method: Bring water and millet to a boil in a covered pot, and then simmer for 20 to 25 minutes (until soft). Allow millet to sit in covered pot for about 5 minutes before serving, fluff with fork, and serve.

BROWN RICE

Brown rice contains fiber, essential fatty acids, minerals, and lots of vitamins. White

rice doesn't. All its happy goodness has been stripped—that's why we always recommend brown. Brown rice is also a great way to add robustness to any meal. There are many varieties of brown rice, and depending on whether it is short or long grain, these cooking times may vary.

Ratio: 1 cup rice to 2 cups water

Cooking time: 45 to 50 minutes

Method: Bring water and rice to a boil in a covered pot, and then simmer for 35 to 40 minutes (until tender). Allow rice to sit in covered pot for about 5 minutes before serving, fluff with fork, and serve.

QUINOA

Quinoa (pronounced KEEN-wah) is the queen of protein in the grain department (even though it's really a seed, it acts more like a grain). Its light texture, quick cooking time, and slightly bittersweet taste make this a no-brainer addition to any pantry (especially for plant-strong eaters!). Quinoa is also second to millet in alkalinity.

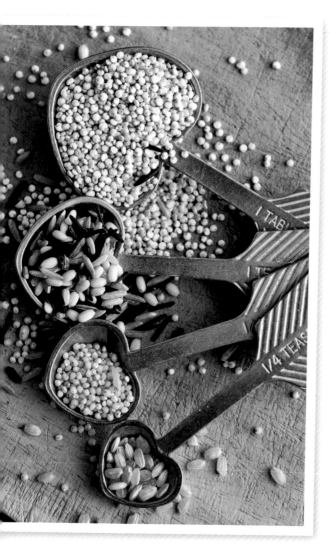

PRESSURE COOKER

Using a pressure cooker will cut cooking time in half, plus by locking in steam and using less water, it preserves more nutrients than stovetop cooking.

Ratio: 1 cup quinoa to 2 cups water

Cooking time: 20 to 25 minutes

Method: Bring water and quinoa to a boil in a covered pot, and then simmer for 20 to 25 minutes (until the spiral or "tail" is visible, the water is absorbed, and the grain is fluffy). Allow the quinoa to sit in a covered pot for about 5 minutes before serving, fluff with fork, and serve.

OATS

In the Crazy Sexy Kitchen, we prefer old-fashioned rolled oats or steel-cut oats—which are high in protein and soluble fiber, help lower cholesterol and stabilize blood sugar, and are great for your heart. (Most instant oats are processed with sugary additives—no, thank you.) When cooked, rolled oats are soft and creamy, while steel-cut oats have a nuttier and chewier texture.

Ratio: 1 cup rolled or steel-cut oats to 2 cups water

Cooking time: Rolled oats: 5 minutes, Steel-cut oats: 30 to 35 minutes or overnight (soaking method)

Method: Rolled oats: Bring water and oats to a boil in an uncovered pot, cook on low for 5 to 10 minutes. Stir and serve. Steel-cut oats: Bring oats and water to a boil in an uncovered pot, cook on low for 30 minutes. Stir and serve. In both cases, add more or less water depending on whether or not you like it creamy. Another way to cook steel-cut oats is to add 1 cup of oats to 3 cups of boiling water, stir, and turn off the heat. Cover the pot and let it sit overnight. Oats will be ready to eat in the morning!

BEANS

Just about all dry beans have a similar cooking method. Start with cold water and beans in a large pot. Bring to a boil and then turn down to a simmer. Cover the pot, leaving the lid tilted just enough to allow some steam to escape. Beans are done when they are tender and the skin is still intact.

BLACK BEANS

These small, sturdy beans have an earthy and sweet flavor. They hold up well during cooking and are popular in Latin American and Caribbean cuisines.

Ratio: 1 cup black beans to 4 cups water

Cooking time: After soaking overnight, 60 to 75 minutes

CHICKPEAS (GARBANZOS)

The nutty, full-bodied flavor of these adorable round beans is popular in Indian and Mediterranean dishes.

Ratio: 1 cup chickpeas to 4 cups water

Cooking time: After soaking overnight, 75 to 90 minutes

WHITE BEANS (GREAT NORTHERN BEANS)

White beans are flexible fellas that take on the flavors of every ingredient they meet. Their creamy texture is perfect for dips and spreads.

Ratio: 1 cup white beans to 3½ cups water

Cooking time: After soaking overnight, 90 minutes

KIDNEY

This tender bean is also one of the most protein-rich in its crew.

Ratio: 1 cup kidney beans to 3 cups water

Cooking time: After soaking overnight, 1 hour

PINTO

Especially well-known in Tex-Mex and Native American cuisine, pinto beans pair well with full-flavored sauces and dishes.

Ratio: 1 cup pinto beans to 3 cups water

Cooking time: After soaking overnight, 75 to 90 minutes

FAVA

These larger, flat beans deliver a strong, tart flavor. Their tough skins are often removed after cooking. Fava beans are native to Africa and Asia and are most often used in soups, stews, and spreads.

Ratio: 1 cup fava beans to 3 cups water

Cooking time: After soaking overnight, 40 to 50 minutes

LIMA

This kidney-shaped bean has a smooth, buttery texture and pairs well with herbs.

Ratio: 1 cup lima beans to 4 cups water

Cooking time: After soaking overnight, 1 hour

KNIFE 101

Working in a plant-empowered kitchen means that you'll be doing lots of chopping, slicing, and dicing. Your knife is your food prep partner (the Bogie to your Bacall). Choose your knives like you would choose a lover; it's the quality, not the quantity, that matters.

Owning excellent knives is a valuable investment in your Crazy Sexy Kitchen. They'll save you time, frustration, sweat, and tears (although not from onions, unfortunately). Once you're equipped with some basic skills; a few sharp, comfortable knives; and a couple of sturdy cutting boards, you'll be prepping your meals like a pro.

CHOOSING YOUR KNIFE

Picking the best knife is as simple as holding the knife and asking yourself: Does it fit well in my hand? Is it comfortable to hold and use? Does the weight of the knife feel balanced when using it? Do I look cool and dangerous? If your answer is yes to these questions, then you're on the right track.

You don't need as many knives as you might think. Although quality knives are moderately expensive, after you've purchased these four basic knives, you'll be set for years to come (as long as you take care of them!). Plus, you'll be so much happier with your daily cooking experience. If you only buy one, make it the chef's knife, since it's the most versatile.

Stainless-steel knives are popular because they don't rust or react chemically with foods. Carbon-steel knives slice well and sharpen easily, but they can stain some foods and need to be washed and dried immediately after use. If you like using light knives with a thin blade, Japanese-style will suit you well. Global, MAC, and NHS (my fave!) are all trusted brands. If you prefer a heavier knife with a thicker blade, go for the German-style brands—Henkel and Wüsthof won't let you down. Hybrid knives have the weight of a German knife and the thinness of a Japanese knife. Shun is one of the best hybrid brands and happens to be Chef Chad's favorite.

RECOMMENDED KNIVES

CHEF'S KNIFE

THE MOTHERSHIP: The chef knife's straight edge cuts as it's pushed through the food. You can perform any cut with a chef's knife. It has a triangular blade, pointed tip, and wide base, which give your cutting hand plenty of space to get busy. Although the length ranges from 6 to 14 inches, you're best off with an 8- to 10-incher.

PARING KNIFE

THE SIDEKICK: This little guy was created for delightful details, from scraping a vanilla bean to peeling an apple or slicing a garlic clove. The 2.5- to 5-inch blade is approximately the same size as its small, maneuverable handle.

SERRATED KNIFE

THE BIG MOUTH: The serrated knife's toothy edge cuts as it is dragged back and forth across the food's surface and gradually pushed through. Perfect for slicing bread, tender fruits, and soft veggies. It's also excellent for cutting your sushi (make sure to lightly dip it in water before making the cut, this way the nori sheet won't stick and tear). Most serrated knives are 8 to 10 inches in length.

CUTTING BOARDS

You're a culinary artist, so give yourself some room to work with your muse. I recommend having two spacious wood or bamboo cutting boards on hand. Wash and dry your boards after each use to prevent warping and mold. If possible, reserve one side of a particular cutting board for garlic and onions. This will ensure that other ingredients are safe from absorbing their pungent odor and taste. To keep your cutting boards from slipping, place a dish towel underneath for extra grip.

CLEAVER

THE TOUGH GUY: The cleaver's heavy, thick, rectangular blade cuts through dense foods that would bend or damage other knives. Superb for cracking coconuts and cutting dense winter veggies. See page 90 for tips on how the heck to open a coconut.

CARING FOR YOUR KNIFE

crazy sexy kitchen **PSA** Dull knives are dangerous. Keep your knives sharp at all times to avoid rogue blades and wounded digits!

The sharpening steel that accompanies most knife sets is for fine-tuning your blade each time it's used, not for sharpening an already dull blade. If you only buy one knife, consider purchasing a sharpening steel for regular maintenance. Chef Chad prefers ceramic steels. To sharpen your knife, there are a couple of inexpensive, speedy methods. A whetstone is a coarse, double-sided block. Pressure is used to sharpen the blade at an angle against the block. Some find this method challenging, however, and opt for a manual sharpener. The AccuSharp Knife and Tool Sharpener is only $8 and will sharpen your knife in a couple of minutes. If your knife is in really poor shape (dings and notches in the blade), you can send it back to the manufacturer for sharpening or you can purchase an electric sharpener. Most kitchen

stores, such as Williams-Sonoma, offer knife-sharpening services, which will make your knives seem new again.

Your knives will dull quickly if left rattling around with other utensils in a drawer. Store your knives properly in a wooden knife block, a drawer knife tray, or on a wall-mounted magnetic strip. If you'd prefer drawer storage sans tray, get a sheath to cover the blade and ensure the longevity of the edge. Also, be sure to hand-wash and hand-dry your knives after each use to avoid rusting (no dishwashers please).

tip Scrub pads will wear away at the knife blade finish. Instead, try using a wine cork to clean gunk off the blade before giving it a hot, soapy rinse.

KNIFE SKILLS

How to hold and wield your blade—watch out, world!

HOLDING YOUR KNIFE: Use your thumb and first finger to pinch the blade where it meets the handle (the "heel"). Then, wrap your other three fingers around the handle. Although this hold may feel awkward at first, it will give you control and steadiness while cutting.

GUIDE HAND: Place the fingertips of your free hand on top of the food to hold it firmly in place. Tuck your thumb behind your fingers (thumbs are useful, keep them). Your food should have a flat base resting against the cutting board so that it's stable. Your fingertips should be curved under your knuckles (a.k.a. the claw grip) to protect your cute digits. Use the flat part of your knuckles to guide the cut.

BASIC CUTTING METHOD: Hold the knife in your dominant hand and steady the food with your guide hand. Use a rocking motion to cut through the food with your knife. The tip of your knife should remain on the cutting surface, pointing downward as the rest of the blade rocks up and down. The side of your blade rests against your knuckles on your guide hand. If your knife is sharp, you should be able to cut through your food in one fluid motion. Your guide hand will gradually move back as the knife cuts through the food.

BASIC CUTTING TECHNIQUES

CHOP: Chopped foods have been cut into pieces that do not need to be uniform in size or shape. To chop, first cut the food lengthwise, and then turn the food 90 degrees and cut crosswise.

DICE (COARSE & FINE): Diced foods have been cut into uniform, cube-shaped pieces. The width of your first cuts will determine the size of your final pieces, so plan accordingly. To dice, first cut the food lengthwise into even strips. Then, cut the strips crosswise to create uniform cubes. Coarsely diced pieces are approximately ¾ inch in size, and finely diced pieces are about ¼ inch in size.

MINCE: Minced foods have been cut into tiny pieces (smaller than diced or chopped). This technique is most commonly used with onions, garlic, and strong herbs. To mince, cut the food lengthwise, repeatedly stacking the strips. Then, turn the thin strips 90 degrees and cut crosswise, rocking the knife back and forth until only tiny pieces remain.

JULIENNE: Julienned foods have been cut into long, slender strips (matchstick size). To julienne, first cut food into 2- to 3-inch-long pieces. Then, slice the food at a 45-degree angle to create flat pieces. Stack 2 to 3 pieces and cut lengthwise to make thin strips. Julienned vegetables are used in dishes such as stir-fries, raw salads, and as garnishes.

CHIFFONADE: Chiffonaded foods, usually leafy greens and herbs, have been sliced into super-fine strips. To chiffonade, stack your greens and roll into a cigarlike shape. Thinly slice the roll crosswise to create wispy strips. This is a great technique when cutting basil for garnish.

RECIPE
SYMBOL LEGEND

To help you decide what recipes to make (or adapt)
we've included these symbols where appropriate.

DIFFICULTY LEVEL

1 EASY BREEZY

Perfect for beginners or
for when you want to keep
it light, bright, and easy as
pie . . . no previous cooking experience required.

2 CHEFFY

For the more adventur-
ous kitchen voyager
who loves to impress
their hot date or
mother-in-law.

TIME SAVER

Q CRAZY SEXY QUICKIE

(less than 45 minutes)

Everyone loves a good, down
and dirty quickie. Need I say
more? 'Cause you know I will.

DIETARY PREFERENCES

GF GLUTEN-FREE

If you have an issue with gluten, look
for recipes with this symbol. Feel
free to make any of our recipes belly
friendly by swapping out the wheat
with a gluten-free grain.

R RAW

Just like it says. Raw. No fire, tons of
desire. If a recipe is labeled as raw, that
means we use 100 percent raw ingredients, with the exception of an occasional,
small amount of toasted sesame oil, miso,
or heated spices.

SF SOY-FREE

Not everyone loves soy. If you're not a
fan, we've got the plan. Use this symbol to identify the soy-free recipes.

KF KID-FRIENDLY

These recipes are especially fun and
tasty choices for the kiddos, plus it's
easy to involve them while cooking!

TIPS FOR *gastronomic delight*

- ○ Set the scene. Mood = magic.
- ○ Play music (jazz, reggae, classical, spiritual jams, sexy mellow electronic . . .).
- ○ Light candles.
- ○ Don't fight.
- ○ Don't eat when you're upset.
- ○ Make it mindful.
- ○ Chew!
- ○ Don't go to bed on a full stomach.
- ○ Turn off your cell phone (better yet, leave it in another room!).
- ○ Don't check e-mail, Facebook, Twitter, you get the point . . .
- ○ Invite friends and family—especially plant-empowered newbies.
- ○ Pick a lively topic for dinner conversation (not politics!).
- ○ Ambience, essence, tone, and sensuality matter.
- ○ Checkered or vintage tablecloths are ritzy.
- ○ Cloth napkins are adorable and super green!
- ○ Mixed plates and glasses via flea markets add kitschy elegance.
- ○ Open the windows.
- ○ Eat outside (a bench, blanket, or just the earth will do as your table).
- ○ Give thanks/make a toast.

the FOURTH COURSE

crazy *sexy* RECIPES

JUICES

Sweet
GREENS

1 GF R SF KF Q

Serves 2

- 3 green apples, quartered
- 2 kiwis, quartered
- 3 cucumbers
- 5 kale leaves (with stems)
- 8 romaine leaves
- 1½ cups dandelion greens (or spinach if milder green taste is preferred)

The mild sweetness in this chlorophyll-packed juice takes the mean out of green. Plus, dandelion contains choline, which stimulates your liver—a detox powerhouse.

1   Wash and prep all ingredients.

2   Juice all ingredients.

Immune
ME

1 GF R SF KF Q

Serves 2

- 2 green apples, quartered
- 4 cucumbers
- 1-inch piece ginger root
- 1 lemon, peeled and quartered
- 8 romaine leaves

Juice this bad boy when you feel a pesky cold coming on. For extra immune-boosting zing, double the ginger, which has antiviral and antifungal properties. In addition, ginger is an anti-inflammatory (great for arthritis pain relief) and it stimulates circulation.

1   Wash and prep all ingredients.

2   Juice all ingredients.

Fennel
and FRUITS

1 GF R SF KF Q

Serves 2

8 stalks celery

2 fennel bulbs, with stems and fronds, chopped

2 green apples, quartered

1 pear, quartered

½ lemon, peeled and quartered

1-inch piece ginger root

1 cup loosely packed spinach

Here's a spectacular spin on one of Chef Chad's favorite salads. The fresh fennel adds a hint of anise or licorice-like flavor. You might assume that lemon is acidic, but it actually falls on the alkaline side of the pH scale.

1   Wash and prep all ingredients.

2   Juice all ingredients.

Iron
MACHINE

1 GF R SF Q

Serves 2

2 beets, peeled and quartered

8 carrots

2 stalks celery

1 long piece of burdock root (carrot size), scrubbed or peeled

½ cup loosely packed parsley

1 cup loosely packed spinach

The star of this recipe is burdock root—an iron tour de force and blood purifier. Burdock is a thin Japanese root with a woodsy, earthy taste. The younger the root, the sweeter the flavor. Carrots are the perfect complement to burdock in this recipe, since their vitamin C content helps your body absorb iron more efficiently.

1   Wash and prep all ingredients.

2   Juice all ingredients.

THE
Sicilian

6 carrots

3 large tomatoes

2 red bell peppers

4 cloves garlic

4 stalks celery

1 cup watercress

1 cup loosely packed spinach

1 red jalapeño, seeded
(optional)

Even your dear Italian grandmother will guzzle down this spicy drink. It's hearty, savory, and hits the spot when your tummy is grumbling. Celery's fabulous phytochemical, phthalide, makes this veggie a heart helper. Phthalide relaxes the smooth muscles of the arteries, which helps to lower blood pressure. Ahhh . . .

1   Wash and prep all ingredients.

2   Juice all ingredients.

MORNING
Glorious

1 GF R SF KF Q

Serves 2

1 large cucumber

A fistful kale

A fistful romaine

2 or 3 stalks celery

1 big broccoli stem

1 green apple, quartered

½ peeled lemon, quartered

It's our motto and our morning beverage. Green juice is the rock-solid foundation of my crazy sexy life. Almost all of my juice recipes start with one or two cukes. Cucumber is the perfect base since it yields lots of mild and refreshing juice and minerals, and it's a fountain of alkalinity. Vive la révolution!

1   Wash and prep all ingredients.

2   Juice all ingredients.

THE Gardener

1 GF R SF KF Q

Serves 2

8 carrots

2 red bell peppers

1 orange, peeled

½ cup red radishes

6 kale leaves (with stems)

Radish gives this juice a sassy, sharp bite. Make sure to include the radish leaves, since they're also rich in vitamin C, potassium, and folic acid. Feel free to substitute your favorite greens in place of the kale.

1   Wash and prep all ingredients.

2   Juice all ingredients.

Jolly GREEN

1 GF R SF Q

Serves 1

6 celery stalks

3 cucumbers

3 large broccoli stems

½ cup loosely packed parsley

1½ lemons, peeled and quartered

Did you know that broccoli stems are surprisingly sweet and fabulous for juicing? Broccoli is a VIP in the cruciferous family, since its vitamin C and K levels are off the charts (more than our daily value needs are in one cup!). Save the stems next time you're preparing a stir-fry or salad, especially since they're an excellent source of calcium.

1   Wash and prep all ingredients.

2   Juice all ingredients.

SMOOTHIES

Serves 2

1 avocado*

1 banana

1 cup blueberries

1 cucumber

A fistful of kale or romaine or spinach

Coconut water (or purified water)

Stevia, to taste, and/or a sprinkle of cinnamon or some cacao (optional)

* If desired, use coconut meat, raw almond butter, or nut milk in place of avocado. You can also add superfoods like cacao (to taste) and/or 1 to 2 table-spoons of E3Live.

CRAZY SEXY GODDESS
Smoothie

This is a smoothie staple in the Carr-Fassett household. The avocado, cucumber, greens, and coconut water will shower your cells in alkalinizing goodness. An alkaline inner environment helps your body's systems operate optimally.

1   In high-speed blender, blend all ingredients until smooth.

A.J.'s POWER SMOOTHIE

Serves 2

3 cups almond or nondairy milk of choice

½ cup fresh or frozen berries

½ cup frozen mango

2 tablespoons raw almond butter

Sprinkle of cinnamon

4 or 5 kale leaves

Handful of spinach

Chad's daughter gives this smoothie two thumbs up! The almond butter provides a protein punch that'll fuel you and your kids with long-lasting energy.

1   In high-speed blender, blend all ingredients until smooth.

note FROM CHAD

Serve this green smoothie to kids (or adults) who may be a bit spooked by its green color. It's so tasty; they'll never dodge a green drink again!

Vanilla
MYSTIC

1 GF R SF KF Q

Serves 2

----

3 cups almond or nondairy milk of choice

1 cup young coconut meat (alternative: ⅓ cup raw cashews soaked in water to soften)

1 whole vanilla bean, scraped, or ¾ teaspoon vanilla extract

1 tablespoon coconut butter

2 tablespoons agave or other sweetener of choice

The Vanilla Mystic was Chad's most popular smoothie at his Woodstock, NY raw-food joint (I would often overdose on them). Give this drink unicorn wings by adding your favorite greens.

1   In high-speed blender, blend all ingredients until smooth.

tip **HOW TO SCRAPE A VANILLA BEAN**   Slice the vanilla bean lengthwise with a knife. Open the pod and use the tip of the knife to scrape out the seeds. But don't toss that pod. Infuse liquids such as syrups, vinegars, and oils (or vodka!) with a va-va-vanilla flavor by adding the pod and letting it sit for a few days. The flavor will intensify with time.

CRACKING OPEN YOUNG THAI COCONUTS

You'll find these baby coconuts at most health-food stores, or by the case in Chinatown. They look intimidating, but all you need is a cleaver to open them. Clear some space on the counter and hit the top of the coconut 4 times around the tip to create the square opening (watch your fingers!). Pour out the electrolyte-rich water. It's hydrating and sweet on its own, in a smoothie, or as a substitute for water in a variety of recipes. If you'd like to use the meat as noodles or in a smoothie, whack the empty coconut on the top center and it'll split right open. Scrape the inside with a large serving spoon. Some of the hard shell might stick to the meat, so give it a good rinse before use.

GREEN
Colada

1 GF R SF KF Q

Serves 2

- 2 cups cashew or nondairy milk of choice
- ½ cup pineapple chunks
- 1 orange, peeled
- 1 banana
- ½ cup loosely packed spinach

The Crazy Sexy–fied piña colada will have your cells thanking you rather than cursing you in the morning. The half-cup of raw spinach in this smoothie provides 100 percent of your daily vitamin K needs. Did you know that vitamin K helps keep your bones healthy and strong? Spinach is also high in calcium and magnesium—no wonder Popeye kicked ass!

1   In high-speed blender, blend all ingredients until smooth.

Chai
LATTE

1 GF R SF Q

Serves 2

- 3 cups almond or nondairy milk of choice
- ½ tablespoon ginger, finely minced or grated
- ½ tablespoon cinnamon
- ½ teaspoon cardamom
- 1 teaspoon vanilla extract
- 2 dates pitted or 2 tablespoons maple syrup (if using dates, you may want to soak them first to ensure they blend smoothly, and don't turn out gritty)
- Sea salt, to taste

Take your palate on an exotic trip to the Far East with this spicy chai. You might be surprised by the slightly citrus and strong taste, thanks to the cardamom (keep in mind that a little goes a long way). A pinch of sea salt will bring out the full flavor of each spice. Add some oomph and body to your shake with a dollop of almond butter. Blend it with ice for a phenomenal chai frappuccino! Zing!

1   In high-speed blender, blend all ingredients until smooth.

note **FROM CHAD**
For an added energy kick, sub out half the amount of nondairy milk for freshly brewed black or green tea.

Basic
NUT/SEED MILK

1 GF R SF KF Q

Yields 3+ cups of
nondairy milk

1 cup raw nuts/seeds of
your choice, soaked 10 to 12
hours in water

3 cups filtered water

note FROM CHAD
Try making homemade
pecan milk with a touch
of cinnamon, vanilla, and
cocoa powder for a
delicious treat.

Almond milk is a megahit in the Crazy Sexy Kitchen, especially since it's a fantastic source of protein and contains antioxidant vitamin E, which nourishes your glowing skin. Nut/seed milk is a versatile vixen—pour it over diced fruit and granola, use it as the base of your smoothies, or substitute your freshly made nut/seed nectar for moo juice in any recipe.

1   In blender, blend all ingredients until smooth.

2   Pour milk mixture into nut milk bag (check out Nut Milk Bag in The Tools on page 59) or cheesecloth. Place bowl or pitcher underneath to catch the "milk."

3   Squeeze the bag or cheesecloth to pull out remaining liquid from the pulp.

NUT PULP = NUT FLOUR

Nut flour is a gluten-free alternative to traditional grain flours. Simply crumble the nut pulp in a thin layer on a dehydrator sheet and dehydrate for 4 to 6 hours, or until crisp. Then, blend the dehydrated nut pulp in a food processor or blender. If you prefer a superfine texture, sift the flour after blending.

Greensicle
SMOOTHIE

1 GF R SF KF Q

Serves 2

- -

3 cups cashew or nondairy milk of your choice

2 small oranges, peeled

1 vanilla bean, scraped

3 tablespoons yacón or agave syrup

1 cup loosely packed spinach

4 romaine leaves

Savor this dreamy creamsicle, green-style. Yacón syrup comes from the roots of the yacón plant, native to South America. Its caramelized sugary flavor is even sweeter than it tastes, because it won't raise your glucose levels. Beautiful health, without compromise. Cheers!

1   In high-speed blender, blend all ingredients until smooth.

FIERCE FATS

Fat isn't taboo, especially when you're choosing the healthy, whole guys. Good fats increase your metabolism, boost your immune system, support brain function, and help your body absorb and transport vitamins. And that's only the beginning of their glorious graces! Just avoid saturated and partially hydrogenated fats (a.k.a. trans fats), while consuming beneficial fats in moderation. Feel free to swap out the fat ingredient in your smoothies to fit your taste and mood. Avocado, coconut meat, or raw nut butter are all smart choices.

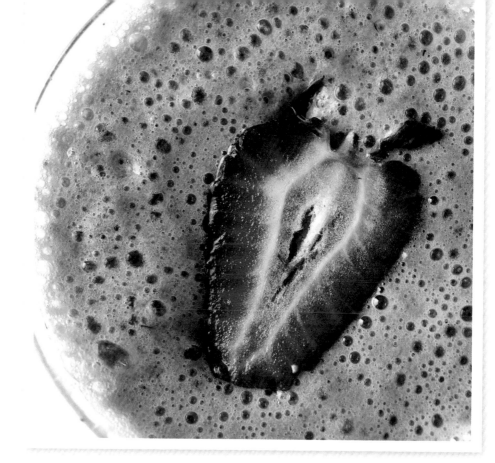

Strawberry Fields
SMOOTHIE

1 GF R SF KF Q

Serves 2

3 cups cashew or nondairy milk of your choice

2 cups fresh strawberries

1 tablespoon lemon zest

1 small orange, peeled

1 banana

1½ cups loosely packed spinach

Now you can enjoy the nostalgic tastiness of strawberry milk sans moo juice or powdered junk. Strawberries are phytonutrient factories, supplying your body with a bounty of anti-inflammatory and antioxidant nutrients. John Lennon would be pleased.

1   In high-speed blender, blend all ingredients until smooth.

Aztec
SPIRIT

1 GF R SF Q

Serves 2

- -

3 cups brazil nut or nondairy milk of choice

⅓ cup cacao powder

1 vanilla bean, scraped or ¾ teaspoon vanilla extract

2 shots of espresso or very strong coffee (optional)

2 tablespoons agave or maple syrup (or stevia, to taste)

3 kale leaves, stripped from the stem

Pinch of cayenne

This chocolatey, fiery superdrink disguises kale in pure deliciousness. If you don't have an espresso machine, brew some superstrong coffee instead (even in the CSK, java's okay once in a while). Cayenne is a known aphrodisiac, so share this smoothie with someone you love. Ooh la la!

1 In high-speed blender, blend all ingredients until smooth.

STELLAR STEVIA

Stevia is new to America's sweetie scene, although this herb has been used for ages in South America and other parts of the world. The fact that stevia does not spike your blood glucose level is one reason this sugar substitute is a healthy alternative. You can decrease the amount of higher-GI fruits and sweeteners by adding stevia to your smoothies and treats. It's 300 times sweeter than white sugar, so sprinkle conservatively and experiment with recipes to find the tastiest amount. You'll find stevia (SweetLeaf is a popular brand) in most grocery stores. It comes in powder and liquid form.

FOR THE LOVE
of Nog!

1 GF R SF KF Q

Serves 2

----

3 cups almond or nondairy
milk of choice

1 banana

½ teaspoon freshly grated
 nutmeg (using Microplane or
other grater)

½ tablespoon cinnamon

1 teaspoon almond extract

2 dates, pitted

You'll be the most popular and holistically swanky guest at your holiday festivities with this irresistible nog. Nutmeg is a tummy soother, making it a secret weapon while indulging. Um, unless you add booze to it. Then all bets are off—though it's still healthier than the average nog!

1   In high-speed blender, blend all ingredients until smooth.

BREAKING
the FAST

Mango *and* Coconut Millet

Tofu Country Scramble

Smoky Sweet Potato Hash

Mango-Raspberry Parfait
with Vanilla Crème

French Toast
with Amaretto Crème

Crazy Sexy Breakfast Tacos

Green "Paint"
with Assorted Fruits

Cornmeal Banana Walnut Pancakes
by CHEF FRAN COSTIGAN

Morning Glory Gluten-free
Pancake Variation
by CHEF FRAN COSTIGAN

Chickpea Crêpe (Farinata)
with Mushrooms *and* Artichokes

Cinnamon-Cherry Granola
by PETER A. CERVONI

Avo Toasts

MANGO and COCONUT
Millet

1 GF SF KF Q

Serves 4

1 cup millet or your favorite whole grain (quinoa, brown rice, or buckwheat)

1½ cups almond or nondairy milk of your choice

One 12-ounce can of coconut milk

3 tablespoons agave or sweetener of your choice

1 vanilla bean or ¾ teaspoon vanilla extract

1 cup frozen or fresh mango or peaches

A Crazy Sexy tropical twist on Mr. Quaker's favorite morning meal. Millet is a nutty, chewy grain that's chock-full of fiber and B vitamins. Plus, it's alkaline!

1   Combine millet with nondairy milk, coconut milk, agave, and vanilla bean in a medium pot. (Note: Slice the vanilla bean lengthwise and scrape out the seeds. Use the pod as well while cooking, but discard before serving.)

2   Bring to a boil, then reduce heat to low and simmer for 10 to 12 minutes (or until the millet has absorbed most of the liquid), making sure to stir occasionally to avoid quick reduction or burning.

3   Add the frozen mango or peaches. Stir.

4   Cook on low heat for 3 to 4 minutes.

5   Remove pot from heat and discard vanilla bean pod.

tip **MORNING FRUIT AND GRAIN BOWLS**   Begin your day with a swift and satisfying grain bowl. Start with your favorite grain (oatmeal, millet, quinoa) cooked with a nondairy milk of your choice. Add a little more than double the amount of milk to the amount of grain. Heartier grains such as wild rice, wheat berries, faro, and barley will absorb the milk more slowly, so you will need to adjust accordingly, adding more nondairy milk as needed while cooking. Top with dried fruits, nuts, seeds, and your favorite diced fresh fruits. Wanna spice it up? Sprinkle some cinnamon, cacao powder, stevia, or carob on top.

Tofu
COUNTRY SCRAMBLE

I GF KF Q

Serves 4

- - - - - - - - - - - - - - -

2 tablespoons olive oil

1 cup finely diced white onion

½ bunch of asparagus, tips only, cut 2 inches in length

2l ounces extra-firm tofu (1½ blocks), crumbled

¼ cup sun-dried tomatoes packed in oil, diced (or dried and softened in water)

3 tablespoons nutritional yeast

2 tablespoons wheat-free tamari

Pinch of sea salt

½ tablespoon turmeric

Freshly ground black pepper, to taste

¼ cup coarsely chopped basil

This filling dish is chock-full of cozy comfort. Serve it with Smoky Sweet Potato Hash (page 102). Turmeric gives your scramble a yellow egglike color, but more importantly contains cancer-fighting and immune-boosting properties. Feel free to swap out the suggested veggies with anything you have handy. We also love broccoli, onion, and avocado in this dish.

1   Add oil to hot sauté pan. Add onion and reduce heat to medium. Sauté until onion is translucent and golden.

2   Add asparagus, sun-dried tomatoes, and crumbled tofu, and cook on high heat for 3 minutes.

3   Add nutritional yeast, tamari, sea salt, turmeric, and black pepper. Continue to cook on medium heat for 3 to 5 minutes.

4   Right before serving, add the handful of chopped fresh basil.

tip **HOW TO PRESS TOFU**   For a firmer texture and maximum flavor, press tofu before using it (even extra-firm tofu can be pressed). Place the tofu in a colander or strainer with a small plate on top. Put a weight such as a large can or pitcher of water on the plate. Allow it to sit for 15 minutes to drain the excess water from the tofu. Once the tofu is pressed, decreasing its water content, it will act like a sponge, allowing more flavors from sauces, marinades, herbs, and spices to be absorbed.

note FROM CHAD

If you have some extra prep time, marinate the tofu to deeply intensify the flavors. Here's how: Once your tofu is pressed, crumble and mix in the turmeric, tamari, black pepper, and nutritional yeast. Allow it to sit for at least an hour, although overnight is even better.

Smoky
SWEET POTATO HASH

1 GF KF Q

Serves 4 to 6

- -

2 sweet potatoes or 3 red russet potatoes, cut into small cubes (yields about 3 cups)

½ yellow bell pepper, finely diced

½ red bell pepper, finely diced

1 small red onion, finely minced (about ½ cup)

1 pack of Lightlife Fakin' Bacon finely diced (or one 8-ounce package of smoked tofu)

2 teaspoons smoked paprika

3 tablespoons olive oil

Coarse sea salt, to taste

Freshly ground pepper, to taste

¼ cup chopped parsley

Hash aficionados will sprint to your breakfast table for a serving (or two) of this mouthwatering, smoky-flavored delight. Serve hot with Tofu Country Scramble (page 101), or wrap it with your favorite salsa and sliced avocado in a gluten-free, whole- or sprouted-grain tortilla.

1   Preheat oven to 375°F.

2   Mix all ingredients, except the parsley, in bowl by tossing with hands or two large spoons. Season to taste with salt and pepper.

3   Pour the mixture onto a baking sheet. Cook for 15 to 20 minutes, until potatoes are tender, browned, and crispy around the edges.

4   Once hash is cooked, remove from oven and sprinkle with parsley.

SMOKED PAPRIKA

Smoked paprika's robust flavor is perfect for Spanish-influenced dishes. Olé! Typically, all varieties of paprika are slightly sweet, but you can also find a hotter variety to give your dishes a bite.

MANGO-RASPBERRY
Parfait
with VANILLA CRÈME

1 GF R SF KF Q

Serves 6

- - - - - - - - - - - - - - -

VANILLA CRÈME
1 cup raw cashews, soaked in water for a few hours or overnight, to soften

One 12-ounce can of coconut milk (for raw version, blend ½ cup young Thai coconut meat with ¾ cup coconut water)

½ cup water

1 tablespoon vanilla extract or 1 vanilla bean, scraped

¼ cup agave

Sea salt, to taste

MANGO JAM
1 cup dried mangos

BUCKWHEAT CRUNCHIES
1 cup raw hulled buckwheat groats, soaked in water overnight to germinate (see tip)

½ tablespoon cinnamon

½ teaspoon sea salt

GARNISH
½ cup fresh raspberries

Mint sprigs

Parfaits are a fresh, raw way to kick off your day. They're also ideal as a light ending to your meal. Use this recipe as a blueprint for your own parfait creations. For a chocolatey pow, add a dash of cacao powder to the crème. Mix up the layers with granola or your favorite fresh fruits.

1   *Prepare Vanilla Crème:* Blend all crème ingredients in a blender. Scrape the sides of the blender with a rubber spatula while blending to ensure that the crème is silky smooth.

2   *Prepare Mango Jam:* Soak the dried mangos for 15 minutes to 1 hour in warm water to rehydrate and soften them. When they are soft, drain water and put mangos in food processor or blender. Blend until you have a thick jam consistency.

3   *Prepare Buckwheat Crunchies:* Once buckwheat is germinated and softened, strain well and rinse. Mix buckwheat, cinnamon, and sea salt in a medium bowl. Spread mixture on a dehydrator sheet and dry in dehydrator until crisp, for about 6 to 8 hours. If using oven, spread mixture on a baking sheet that is covered with a piece of parchment paper and bake on the lowest temperature until crisp, about 40 minutes.

4   *Assemble Parfaits:* Using short tumbler glasses, or glass of choice (wineglasses are très élégant), layer each parfait in the following order: Buckwheat Crunchies, fresh raspberries, Mango Jam, Vanilla Crème, Mango Jam, fresh raspberries, Buckwheat Crunchies, Vanilla Crème. Garnish with berries or fresh mango and mint sprig. Serve chilled.

tip **HOW TO GERMINATE BUCKWHEAT GROATS** To germinate buckwheat, add raw, hulled buckwheat groats to a bowl or jar with 2 to 3 times the amount of cool water. The groats will absorb most of the water within 6 to 8 hours. Once soaked, these little buggers are very starchy and the water will look a bit foggy. Don't fret. Simply pour the germinated buckwheat into a fine strainer and rinse thoroughly. The buckwheat is now ready to season and dehydrate for the Buckwheat Crunchies. You can also enjoy them as a cereal with nondairy milk.

1 SF Q

Serves 6

AMARETTO CRÈME

1 cup raw cashews, soaked for a few hours to overnight in water (to soften)

1 can coconut milk (for raw version, blend ½ cup coconut meat with 1 cup coconut water)

½ cup nondairy milk of choice

½ cup amaretto liquor

½ tablespoon vanilla extract or 1 vanilla bean, scraped

¼ cup agave

Pinch of sea salt

FRENCH TOAST

½ cup raw almond butter or cashew butter

1½ cups vanilla almond milk

¼ cup whole spelt flour

2 tablespoons nutritional yeast (optional)

1 tablespoon cinnamon

¼ cup maple syrup or date paste

¼ teaspoon nutmeg powder

½ tablespoon vanilla extract

Sea salt, to taste

Whole-grain baguette or your favorite whole-grain bread (whole-grain cinnamon raisin bread is superb as well)

3 tablespoons Earth Balance or any vegan butter

GARNISH

Fresh berries

Toasted pecans or Maple Candied Pecans (page 252, optional)

French Toast
with AMARETTO CRÈME

Morning decadence at its best—vegan-style. Simplify this recipe by skipping the Amaretto Crème and serving it with fresh berries and a bit of maple syrup. Although, if you're a sucker for anything almond-flavored, the crème is a must.

1. *Prepare Amaretto Crème:* In a high-speed blender, blend all ingredients until smooth.

2. *Prepare French Toast:* In a medium bowl, whisk the almond butter, almond milk, flour, yeast, cinnamon, maple syrup, nutmeg, vanilla, and salt to make the batter, or blend ingredients in blender until smooth. Set aside.

3. Slice the baguette or other bread in thick slices. Dip bread slices into batter. Allow each slice to sit in the batter for a minute, which helps it absorb more.

4. Add ½ tablespoon vegan butter to a flat pan, flat grill, or large saute pan on medium heat. Once melted, add battered bread slice. Add additional ½ tablespoon of vegan butter for each bread slice. (It's okay if the slices are wet with lots of batter—this is what creates the delicious crust.)

5. Cook on medium heat for 2 to 3 minutes. Flip with spatula, and cook other side until lightly golden.

6. *Serve:* Drizzle Amaretto Crème on while French Toast is still warm and top with a generous handful of fresh berries and pecans.

tip **HOW TO MAKE DATE PASTE** Blend 1 cup of pitted dates with 1 cup filtered water until a thick paste forms. The paste will keep in the fridge for two weeks. Dates add a sweet kiss to smoothies, dressings, sauces, or desserts, without adding refined sugar.

4 small whole-grain or gluten-free tortillas (gently warm over a burner or in oven for one minute)

1 cup Crazy Sexy Refried Pinto Beans (page 215) or one 16-ounce can of organic vegetarian refried beans

1 cup chopped baby spinach or romaine leaves

½ cup of your favorite salsa or Sprouted Lentil and Heirloom Salsa (page 242)

1 avocado, sliced

Hot sauce (optional)

CRAZY SEXY
Breakfast Tacos

Here's a Crazy Sexy "south of the border" delight that'll have your taste buds singing "La Bamba" in no time. Your wrap is your palette, so get creative and mix things up by pairing Tofu Country Scramble (page 101) or Smoky Sweet Potato Hash (page 102) with some crisp greens. Use corn or brown-rice tortillas with collards or romaine leaves to bring your masterpiece together in a gluten-free package.

1   Using warm tortillas as your base, layer all ingredients on top in the following order: beans, greens, salsa, avocado, and hot sauce.

2   Wrap it up and enjoy!

SUPERFOOD BENEFITS

Superfoods are packed with phytochemicals—disease-fighting chemicals found in plants. Many superfoods can be found in powdered form at health-food stores and online. Check out the Navitas Naturals website at: www.navitasnaturals.com.

Spirulina: This blue-green algae is rich in carotenoids—antioxidants that protect cells from damage. Spirulina also nourishes the body with vitamin B complex, beta-carotene, vitamin E, manganese, zinc, copper, iron, selenium, and gamma linolenic acid (an essential fatty acid).

Maca: Maca root contains certain alkaloids that benefit your endocrine system, which regulates your hormones. This is especially helpful to those who want to increase stamina and energy levels. When your endocrine system is functioning optimally, your body can adapt more easily to stress.

Mesquite: This seed-filled pod helps balance blood-sugar levels and is a good source of protein, calcium, magnesium, potassium, iron, and zinc.

Tocotrienol: Tocotrienols are part of the vitamin E family. They are a powerful antioxidant and have been shown to reduce cholesterol.

Cacao: This superfood not only gives you an energy boost, it also supplies your body with fiber, magnesium, and iron.

Green "Paint"
with ASSORTED FRUITS

1 GF R SF KF Q

Serves 2

- - - - - - - - - - - - - - - - - -

1 cup of your favorite raw nut butter (cashew or almond are great!)

3 tablespoons spirulina or your favorite green powder

¼ cup agave or sweetener of your choice (yacón, maple syrup, date paste, or stevia)

¼ cup almond milk, or nondairy milk of your choice

1 teaspoon vanilla extract

Fruits are even more tempting and tasty when dipped in this vibrant cloak of chlorophyll. For a superfoods boost, add 2 tablespoons of maca powder, mesquite meal, tocotrienols, or cacao powder.

1   Mix all ingredients in a medium bowl using a small whisk, until you have a dark green, smooth, paintlike texture.

2   Serve as a dip with your favorite sliced fruits or on whole-grain bread with fresh berries.

note FROM CHAD

While working on a film with Woody Harrelson, his wonderful wife Laura introduced me to this simple snack. Since then, I've been whipping up my take on Laura's recipe when I'm looking for a quick bite for my daughter and me.

guest chef
FRAN COSTIGAN

CORNMEAL BANANA WALNUT
Pancakes

2 SF KF Q

Serves 2 to 3

- ½ cup fresh, fine-, or medium-grind yellow cornmeal
- ¼ cup whole spelt flour, or use whole-wheat pastry flour
- ¼ cup light spelt flour, or use whole-wheat pastry flour
- 2¼ teaspoons aluminum-free baking powder
- ½ teaspoon ground cinnamon
- ⅛ teaspoon fine sea salt
- ⅔ cup to ¾ cup almond or other nondairy milk
- 2 tablespoons real maple syrup, grade B or dark amber, or use agave syrup
- 1 tablespoon extra-virgin olive oil or melted coconut oil, plus more for the griddle
- 2 teaspoons pure or non-alcoholic vanilla extract
- ½ teaspoon apple cider vinegar
- ½ cup (about ½ medium) diced banana; reserve the balance for serving
- ¼ cup lightly toasted walnuts, coarsely chopped, plus more for serving
- 2 to 3 tablespoons maple or agave syrup
- Apple cider, to taste

Pancakes made with typical white flour, white sugar, and eggs can be superheavy and flavorless. However, this whole-grain, egg-free, hearty but not heavy pancake will have you hooked at first bite. Note that pancake batter, particularly when made with whole-grain flours, tends to thicken as it sits. Add more liquid, if needed, so that the batter spreads on the hot griddle.

1 Begin heating a heavy griddle or well-seasoned cast-iron pan on low heat.

2 Place a wire mesh strainer over a medium bowl. Add the cornmeal, both of the spelt flours (or pastry flour, if using), baking powder, cinnamon, and salt to the strainer. Stir with a wire whisk to sift the ingredients into the bowl. Add any cornmeal left in the strainer into the bowl. Whisk to aerate the mixture.

3 In a separate medium bowl, whisk the almond milk, maple syrup, oil, vanilla, and apple cider vinegar until thoroughly combined. Pour into the dry mixture and stir with a silicone spatula, only until the batter is smooth. The batter may increase and thicken at this point. Wait half a minute and stir with a fork. Add a scant ½ cup of the diced banana and the nuts. Adjust the consistency of the batter if needed so that it falls off a spoon in heavy puddles.

4 Oil the griddle. Increase the heat to medium. When a few drops of water dance on the griddle, begin making the pancakes. Adjust the heat as needed to ensure the pancakes brown but don't burn.

5   Pour a scant ¼ cup of batter on the griddle, leaving about 2 inches between pancakes. Cook the first side for about 2 minutes. Resist any urge to move them. Bubbles will form on the top side of the pancakes and the edges will set. Slip a thin, flexible, wide spatula under the edges to loosen the edges, then flip. Cook the second side for about 1 minute. Don't worry; this side never cooks as evenly as the first side.

6   Top each pancake serving with some of the reserved bananas and more nuts. Warm and mix maple syrup and apple cider. Drizzle the warm syrup over the pancakes, bearing in mind that a little (1 tablespoon) is enough. Pancakes taste best when served straight from the griddle but these can be held in a low-heat (200°F) oven for 5 to 10 minutes. Cover with parchment.

Recipe contributed by pastry chef Fran Costigan, creator of The Vegan Baking Boot Camp Intensive® and is adapted from her cookbook, More Great Good Dairy-Free Desserts Naturally. *www.francostigan.com*

Morning Glory
GLUTEN-FREE PANCAKE VARIATION

guest chef
FRAN COSTIGAN

1 GF KF Q

Serves 2 to 3

9 tablespoons gluten-free all-purpose baking mix (suggestion: Bob's Red Mill All-Purpose Gluten-Free mix)

4 tablespoons fresh, fine-grind cornmeal

¾ teaspoon aluminum-free baking powder

⅛ teaspoon fine sea salt

7 tablespoons almond milk or other nondairy milk

¼ teaspoon guar gum (alternative: xanthan gum)

2 tablespoons agave or maple syrup, grade B or dark amber

1 tablespoon extra-virgin olive oil or melted coconut oil

1 teaspoon pure or non-alcoholic vanilla extract

¼ teaspoon apple cider vinegar

¼ cup diced banana, plus more for serving

¼ cup chopped nuts, plus more for serving

2 to 3 tablespoons maple or agave syrup

Apple cider, to taste

Gluten-free does not mean pancake-free. While as scrumptious, delicious, and easy to make as the preceding wheat-flour pancakes, the gluten-free variety does not hold or reheat well. Make these à la minute—griddle to plate is the rule.

1   Whisk the dry ingredients (baking mix, cornmeal, baking powder, and salt) in a medium bowl. Set aside.

2   Mix the almond milk and guar gum thoroughly in a separate small bowl. Add the rest of the ingredients (except for the topping). Whisk until foamy. Pour into the dry mixture and whisk until combined. Let the batter rest for 10 minutes. Preheat the griddle.

3   Pour a scant ¼ cup of batter on the griddle, leaving about 2 inches between pancakes. Cook the first side for about 2 minutes. Resist any urge to move them. Bubbles will form on the top side of the pancakes and the edges will set. Slip a thin, flexible, wide spatula under the edges to loosen the edges, then flip. Cook the second side for about 1 minute. Don't worry; this side never cooks as evenly as the first.

4   Top each pancake serving with some of the reserved bananas and more nuts. Warm and mix maple syrup and apple cider. Drizzle the warm syrup o--- the pancakes, bearing in mind that a little (1 tablespoon) ---- ugh.

Recipe contribute--- ---f Fran Costigan, creator of The Vegan Baking Boot Cam--- ---and is adapted from her cookbook, More Great Good Dairy-Free Desserts Naturally. *www.francostigan.com*

Chickpea Crêpe (Farinata)
with MUSHROOMS and ARTICHOKES

2 GF KF

Serves 4 to 5

ARTICHOKE AIOLI

1 cup raw cashews, soaked in water for 4 or more hours to soften

⅛ cup water, to blend

1 tablespoon olive oil

1½ teaspoons apple cider vinegar

2¼ teaspoons lemon juice

1½ teaspoons agave

1 clove garlic

½ teaspoon sea salt

¼ cup jarred artichoke hearts, coarsely chopped

2 tablespoons chopped tarragon

2 tablespoons chopped parsley

1½ tablespoons minced shallot

1 tablespoon lemon zest

FARINATA BATTER

1½ cups water

½ cup olive oil

1 teaspoon sea salt

Freshly ground black pepper, to taste

1⅓ cups chickpea flour

2 tablespoons chopped fresh rosemary

This is the Crazy Sexy version of Italy's popular chickpea crêpe—one of Chad's most popular brunch items in his European restaurants. Chickpea flour is gluten-free and particularly high in folate. Folate helps our bodies produce and maintain new cells, making it especially important for pregnant ladies and their growing babes.

1   *Prepare Artichoke Aioli:* In a high-speed blender, blend cashews, water, olive oil, vinegar, lemon juice, agave, garlic, and salt until smooth. Add water as needed to reach desired thick, mayo-type consistency. Move mixture to bowl and whisk in artichoke hearts, tarragon, parsley, shallots, and lemon zest.

2   Preheat the oven to 300°F.

3   *Prepare Farinata Batter:* In a blender, combine water with the oil, salt, pepper, and chickpea flour. Blend until smooth. Add more flour, if necessary, until the mixture is the consistency of pancake batter. Lastly add the fresh rosemary and pulse, to ensure there are pieces of rosemary scattered in the batter. Set aside.

4   *Prepare Roasted Tomatoes:* Put the tomatoes and thyme on a baking dish and drizzle with a bit of oil. Season with salt and pepper to taste, and toss to lightly coat the tomatoes. Roast in oven for about 10 minutes, until the tomato skins crack.

5   *Prepare Mushrooms:* Place a large sauté pan over medium heat. Melt the vegan butter, being careful not to let it burn. Add the mushrooms and garlic and sauté until the mushrooms have released their liquid and the pan is almost dry, about 4 minutes. Gently stir in the chives and remove from the heat.

6   *Prepare Farinata:* Place a crêpe pan or griddle over medium heat and add enough vegan butter to lightly coat the bottom. Ladle about ¾ cup of the Farinata Batter into the center of the pan. Tilt the pan to spread the batter into a thin circle. The crêpe should be thinner than a pancake in order to be able to fold it later. Cook until golden brown on the bottom, about 3 to 4 minutes, then flip it over and brown the other side. Set aside on a plate and cover to keep warm while you cook the remaining crêpes, using the rest of the batter and more vegan butter as necessary. Remember when making crêpes, it's very common for the first one or two to not turn out so well while the pan is heating to the right temperature.

7   *Serve:* Cover half of each crêpe with a heaping spoonful of the Mushrooms, drizzle with 2 tablespoons of the Artichoke Aioli, and then fold it closed. Garnish with a dollop of Artichoke Aioli, some Roasted Tomatoes, and freshly ground black pepper. Serve immediately.

ROASTED TOMATOES

8 ounces cherry tomatoes (on-the-vine is best)

3 sprigs fresh thyme

1 tablespoon olive oil

Sea salt, to taste

Freshly ground black pepper, to taste

MUSHROOMS

2 tablespoons Earth Balance or other vegan butter

1½ cups loosely packed wild mushrooms, preferably chanterelles, or baby bellas

2 garlic cloves, minced

2 tablespoons minced fresh chives

note **FROM CHAD**

I first worked with this recipe during the relaunch of Counter Restaurant in NYC, and have used variations of it in just about all of my restaurants. The farinata is a traditional Italian flatbread, usually served as a crispy baked snack. To make: Preheat oven to 400°F. In a well-seasoned cast-iron pan, pour in batter about 1-inch thick and bake for 25 to 30 minutes until golden and crisp. Sprinkle with coarse sea salt before serving. This is also a great gluten-free pizza crust.

AIOLI

Traditionally, aioli is a garlic-flavored mayonnaise made of egg yolk, oil, garlic, and seasonings. In the Crazy Sexy Kitchen we've dumped the eggs, but kept all the rich, buttery, garlicky flavors! Check out the Dressings (page 224) section for some exciting spins on basic aioli.

guest chef
PETER A. CERVONI

CINNAMON-CHERRY
Granola

2 GF R SF KF

Serves 8 to 10

- - - - - - - - - - - - - - - - -

1½ cups buckwheat groats, soaked in water

1½ cups sunflower seeds, soaked in water

¾ cup pumpkin seeds, soaked in water

¾ cup hemp seeds, soaked in water

¾ cup almonds, soaked in water

¾ cup pecans, soaked in water

¼ teaspoon sea salt

2½ cups coconut sugar (alternatives: Sucanat, maple sugar, Florida crystals, or date sugar)

1 cup lucuma powder

¼ cup coconut flour

2 tablespoons cinnamon powder

½ tablespoon vanilla powder

1 tablespoon almond flavor (not extract)

2 cups cherries, tart (no added sugar, oil, or sulfites)

You've got to love the versatility and portability of granola: while it makes a terrific sit-down breakfast food, it doubles as a great anytime snack. This granola has loads of protein, good fats, fiber, and minerals. It goes nicely with some homemade hemp milk or even some freshly made coconut milk or coconut yogurt.

1 Place buckwheat groats in a bowl with enough water to cover by several inches. Soak groats for a minimum of 6 hours or overnight. Leave covered in a cool, dry place.

2 Drain and rinse the buckwheat well. Place on a dehydrator sheet and dehydrate for at least 12 hours, until the buckwheat is light, crisp, and devoid of any water or moisture. Use as many dehydrator trays as you need to give them each some "personal space"! When crispy, place in an airtight container and leave in a cool, dry place. Reserve for the next step.

3 Soak all remaining nuts and seeds in enough filtered water to cover. Let the nuts and seeds soak for a minimum of 6 hours and then drain and rinse well.

4 Combine soaked nuts and seeds along with the dehydrated buckwheat and the remaining ingredients, and mix well to ensure they're well coated with seasonings.

5 Place granola mixture on dehydrating trays without a Teflex sheet and dehydrate for a minimum of 18 hours or until super crunchy.

6 After about 4 hours, take trays out and break up large clumps to ensure proper dehydration.

7 You can repeat the last step in another 4 hours to make a smaller "grain" or leave the granola in medium-size clusters. It's completely up to your taste.

tip **ALMOND FLAVOR** The almond flavor is completely optional. If you do opt for this ingredient, make sure it is labeled "flavor," not "extract." Extract is in a carrier base of alcohol, and because we're not baking this granola the alcohol never evaporates and can leave a weird, off-putting flavor.

Avo TOASTS

1 SF KF Q

Serves 1

2 slices of your favorite whole or sprouted grain bread, lightly toasted

½ avocado

½ lime

Red pepper flakes, to taste

Coarse sea salt, to taste

Freshly ground black pepper, to taste

Also known as "earth's butter," velvety avocados add richness to your toast, and their heart-healthy fats will keep you satisfied till lunch. This is a favorite breakfast at Chez Carr-Fassett (my hubby loves it!).

1   Toast bread slices. Slice a ripe avocado in half. Squeeze the meat of the avocado onto the toasted bread and spread it evenly.

2   Cut a lime in half and gently squeeze the juice over the avocado on your slices of toast.

3   Sprinkle red pepper flakes, sea salt, and black pepper to taste.

tip **TOAST TOPPERS** Top your toast with your favorite additions such as: sun-dried tomatoes, Semi-Dried Tomatoes (page 213), thinly sliced cucumbers, cilantro, sprouts, roasted red pepper, sliced olives, sliced fresh chilies, or Sprouted Lentil and Heirloom Salsa (page 242).

SOUPS and STEWS

1½ tablespoons cumin seeds

1 tablespoon coriander seeds

2 tablespoons olive oil

½ red serrano or cayenne pepper

1 small white onion, finely diced

1½ cups red lentils

4 to 5 cups vegetable stock (or water)

One 12-ounce can coconut milk

2 tablespoons minced or grated (not zested) fresh ginger

½ tablespoon black pepper

½ tablespoon sea salt

2 tablespoons lemon zest (1 lemon rind)

2 lemons, juiced (or 5 tablespoons bottled lemon juice)

½ bunch fresh cilantro, chopped, plus more for garnish

Avocado, diced (optional)

COCONUT and RED LENTIL Soup

Thirty percent of the calories in lentils come from protein, which our bodies use to build and repair tissues (pretty important!). This recipe is a creamy, spicy spin on classic Indian dal. Enjoy with a slice of gluten-free or whole-grain seeded bread.

1 Toast cumin and coriander seeds in dry pot on medium heat for 2 minutes until you smell the robust aromas. (This process releases the full flavor of the spices.)

2 Add the olive oil, pepper, and onion. Stir consistently until the onion is golden and translucent.

3 Add the next 6 ingredients.

4 Put on low heat, stir well, and cover. Allow to cook for about 30 to 35 minutes, stirring occasionally, until the lentils have "melted," meaning that they have lost their round shape and have softened. You may need to add more water to get the desired thickness.

5 When soup is done, add the lemon zest, lemon juice, and chopped cilantro.

6 Remove from heat and serve with diced avocado, if using, and cilantro leaves.

COOKING TIME-SAVER

Cut the cooking time in half for the red lentils by soaking them overnight in water. Strain the lentils and discard the soaking water. You can apply this technique to any bean or grain.

CRAZY SEXY
Bean Chili

1 GF SF Q

Serves 8

1½ tablespoons cumin seeds

2 tablespoons olive oil

1 white onion, diced

3 garlic cloves, minced

1 jalapeño, finely diced (for less heat, remove seeds and/or use half the pepper)

2 tablespoons chili powder

1½ cups ground seitan (alternatives: crumbled tempeh [wheat-free] or finely diced mushrooms [soy-free])

1 zucchini, diced

½ cup diced potato (any kind)

Two 15-ounce cans of black beans, rinsed

One 15-ounce can of kidney beans, rinsed

One 14-ounce can of crushed tomatoes (San Marzano recommended)

2 cups water

2 tablespoons maple syrup

1 teaspoon sea salt

½ bunch of fresh cilantro

1 cup kale, chopped

Diced avocado (optional)

Fresh cilantro (optional)

This crowd-pleaser is a go-to dish for potlucks, football-watching shindigs, and no-stress weeknight dinners. Serve over brown rice and pair with a heaping side of steamed greens and corn tortillas. Cumin's nutty, peppery flavor is popular in Mexican and Indian cuisines. Chili powder contains a unique blend of paprika, onion, garlic, oregano, and cayenne, giving your chili the traditional flavor that keeps you coming back for more. Don't sub it out for cayenne alone!

1 Toast cumin seeds in dry soup pot on medium heat, for 2 minutes until you smell the robust aroma. (This process releases the full flavor of the spice.)

2 Add the olive oil, onion, garlic, and jalapeño. Stir consistently until the onion is golden and translucent.

3 Add in the chili powder, seitan, zucchini, and potato, and stir well. Sauté for 3 to 4 minutes, stirring to avoid sticking.

4 Add in black beans, kidney beans, tomatoes, water, maple syrup, sea salt, and cilantro. Cover with a lid, reduce heat to low, and allow to cook for 20 to 25 minutes, or until the potatoes are tender.

5 Remove from heat, and stir in the kale.

6 Serve hot. Garnish with diced avocado and a handful of cilantro, if using.

Vegan
"CLAM" CHOWDER

2 GF SF KF

Serves 12

CASHEW CREAM

4 cups whole raw cashews, rinsed under cold water

KOMBU BROTH

4 pieces kombu seaweed (about 5 by 8 inches)

2 quarts water

SMOKED MUSHROOMS

1 tablespoon small hickory chips

1 heaping cup diced king trumpet mushrooms

CHOWDER ASSEMBLY

1 tablespoon canola oil

1 cup diced white onion

½ cup diced celery

1 cup peeled and diced baking potato

2½ to 3 cups water

1 teaspoon lemon juice, more to taste

½ teaspoon Tabasco or other hot sauce, more to taste

2 teaspoons kosher salt, more to taste

1 teaspoon black pepper, more to taste

Chef Tal developed this clam slam-dunk of a chowder for Lakeside, a seafood restaurant at the Wynn hotel in Las Vegas. A bowl of this soup brings the New England shore to your table.

1   *Prepare Cashew Cream:* Put the cashews in a bowl and cover with water. Cover with plastic wrap and refrigerate to soak overnight.

2   Drain the cashews and rinse under cold water. Place the cashews in a high-speed blender (this will need to be done in a couple of batches) and add enough water to cover by an inch. Purée until completely smooth. If needed, pass the cashew purée through a fine strainer to remove any coarse bits; the final "cream" should have the smooth, thick consistency of heavy dairy cream. This makes about 3 cups cream (consistency will depend on the amount of water added while blending, and can vary from just over 2 cups to about 3½ cups; thin as desired).

3   *Prepare Kombu Broth:* Combine the kombu and water in a medium pot and bring to a simmer. Reduce the heat to a gentle simmer and cook 40 minutes, then strain. This makes about 5 cups kombu broth, more than is needed for the remainder of the recipe. The broth will keep, covered and refrigerated, up to 10 days.

4   *Prepare Smoked Mushrooms:* Prepare a stovetop smoker: Spread the chips in the base of the smoker, directly over the burner. Place the drip pan (if using) over the chips, and a rack on top of the drip pan. Place the diced mushrooms on the rack (be sure to use a rack fine enough so the mushrooms don't fall through) indirectly over the chips (do not place the mushrooms directly over the chips, as this can cause them to oversmoke and turn bitter). Partially cover the smoker with a lid, leaving it open a couple of inches. (If you do not have a commercial stovetop smoker, you can substitute by using a heavy roasting pan, a cake rack, and heavy-duty foil to cover the pan as a lid.)

5   Heat the smoker over medium heat just until you see smoke escaping through the opening. Close the smoker entirely and gently smoke just to infuse the mushrooms with smoke flavor, not to cook, 3 to 5 minutes. Be careful not to oversmoke, or the mushrooms will become bitter.

6   *Assemble Chowder:* Heat the oil in a medium-size soup pot over medium-high heat. Add the onion, celery, and potato. Sweat the ingredients, stirring frequently, until softened, 8 to 10 minutes.

7   Add 1½ cups each of the Kombu Broth, Cashew Cream, and Smoked Mushrooms. Reduce the heat, and cook over low heat, stirring frequently, for 10 to 15 minutes to develop and marry the flavors. The Cashew Cream will thicken as it cooks, and you will need to add water from time to time to thin and adjust the consistency. We added about 3 cups water as the soup cooked.

8   Season with the lemon juice, Tabasco, salt, and pepper. Taste and adjust the seasonings as desired. This makes a generous 2 quarts of soup.

tip **SMOKER SMARTS** This recipe calls for a commercial stovetop smoker, but a heavy-duty roasting pan with a rack and lid can be substituted. This recipe also recommends using small hardwood hickory chips or shavings. The chips are available at select cooking stores and are widely available online. Kombu (dried seaweed) is available at Asian markets and well-stocked supermarkets.

STORING SOUPS & STEWS

Crazy Sexy soups and stews are freezer-friendly. Make a double batch, freeze half (using smaller meal-size containers), and you'll always have a meal that's only a thaw away. Don't fill the container to the tippy top, since the soup/stew will expand when frozen. CSK's soups and stews will keep for about one week in the fridge.

Pumpkin
BISQUE

When this recipe hit *The New York Times* during the holiday season, letters poured in from satisfied soup-makers across the country. Bright orange veggies like pumpkin, butternut squash, and sweet potato contain high levels of beta-carotene, which is a well-known cancer- and disease-fighter. This autumnal celebration in a bowl is sure to win praise and encourage second helpings!

1   Steam or boil the pumpkin (or squash or potatoes) until tender. Set aside.

2   Sauté onions on medium heat in olive oil until translucent.

3   Blend pumpkin, garlic, onions, and next 7 ingredients until smooth in a high-speed blender.

4   Transfer the blended soup to a medium soup pot and place on low-medium heat.

5   Serve warm with garnish of toasted pumpkin seeds and a drizzle of toasted pumpkin-seed oil.

tip **ROASTING GARLIC** Preheat oven to 400°F. Slice off the top end of a bulb of garlic, cutting off tips of garlic cloves, but leave the bulb intact. Place garlic bulb on a piece of tin foil, large enough to wrap the entire head. Drizzle a teaspoon of olive oil over the garlic and wrap in the foil. Place garlic on a baking sheet. Bake in oven for 20 to 25 minutes or until garlic is golden brown. Once roasted, let cool, then the cloves will easily slide out of their skins. Check out the Roasted Herby Goodness recipe (page 230) for an alternative method.

1 GF SF KF Q

Serves 4 to 6

2 cups pumpkin, butternut squash, or sweet potato, peeled and cubed

1½ cups diced white onions

2 tablespoons olive oil

5 cloves roasted garlic (see tip)

3 cups vegetable stock

1½ tablespoons maple syrup

½ teaspoon cinnamon

¼ teaspoon cayenne

¼ cup sherry wine

½ teaspoon sea salt

Freshly ground black pepper, to taste

¼ cup toasted pumpkin seeds (optional)

Drizzle of toasted pumpkin-seed oil (optional)

Split Pea Soup
with DULSE *and* KALE

1 GF SF

Serves 8

2 tablespoons olive oil

1 white onion, diced

4 cloves garlic, minced

3 stalks celery, diced

2 carrots, diced

1½ cups dry split peas

6 cups vegetable stock, no or low sodium

2 tablespoons minced thyme

¼ cup chopped parsley

3 tablespoons nutritional yeast

½ tablespoon sea salt

½ tablespoon coarse black pepper

½ teaspoon red pepper flakes

1½ cups finely shredded kale

¼ cup whole-leaf dulse seaweed, ripped into 1-inch pieces (applewood-smoked preferred)

Fresh parsley (optional)

Lemon wedges (optional)

Gluten-free or whole-grain bread (optional)

This cruelty-free version of split pea soup will take the chill out of any day. In case you don't have access to applewood-smoked dulse—purple seaweed that is filled with minerals, vitamins, and protein—use smoky tempeh bacon or smoked tofu, or a teaspoon of smoked paprika.

1   Heat oil in soup pot on medium heat. Add onion and cook until translucent and golden.

2   Add garlic, celery, and carrots, and continue to stir for a few minutes to sauté slightly.

3   Add split peas, vegetable stock, thyme, parsley, nutritional yeast, sea salt, black pepper, and red pepper flakes. Bring to a simmer, cover, and allow to cook for 45 to 50 minutes, stirring occasionally.

4   When split peas begin to lose their shape, add kale and dulse. Remove from heat and cover. Allow the kale to steam and flavors to settle for 5 minutes before serving.

5   Garnish with fresh parsley and lemon wedge and serve with your favorite bread.

tip **TOASTING NUTS, SEEDS, AND WHOLE SPICES**
This easy extra step will release the natural oils in nuts and seeds, deepening their flavors. Add them to a dry pan on medium heat. Shake or stir the nuts/seeds continuously, until their color has darkened and you can smell their irresistible aromas. Don't let them sit! Those little buggers will burn quickly if neglected.

WILD MUSHROOM, GINGER, *and* MINTED BRUSSELS Pho Show

guest chef
DEREK SARNO

1 KF

Serves 4

- - - - - - - - - - - - - - - - - -

1 tablespoon olive oil or spray oil

½ onion, diced

1 pound Brussels sprouts, trimmed

4 cups low-sodium vegetable broth

1 tablespoon fresh grated ginger

4 ounces shiitake mushrooms, thinly sliced

4 ounces wild mushroom mix (French horns, Maitake, Hon Shimeji)

1 large portobello mushroom, cubed

8 ounces white button mushrooms, quartered

3 heads baby bok choy, chopped

One 5-ounce can baby corn, drained and halved (juice reserved)

One 14-ounce can water chestnuts, sliced (juice reserved)

5 tablespoons light soy sauce

1 star anise

3 limes, juiced

4 tablespoons finely chopped mint

2 tablespoons sesame oil

This feisty flavored pho, which is a Vietnamese noodle soup, will have your buddies begging for another bowl (and the recipe!). Slice the variety of mushrooms in different ways for added texture and appeal. Serve with your favorite brown-rice, buckwheat, or rice noodles.

1   Heat oil in large pot on stove top, on medium high. Add the onion and whole Brussels sprouts and sear for 1 minute, splashing with vegetable broth to slightly steam and blanch.

2   Add ginger and all the mushrooms, mixing together.

3   Add remaining vegetable broth, cooking the mushrooms down a bit and stirring frequently.

4   Add baby bok choy, baby corn, water chestnuts, soy sauce, and star anise. Bring to a slow simmering boil for a few minutes at most.

5   Before serving, remove star anise and add lime juice, mint, and sesame oil to finish. Serve over your favorite grain or noodles!

Miso Soup
with SHIITAKE
and COCONUT NOODLES

1 GF R Q

Serves 4 to 6

- - - - - - - - - - - - - - - - - - - -

2½ tablespoons
dark barley miso

4½ cups coconut water
(or filtered water)

1 tablespoon wheat-free tamari

1 tablespoon toasted sesame oil

2 cloves garlic

1½ tablespoons
chopped fresh ginger

1½ tablespoons chopped
lemongrass

1 carrot, julienned thin

¼ cup snow peas, julienned thin

¼ cup finely diced
red bell pepper

¼ cup shiitake mushrooms,
soaked in water to soften,
stems removed and julienned

⅓ cup coconut meat, julienned
thin to noodle size

2 tablespoons finely diced
spring onion

This warm yet still raw soup is perfect when you want to take the chill out of your day without sacrificing the enzymes in your food. Lemongrass is a Southeast Asian grass with a citrusy taste, often used in Thai dishes. Serve over any combination of veggies and you've got a main course. Partner with Sushi Maki (page 143) and Root Rice (page 145) for a heavenly meal.

1 In high-speed blender, blend the miso, coconut water, tamari, sesame oil, garlic, ginger, and lemongrass until liquefied.

2 Slowly pour the mixture through a fine mesh strainer in an even stream, to avoid creating foam.

3 Combine and mix all veggies, mushrooms, and coconut meat with soup.

4 Add everything to a small soup pot and heat on low (the soup should be warm to the touch, but never simmer to ensure it is kept raw, which preserves enzymes).

tip **CUCKOO FOR COCONUTS** If you can't rustle up a young Thai coconut, simply sub out the coconut water for canned coconut water or filtered water. You can also replace the coconut meat with julienned zucchini noodles. (See box on page 182.)

MARVELOUS MISO

Miso is a fermented bean or grain that has a thick, pasty consistency and is most commonly used in soups, sauces, and spreads. Miso's fermentation produces microflora, which aids digestion. It's also rich in B vitamins, enzymes, and essential amino acids (protein!). There are more than a thousand kinds of miso made in Japan, with just as many flavors and ages. You'll find salty, smoky, sweet, and bitter flavors. Yum!

guest chef
PETER A. CERVONI

Red Thai
COCONUT SOUP

2 GF R SF

Serves 4

- - - - - - - - - - - - - - - - - - -

1 to 2 young Thai coconuts, or 1 cup coconut meat and 2½ cups coconut water

½ tablespoon fresh lime juice

1 cup diced red bell pepper

1 medium-size clove fresh garlic

½ teaspoon minced fresh ginger

1 tablespoon paprika powder

1 tablespoon yellow miso

¼ teaspoon sea salt

⅛ teaspoon cayenne powder

1 tablespoon coconut sugar (alternatives: Sucanat, maple sugar, Florida crystals, or date sugar)

⅛ teaspoon minced fresh kaffir lime leaves (see tip)

2 tablespoons thinly sliced scallions (optional)

2 tablespoons roughly chopped cilantro (optional)

This creamy and satisfying soup has a slight umami tang from the miso and a fragrant floral essence from the kaffir lime. Now you can skip the fish sauce used in traditional Thai soup and keep all the exotic flavor!

1   Carefully open Thai coconuts and separate the meat from the water. Strain the water to remove any shell particles and gently clean the coconut meat with a paring knife to remove any pieces of shell.

2   Place all ingredients, with the exception of the scallion and cilantro garnish, into a high-speed blender such as a Vitamix. Blend on high, for about 20 to 30 seconds, until you achieve a creamy, smooth, and wonderfully red soup. There should be no sign of fat droplets from the coconut meat. If this is the case, blend the soup a little while longer.

3   Fold in the scallions and cilantro and serve!

tip **KAFFIR LIME LEAVES** Kaffir lime leaves are usually available in the refrigerated produce sections of high-end supermarket chains. You may also find them at Indian spice shops. Use the leaves very sparingly. A little goes a long way and a bit too much will turn this soup south!

SANDWICHES and WRAPS

2 cups Cashew Cream Cheese
(page 237)

6 whole-wheat or gluten-free
wraps

¼ cup capers or caper berries,
strained and rinsed

½ cup sun-dried tomatoes,
julienned (if sun-dried tomatoes are too hard, soak them in
hot water for a couple minutes
to soften)

1½ cups baby arugula or baby
spinach

Mediterranean Wrap
with CASHEW CREAM CHEESE

The Mediterranean flair of these wraps comes from sun-dried tomatoes and capers—pickled flower buds of the caper bush, also known as little treasure troves of salty goodness.

1   Place a small scoop of approximately ⅓ cup Cashew Cream Cheese at the center of each wrap and spread evenly.

2   Top with capers, sun-dried tomatoes, and baby arugula.

3   Tuck in the sides of each wrap and roll firmly. Slice in half and serve.

FRUIT and ALMOND
Sandwiches

½ cup raw almond or
cashew butter

1 cup fresh berries

1 banana, thinly sliced

8 pieces whole-grain or
gluten-free bread

¼ cup date paste (see tip on
page 105)

Sprinkling of cinnamon

Check out this tasty upgrade on a childhood lunchbox favorite. Using fresh berries and date paste keeps unwanted refined sugar out of your kid's sandwich, while adding fiber and antioxidants to fight classroom germ fests.

1   Spread the nut butter, berries, and sliced banana on one slice of bread.

2   Spread the date paste and a sprinkling of cinnamon on another slice.

3   Press together and cut in half. Repeat for remaining sandwiches.

guest chef
PAM BROWN

1 GF KF Q

SF *if not using soy sauce*

Serves 4 to 6

----

1 sweet potato, peeled and cut into small 1-inch chunks (about 1 cup)

2 tablespoons canola oil, plus more for sautéing, plus canola spray

Pinch of salt

½ cup finely diced onion

2 cups cooked black beans or one 16-ounce can black beans, rinsed and drained

1 cup cooked brown rice

2 cloves garlic, minced

½ tablespoon ground cumin

1 teaspoon chili powder (optional)

½ teaspoon salt

3 tablespoons tamari

2 teaspoons vegan Worcestershire sauce (optional)

⅛ cup cornmeal

4 whole-wheat buns, toasted

1 tomato, sliced (optional)

1 onion, sliced (optional)

Lettuce (optional)

BLACK BEAN
and ROASTED SWEET POTATO
Burger

These flavor-packed burgers can be eaten on a bun or served as a croquette for an entrée with a salad for dinner. Top the burger with Green Chile Guacamole (page 231) and Sprouted Lentil and Heirloom Salsa (page 242) for even more deliciousness. Make extra and freeze them for a quick meal.

1   Preheat oven to 425°F.

2   Place the potato, 1 tablespoon canola oil, and salt in a bowl and mix well. Spray a small baking pan with oil, and spread the sweet potato out in an even layer. Roast for 20 to 25 minutes or until tender, stirring frequently.

3   Warm a small sauté pan and add remaining tablespoon of oil and the onion. Sauté until the onion is browned, about 5 minutes.

4   Pulse the next 9 ingredients together with the roasted sweet potato and onion in a food processor or stand mixer, being careful not to overmix. Taste for seasoning, then cool in the fridge. Remove after chilled and form six 6-ounce patties.

5   Warm a cast-iron skillet or other heavy pan. Spray pan with canola or olive oil and spray the burgers lightly. Brown both sides.

6   Serve on toasted buns and top with your favorite veggies.

Serves 6

Two 14-ounce packages of firm tofu

¾ cup Vegenaise or Cashew Aioli (page 240)

3 tablespoons finely diced green onions

¼ cup grated carrot

3 tablespoons finely chopped parsley

3 tablespoons finely chopped cilantro

3 tablespoons nutritional yeast

1 tablespoon Dijon mustard

1½ tablespoons curry powder

½ teaspoon sea salt

½ teaspoon black pepper

6 whole-grain tortillas (alternatives: sprouted or gluten-free)

1½ cups watercress or baby arugula

1 tomato, thinly sliced

CURRIED NADA-EGG *with* WATERCRESS Wraps

If you're transitioning to a plant-powered diet, our excellent eggless salad will squelch any cravings you might have for this classic salad-sammie combo. Watercress greens are bursting with beneficial nutrients, including vitamins A and C, beta-carotene, calcium, and folate. And did you know that it grows mostly in spring-fed streams? Cool!

1   Crumble tofu with your hands in a bowl.

2   Add Vegenaise, green onions, carrot, parsley, cilantro, nutritional yeast, Dijon mustard, curry powder, salt, and pepper, and mix thoroughly.

3   Place generous amount of tofu salad in the center of each wrap. Top with watercress and sliced tomatoes.

4   Tuck in the sides of the wraps and roll firmly. Slice in half, and serve.

WRAPPING UP LEFTOVERS

Want a quick meal? Wrap it! Wraps are like hugs for your veggies. Just remember to keep your favorite whole-grain or gluten-free varieties handy. Store a bunch in the freezer and heat them in a skillet or warm in the oven when needed. Wraps are also a fantastic way to repurpose your leftovers. Waste not; want not. Brush your wrap with tasty spreads like Green Chile Guacamole (page 231), tahini, Hummus Two Ways (page 243), your favorite dressing, or even a dab of Vegenaise. Top with greens du jour, wrap 'em up, and voilà!

Pita PIZZAS

1 SF KF Q

Serves 4

1 teaspoon olive oil

4 whole-grain pitas

1 cup Nana's Marinara (page 229) or your favorite jar of organic tomato sauce

1 zucchini, sliced paper-thin

1 tomato, thinly sliced

1 cup chopped baby spinach

1 cup Daiya cheese, or other nondairy cheese

Sprinkling of dried oregano (or fresh, minced)

Kids will jump at the chance to prepare and devour these easy-peasy pizzas. Add any thinly sliced or shredded veggies as toppings (or get stealthy and bury them under the cheese). The words "nutritious" and "pizza" can finally be used in tandem.

1   Preheat oven to 375°F.

2   Place the pitas on a lightly oiled baking sheet. Spread an even layer of sauce, followed by zucchini, tomatoes, and baby spinach on each pita.

3   Top the pitas with an even layer of Daiya cheese and a sprinkling of oregano.

4   Bake for 8 to 10 minutes.

5   Allow to cool for a minute. Slice and serve.

Hummus PINWHEELS

1 KF Q

GF *if using gluten-free wrap*

Serves 4

4 large whole-grain tortillas or gluten-free wraps

¾ cup Hummus Two Ways (page 243)

1 cup chopped baby spinach or butter lettuce

1 cucumber, peeled and thinly sliced

¼ cup sliced kalamata olives

½ cup thinly sliced roasted red peppers

Sea salt, to taste

One of the best ways to educate young'uns on healthy eating is to involve them in food prep. CSK's hummus spread can be made with white beans, which stabilize blood sugar and will give your kids—and you—long-lasting energy.

1   Lay out each tortilla. Spread hummus on the tortilla, and be sure to leave about half an inch around all the edges.

2   Add baby spinach, cucumber, kalamata olives, and roasted red pepper in an even layer across most of the tortilla, and sprinkle with sea salt.

3   Roll and slice in half. For bite-size snacks, roll tightly and slice each wrap into 8 to 10 pinwheel pieces. Enjoy!

CRAZY SEXY
Veggie
QUESADILLA

1 SF KF Q

GF *if using corn tortillas*

Serves 4 to 5

---

1 avocado, cubed

One 15-ounce can of black beans, strained and rinsed well (or Crazy Sexy Refried Pinto Beans, page 215)

4 green onions, diced

1 jalapeño, minced (optional)

½ cup chopped cilantro

2 teaspoons olive oil or spray oil

1 cup thinly sliced crimini mushrooms (or mushrooms of your choice)

Sea salt, to taste

Freshly ground black pepper, to taste

8 to 10 whole-wheat or corn tortillas

1 red bell pepper, roasted or raw, diced

1 cup Daiya cheese or Cashew Cream Cheese, page 237

Who doesn't love a hot, cheesy quesadilla? Create a fiesta in your mouth with this yummy appetizer, by serving it with Sprouted Lentil and Heirloom Salsa (page 242) and Green Chile Guacamole (page 231).

1   Combine the avocado, black beans, green onions, jalapeño, and cilantro in a bowl. Mash with a fork to make a coarse purée.

2   In small sauté pan, add 1 teaspoon olive oil and sauté the mushrooms. Finish with pinch of sea salt and pepper. Set aside.

3   Cover half of tortillas with the avocado-bean mix.

4   Top with cooked mushrooms, diced pepper, and an even layer of Daiya cheese (if using Cashew Cream Cheese, spread an even layer on the tortilla that will top the quesadilla). Cover with the remaining tortillas.

5   Warm a sauté pan on medium heat. Drizzle 1 teaspoon oil, or spray an even coating of oil in the pan. Place quesadilla in pan. Press with a spatula and cook for 2 to 3 minutes, or until golden. Carefully flip and do the same on other side.

6   Slice each quesadilla into 6 to 8 pieces and serve.

SAVE THE
Tuna Salad
on RYE

1 SF KF Q

GF *if using gluten-free bread*

R *if using collard or cabbage leaf as wrap*

Serves 4

1 cup raw almonds, soaked for a few hours or overnight in water

1 cup sunflower seeds, soaked for a few hours or overnight in water

⅓ cup minced celery

¼ cup minced red onion

⅓ cup pickles, diced (Bubbies Pickles are best)

2 tablespoons minced dill

1 tablespoon minced oregano

3 tablespoons lemon juice

1 tablespoon agave

2 tablespoons kelp granules (optional)

½ teaspoon sea salt

Freshly ground black pepper, to taste

Dijon mustard

4 pieces whole-grain rye bread, toasted

4 to 6 butter lettuce leaves

1 vine-ripened tomato, sliced

The combination of the pickles, celery, onions, and lots of black pepper will tickle traditional tuna lovers. For a deep-sea sensation, replace the rye bread with nori (hello, minerals!). This recipe is also delish on top of greens or in a pressed/grilled sandwich with Daiya cheese.

1   Blend the soaked almonds and sunflower seeds in a food processor until finely minced (the finer the better). Transfer into a bowl.

2   Add the celery, onion, pickles, herbs, lemon juice, agave, kelp, salt, and pepper to nut/seed mixture and stir thoroughly. Set aside.

3   Spread Dijon mustard on rye bread. Add butter lettuce and tomato.

4   Using an ice cream scoop or large spoon, scoop a generous helping of "tuna" on each slice of bread.

5   Finish with more black pepper, lettuce, and tomato.

SENSUAL STARTERS

Cucumber Cups *with* Olive Tapenade

Vegetable Sushi Maki Rolls

Crostini *with* Artichoke Purée,
Garlicky Mushrooms, *and* Horseradish

Sesame Root Rice

Truffled Edamame Dumplings
with Shallot Broth

Hearts-of-Palm-Style Crab Cakes
with Rémoulade
by TAL RONNEN

Walnut Falafel

Cucumber Cups
with OLIVE TAPENADE

1 GF R SF Q

Serves 6

- 2 English cucumbers
- ¼ cup capers, rinsed (about one small jar)
- 1¼ cups Kalamata olives, pitted, rinsed
- 3 tablespoons finely diced red onion
- 2 cloves garlic, finely minced
- ½ teaspoon red jalapeño, or red serrano, seeded and minced
- 1 tablespoon lemon zest (½ lemon rind)
- 1 tablespoon finely chopped oregano
- 1½ tablespoons finely chopped tarragon
- 1 tablespoon olive oil

Cucumber cups are crunchy mini-stages for relishes, chutneys, and so much more. English cucumber is best, since its seedbed is a bit tighter and sturdier, which helps these little cuties hold together. You could also try this tapenade as the base for the Semi-Dried Tomatoes (page 213), or as a layer in the Garden Lasagna (page 205).

1   Slice cucumbers into ½-inch-thin rounds. To create the cup, scoop out half the seedbed of each round using a small teaspoon. Make sure not to cut all the way through. Set aside.

2   Mince the capers and olives and mix with onion, garlic, jalapeño, lemon zest, oregano, tarragon, and oil in small mixing bowl to make the tapenade.

3   Fill each cup with a heaping tablespoon of tapenade.

4   Garnish each filled cucumber cup with any leftover herbs you may have and serve.

VEGETABLE SUSHI
Maki Rolls

1 GF R SF KF Q

Serves 1

- - - - - - - - - - - - - - - - - - - -

1 nori sheet

¼ cup Sesame Root Rice (page 145) (or cooked short-grain brown rice)

1 red pepper, julienned

¼ cup daikon sprouts

1 cup shiitake mushrooms, thinly sliced and marinated for a few minutes (equal parts wheat-free tamari and olive oil)

A mineral-rich nori sheet is the Batmobile of wraps for your sushi fixings, especially since nori is a strong source of calcium and iron. Your first roll might be a little tricky, but with practice you'll be a sushi master in no time. Dip these delicious rolls in Basic Asian Marinade (page 226) or your favorite wheat-free tamari. You can also spice them up with a little wasabi, if you so desire.

1   Place nori on a sushi mat. Spread the root rice evenly on a nori sheet, but be sure to leave about half an inch around all the edges. Press the root rice firmly against the nori.

2   Stack red peppers, daikon sprouts, and shiitake mushrooms over the root rice in one long strip across the center.

3   Now it's time to rock and roll. Starting at the edge closest to you, begin rolling up the mat with nori using both hands. As you roll, tuck and press the nori with your fingertips to keep the roll tight.

4   Roll until you've reached the last inch of bare nori, wet the nori with a dab of water, and press the edge to seal your roll.

5   Slice each maki roll in 6 to 8 pieces.

tip **MAGICAL MAKI** Maki is a cylindrical roll that has been cut into 6 to 8 pieces. It's usually made with a nori (seaweed) wrap, rice, and one or more veggies, tofu, sprouts, or other fillings stacked in the center before rolling. When it's time to cut your roll, dip the knife in water first—otherwise the nori may tear. Also, if you opt for brown rice, keep a small bowl of water nearby for periodically wetting your fingertips (prevents sticking while rolling!). Feel free to let your creative juices flow and substitute the core ingredients of the roll with your nearest and dearest vegetables, plant protein, salads, grain, or tempeh dishes. Leftovers work great!

Crostini
with ARTICHOKE PURÉE, GARLICKY MUSHROOMS, and HORSERADISH

1 R Q

GF *if using rice crackers*

Makes 12 crostini

2 cups jarred artichoke hearts, rinsed

½ cup pine nuts, toasted

2 tablespoons lemon zest (1 lemon rind)

2 tablespoons olive oil

3 tablespoons minced chives

¼ teaspoon sea salt

Freshly ground black pepper, to taste

1 whole-grain baguette, or your favorite toasted bread sliced into small crostini-size pieces or 12 to 15 gluten-free crackers

Garlicky Mushrooms (page 207)

3- to 4-inch fresh horseradish root, peeled and grated

Get ready for the holy topping trinity of the crunchy crostini world. The fresh, creamy artichoke purée, savory Garlicky Mushrooms, and kick of fresh horseradish create a big AMEN!

1   Strain and rinse artichoke hearts well. Using a food processor, pulse artichoke, pine nuts, lemon zest, and oil into a coarse purée. Transfer into a small mixing bowl and mix in the chives, seasoning to taste with salt and pepper.

2   To assemble, lay out crostini and place 1 or 2 tablespoons of the artichoke purée on each piece.

3   Top with a dollop of Garlicky Mushrooms and finish with fresh grated horseradish root, using a Microplane or other grater.

note **FROM CHAD**
I've been making this recipe on New Year's Eve for over a decade, whether at home or in the belly of a restaurant kitchen. It's an elegant and satisfying way to kick off any special event.

SESAME ROOT
Rice

1 GF R SF KF Q

Serves 4 to 6

- -

2 cups peeled and chopped parsnips (other options: carrots, kohlrabi, beets, jicama, or cauliflower)

¾ cup raw pine nuts

1½ tablespoons flax oil

1 tablespoon toasted sesame oil

½ teaspoon sea salt

½ teaspoon black pepper

3 tablespoons minced green onion or chives

2 tablespoons black sesame seeds

Root rice is a fresh and raw alternative to traditional white sushi rice. If you don't want to go through the extra steps of making root rice, use a short-grain brown rice. A serving of parsnips provides almost your entire daily requirement for copper, which helps to build hemoglobin—keeping your bones, nerves, and blood vessels vibrant. Serve with Vegetable Sushi Maki Rolls (page 143) or simply as a side dish.

1   In food processor, pulse the parsnips and pine nuts until finely minced (white rice consistency).

2   Pour mixture in bowl, and add flax oil, sesame oil, salt, pepper, onion, and sesame seeds, mixing well.

VEGGIE SUSHI BASH

Let's get rowdy with some plant-sassy sushi! Make a batch of root rice, grab a large platter, roll up some maki rolls, pour the sake, and get ready to par-tay.

TRUFFLED
Edamame
Dumplings
with SHALLOT BROTH

2

Makes 25 or more dumplings

SHALLOT BROTH

2 tablespoons olive oil

1½ cups finely minced shallots or white onions

2 cloves garlic, minced

2 cups vegetable stock

2 sprigs of thyme

1 cup Sauternes wine (preferred) or sweet cooking sherry

Freshly ground black pepper, to taste

Chad loves the challenge of veganizing popular nonvegan dishes (and making them even better!). These indulgent gourmet dumplings were inspired by his visit to a sizzling NYC hot spot. Edamame is tofu's mama, a green pod filled with stupendous soybeans. In one serving of edamame, your body receives 11 grams of complete protein and 9 grams of feisty fiber. If you're in a hurry, you can save time by simply making the dumplings and using wheat-free tamari instead of the Shallot Broth. Or if you just want a different taste sensation, pair these dumplings with the Basic Asian Marinade (page 226).

1   *Prepare Shallot Broth:* In sauté pan, heat oil on medium heat. Add shallots and garlic and sauté until golden and translucent. Continue to caramelize and add a touch of the vegetable stock to brown the onions more.

2   Add the thyme, and continue to sauté the onions for 10 minutes, stirring frequently, to caramelize. Add wine to deglaze. Simmer for 8 minutes or until the liquid is reduced by about half.

3   Add the rest of the vegetable stock and pepper and continue to cook down until reduced by half, which will take about another 15 minutes.

4   Remove from heat.

DUMPLINGS

2 cups frozen shelled
edamame, thawed

¼ cup raw cashews, soaked
for a few hours or overnight in
water, to soften

¾ cup unsweetened soy milk
or nondairy milk of choice

¼ cup truffle oil

2 cloves garlic

3 tablespoons Earth Balance
or other vegan butter

½ teaspoon sea salt

White pepper, or freshly
ground black pepper, to taste

1 pack of vegan round dumpling skins (You can find these
in many health-food stores
or Asian markets. Read the
ingredients to ensure they are
vegan—many of these have
eggs.)

1 teaspoon flour or cornstarch

5   Strain the broth using a fine-mesh strainer until it is clear.

6   *Prepare Dumplings:* In a blender or food processor, add all ingredients, except the dumpling skins and flour or cornstarch. Blend until the mixture has a coarse texture.

7   Transfer dumpling filling to a bowl and place it on a work surface alongside a cup of water, dumpling skins, and a sheet pan. Lightly sprinkle flour or cornstarch over the sheet pan (this will keep your dumplings from sticking to the pan during assembly).

8   Place about a tablespoon of filling in the center of each skin. Dip your finger in water and trace a half circle around one side of the dumpling skin. Pick up the dumpling and fold it into a taco. Starting with one corner, crimp around the edge (see the picture). Place on sheet pan and continue until all dumplings are assembled.

9   *Cook the Dumplings:* In a sauté pan on medium heat, add small amount of oil, or spray oil on pan, and sear dumplings until golden on the bottom. Don't crowd the pan or the dumplings may stick to one another.

10 Steaming time! Using a bamboo steamer basket, or your favorite steamer, place a few leaves of cabbage, or other leafy green, on the bottom of the steamer. This will keep your dumplings from sticking.

11 Bring water to a boil, and place the dumplings in the steamer. Steam for about 3 minutes. Remove from heat.

12 *Serve:* Place 4 to 6 dumplings in shallow bowl. Pour about ¼ cup Shallot Broth over the dumplings. Serve with a spoon and enjoy.

---

note FROM CHAD

Once you get the hang of crimping your own dumplings, stock up for future meals by making large batches and popping them in the freezer. Just pull 'em out later, add a little more steaming time while cooking them up, and you've got a taste of gourmet on the fly.

BAMBOO STEAM DREAM

Why use a bamboo steamer? A bamboo steamer helps create lickety-split, easy meals. The steamer's tiered structure allows you to cook layers of veggies. For best results, cut veggies into cubes or small florets, and coarsely chop greens. Keep the more delicate greens or vegetables on the top layer, and the firmer ones, such as carrots, Brussels sprouts, and potatoes, on the bottom layer.

extra tip Line the bottom of each tray with lettuce leaves to prevent contents from sticking.

How do you use a bamboo steamer? Fill a wok, deep sauté pan, or large pot with a few inches of water and place the steamer either in the water (if using a wok or sauté), or on the rim of the pot (must be the same diameter as your steamer or else it might burn). Bring water to a boil. Once the water comes to a boil, your veggies will be steamed to perfection in about 1 to 4 minutes. Time will vary depending on the type of veggies you choose, so make sure to keep an eye on them.

guest chef
TAL RONNEN

HEARTS-OF-PALM-STYLE
Crab Cakes
with RÉMOULADE

2 KF Q

Serves 4

- - - - - - - - - - - - - - - - -

RÉMOULADE

1 cup vegan mayonnaise

1 tablespoon ketchup

1 tablespoon Dijon mustard

1 teaspoon hot sauce

1 teaspoon vegan Worcester-shire sauce

1 tablespoon freshly squeezed lemon juice

¼ teaspoon sea salt

2 teaspoons minced capers

2 teaspoons minced shallot

1 teaspoon minced fresh parsley

2 teaspoons minced red bell pepper

CRAB CAKES

1 sheet of nori, or 2 teaspoons toasted nori flakes

Two 14-ounce cans hearts of palm

½ cup canola oil, more if needed (alternative: reduce to ¼ cup oil if using small sauté pan)

The hearts of palm in this dish provide a "crabby" texture while the nori and Old Bay will remind you of a Maryland-style crab cake. They're so good you won't even think about tartar sauce!

1   *Prepare Rémoulade:* Place all rémoulade ingredients in a food processor or blender and blend on high for 1 minute. Set aside or store, covered, in the refrigerator for up to 1 week.

2   *Prepare Crab Cakes:* Toast nori sheet by holding it with tongs and fanning it over a low gas flame or electric burner. Be careful not to let it burn. Turn the sheet frequently, so that it toasts evenly.

3   Grind the nori using a spice grinder or a coffee grinder that you use exclusively for spices. Break the nori into pieces, place it in the grinder, and pulse until powdered. Alternatively, crumble it as finely as you can with your hands or pulverize it with a mortar and pestle.

4   Drain the hearts of palm and press in a towel to dry them. In a food processor, pulse gently until it looks like the consistency of crabmeat.

5   Place a small sauté pan on medium heat. Add 1 teaspoon of oil and heat for 30 seconds, being careful not to let it smoke. Sauté the onion and bell pepper until soft, 3 to 5 minutes.

6   In a large bowl, combine the hearts of palm, onion, bell pepper, Vegenaise, 1 teaspoon Old Bay seasoning, nori flakes, nutritional yeast flakes, arrowroot or cornstarch, and salt and pepper. Mix until incorporated. Cover and refrigerate for 30 minutes.

¼ cup finely diced red onion

¼ cup finely diced red bell pepper

3 tablespoons Vegenaise or other vegan mayonnaise

2 teaspoons Old Bay seasoning

1 tablespoon nutritional yeast flakes

2 teaspoons arrowroot or cornstarch

Sea salt and freshly ground black pepper, to taste

1 cup panko breadcrumbs

7   Scoop with an ice cream scoop or a large tablespoon to portion into small cakes. Combine breadcrumbs with 1 teaspoon Old Bay seasoning. Coat the small cakes with breadcrumbs. Form and let sit in the refrigerator for 1 hour or until firm.

8   *Cook Crab Cakes:* Place a sauté pan on medium-high heat. Add some canola oil and heat for 2 minutes. Working in batches, sauté the cakes (make certain that the oil comes about half-way up the sides of the cakes) until browned on both sides and heated through, 2 to 3 minutes on each side.

9   Remove the cakes to a baking sheet lined with parchment paper and place in a warm oven (200°F) until you finish all of the cakes.

10   *Serve:* Place the cakes on a plate and garnish with Rémoulade.

Walnut
FALAFEL

2 GF R SF KF

Makes 25 small falafels

1 cup raw almonds, soaked for a few hours or overnight in water, to soften

1 cup raw walnuts, soaked for a few hours or overnight in water, to soften

2 dates, pitted

¾ cup sesame seeds, finely ground

½ cup minced parsley

¼ cup minced cilantro

3 cloves garlic, minced

3 tablespoons minced fresh oregano

2 tablespoons olive oil

2 tablespoons lemon juice

½ tablespoon cumin powder

½ teaspoon black pepper

1 teaspoon sea salt

5 to 6 leaves of butter lettuce

Crazy Sexy Kitchen's falafel will fill you up, although it's much lighter and healthier than the traditional fried version. These are great wrapped in a collard leaf, stuffed in a pita, or on top of a salad. For the full Mediterranean experience, serve with Fresh Minted Tabouli (page 207) or Garlic Tahini Dressing (page 227).

1   If using oven, preheat to 250°F.

2   In a Champion Juicer or other juicer with a solid plate, homogenize the almonds, walnuts, and dates to a thick purée. Alternatively you could use a food processor to purée until fine as possible.

3   In mixing bowl, add remaining ingredients (except butter lettuce) to the nut purée and mix by hand.

4   When thoroughly mixed, form into small half-dollar-size thumbprints by forming a ball and pressing with your thumb in center. Dehydrate for 3 to 4 hours in dehydrator at 115°F or in the oven at 250°F for 30 to 35 minutes.

5   Once the walnut falafel is crisp and/or golden if using an oven, serve 4 or 5 on a bed of butter lettuce or your favorite delicate greens, with a side of Fresh Minted Tabouli and Garlic Tahini Dressing.

SYMPHONIC SALADS

Cabbage Hemp Salad

Simply Green

Greens *and* Berries

Lettuces *and* Citrus

Crazy Sexy Kale

the Herb Garden

Cucumber Sesame Salad

Fennel *and* Fruits
with Mandarin Champagne Vinaigrette

Corn and Heirloom Tomato Salad
with Creamy Poblano Vinaigrette
by JOY PIERSON, JORGE PINEDA, AND ANGEL RAMOS

Tomatoes *and* Herbs

Crazy Sexy Summer Salad

Warm Kale *and* Quinoa Salad

Chopped Salad

the True Crunchy

Super Sprout Salad

Farmer's Salad

Asian Noodles *with* Black Vinaigrette

Caesar Pleaser Salad
by PAM BROWN

Roasted Rutabaga Salad
with Pistachio *and* Charred Onion
by RICHARD LANDAU

Sea Veggie Salad

Cabbage
HEMP SALAD

1 GF R SF Q

Serves 2 to 3

3 cups finely shredded cabbage (mix of purple and green)

¼ cup diced red and yellow pepper

1½ avocados, pit removed and diced

3 tablespoons hemp oil (or flax oil)

1½ tablespoons lime juice

2 tablespoons diced green onion

¼ cup hemp seeds

3 tablespoons chopped cilantro

Hemp's omega-3 fatty acids make this nutty-flavored seed a big hit in the Crazy Sexy Kitchen, especially since omega-3s support healthy brain function. Crunchy cabbage paired with creamy avocado makes this salad a tongue-titillating success.

1   Combine all ingredients in a bowl. Massage and mix with your hands to tenderize the cabbage and cream the avocado, and serve.

SIMPLY Green

1 GF SF Q

R *if not toasting pine nuts*

Serves 2

3 cups baby arugula

½ cup cherry tomatoes, halved

2 tablespoons lemon zest

¼ cup pine nuts, toasted or raw

3 tablespoons Lemon Oil (page 227)

Freshly ground black pepper, to taste

Arugula is center stage in this simple, citrusy salad. This spicy leafy is a detox diva due to its glucosinolate content, which stimulates natural cleansing enzymes.

1   Combine all ingredients in a bowl and toss gently by hand. Serve immediately to prevent arugula from wilting.

---

note FROM CHAD
Some of the most beautiful things in life are simple. These uncomplicated ingredients exude freshness. Wanna impress your guests, but don't have a lot of time? This will save the day.

Greens
and BERRIES

1 GF R SF KF Q

Serves 3 to 4

---

3 cups baby spinach

½ cup strawberries, quartered

¼ cup walnuts, toasted
(or Maple Candied Pecans
page 252)

2 tablespoons balsamic
vinegar

1½ tablespoons flax oil

Sea salt, to taste

Walnuts (optional)

Strawberries (optional)

Balsamic and berries are like Fred and Ginger—they dance beautifully together, especially if you're using a quality aged balsamic. By adding walnuts to your salad, you'll benefit from their omega-3s, which have been shown to improve cholesterol levels and reduce the risk of heart disease.

1   Combine all ingredients in a bowl, toss gently, and serve.

2   Before serving, garnish with walnuts and strawberries, if using.

tip **WATERMELON SWAP** During watermelon season, replace the strawberries with cubed watermelon and toss in a small handful of mint leaves for the ultimate lazy summer picnic salad.

BALSAMIC VINEGAR

Bottles range from $5 into the $100s, so how do you choose a decent balsamic without breaking the bank? Balsamic vinegar becomes sweeter, thicker, and more delicious with age. You can still find a reasonably priced, quality balsamic for about $15. A little balsamic goes a long way, so one bottle will last awhile. Just check the ingredients to make sure there is no added sugar, artificial flavors, or colors. Also, aim to buy one that has aged at least three years.

Lettuces
and CITRUS

1 GF R SF KF Q

Serves 3 to 4

- - - - - - - - - - - - - - - - -

3 cups butter lettuce, ripped

½ cup orange or grapefruit
segments

¼ cup pecans, raw or toasted
and chopped

½ tablespoon minced red chile,
or red pepper flakes

1 tablespoon olive oil

1½ tablespoons white wine
vinegar

Freshly ground black pepper,
to taste

Squeeze of lemon

Pecans (raw or toasted), for
garnish (optional)

Extra orange or grapefruit
segments, for garnish
(optional)

Oranges and pecans mixed with spicy chile bring warm,
festive flavors to your holiday table. In addition to tango-
ing with your taste buds, the vitamin C in the red chile
peppers and oranges help your body absorb the iron in
the pecans.

1   Combine all ingredients in a bowl, toss gently, and serve.

2   Before serving, garnish with a few pecans and citrus segments,
    if you like.

CRAZY SEXY
Kale

1 GF R SF KF Q

Serves 2 to 3

1 bunch kale, any variety, shredded by hand

1 cup diced bell peppers, red, yellow, or orange

¼ cup chopped parsley

1½ avocados, pit removed and chopped

2 tablespoons flax oil

1½ tablespoons lemon juice

Sea salt, to taste

Pinch of cayenne, to taste

Kale is the supreme king of the leafies and the ruler of this prevention-rocks salad. Serve it solo, with your favorite cooked grain, or wrapped in nori or a gluten-free tortilla. Crown your kale creation by adding chopped fresh herbs or your choice of diced vegetables. If you want to be fancy, serve the salad wrapped in a cucumber slice.

1   In a medium mixing bowl, combine all ingredients. Massage and mix with your hands to "wilt" the kale and cream the avocado (this should only take a minute or two), and serve.

note FROM CHAD
Many of my recipes have been influenced by cultural experiences, twists on favorite childhood meals, or newly discovered ingredients. Few dishes have proven to be as timeless and beloved as this kale salad.

the HERB
Garden

1 GF R SF Q

Serves 2 to 3

- - - - - - - - - - - - - - - -

3 cups mesclun mix

Handful of your favorite mixed fresh herbs (parsley, dill, and mint are a great combo)

1½ tablespoons lemon juice

1½ tablespoons flax oil

Freshly ground black pepper, to taste

Sea salt, to taste

Showcasing herbs in a simple salad will elevate your greens from snore to encore! And by the by, dill isn't just for pickles—this feathery fellow contains calcium and antibacterial properties.

1   Combine all ingredients in a bowl, toss gently, and serve.

FRESH HERB MIXES

Give your dishes some added herb excellence with one of these harmonious combos:

Italian: basil, parsley, sage

Thai: basil, cilantro, mint

Mexican: cilantro, oregano, and chives

extra tip Rip the leaves rather than cutting them to prevent browning.

Cucumber
SESAME SALAD

1 GF R SF Q

Serves 3 to 4

- - - - - - - - - - - - - - - - - -

3 cups peeled and thinly sliced cucumber

½ teaspoon sea salt

1 cup baby spinach or baby tatsoi

3 tablespoons sesame seeds, raw or toasted

1 tablespoon toasted sesame oil

1 tablespoon flax oil

1 tablespoon lime juice

For an incredibly crunchy cuke, take 15 extra minutes to wilt your cucumbers before adding them to this already delectable salad. When cukes are pressed with a dash of salt, much of the water is removed, making them an incredibly crunchy addition to any salad. Add some mint for a karate kick of freshness. It pairs perfectly with any Asian-influenced meal.

1   Place the thinly sliced cucumbers in a mixing bowl and sprinkle with sea salt. Gently massage with salt for about 3 minutes. Press the mixture with a small plate with any weight on top, and set aside for 15 minutes to allow the water to be released. Strain and discard the water.

2   Combine wilted cucumbers in a bowl with remaining ingredients, toss gently, and serve.

Fennel and Fruits
with MANDARIN CHAMPAGNE VINAIGRETTE

1 GF R SF Q

Serves 4

1 cup fennel bulb, sliced paper thin

1 cup green apple, sliced into paper-thin half moons

2 cups baby arugula

¼ cup pistachio nuts (shelled), raw or dry roasted

1 tablespoon lemon zest

1 teaspoon minced thyme

1 teaspoon red jalapeño, seeded and finely minced

Freshly ground black pepper, to taste

¼ cup Mandarin Champagne Vinaigrette (page 239)

Spicy jalapeño, arugula, sweet fennel, and sour green apple get frisky in this salad to create a total taste-gasm. Switch things up once in a while by swapping out the apples and adding tangerine, clementine, or pear slices. Fennel is a fountain of phytonutrients, which are Crazy Sexy spectacular for reducing inflammation.

1   Gently toss all ingredients, including the Mandarin Champagne Vinaigrette, in a mixing bowl, and serve.

nutritionist
JOY PIERSON
guest chefs
ANGEL RAMOS
JORGE PINEDA

1 GF SF Q

Serves 6

- - - - - - - - - - - - - - - - - - -

CREAMY POBLANO VINAIGRETTE

2 small poblano peppers

½ teaspoon olive oil

1 tablespoon diced shallots

½ avocado

¼ cup white wine vinegar

½ cup water

1 tablespoon diced jalapeño

1 teaspoon chopped parsley

1 teaspoon chopped chives

1 tablespoon chopped basil

MIXED GREEN SALAD

2 ears of fresh corn, husked and the kernels cut off the cobs

1 cucumber, peeled, trimmed, seeded, and thinly sliced

1 small red onion, thinly sliced

Sea salt, to taste

Freshly ground pepper, to taste

2 cups heirloom tomatoes, sliced in wedges

½ pound mixed greens

GARNISH

2 large ripe avocados, peeled, pitted, and cut in lengthwise slices

2 tablespoons hemp seeds

CORN AND HEIRLOOM
Tomato Salad
with CREAMY POBLANO VINAIGRETTE

This salad takes full advantage of summer corn, tomatoes, and cucumbers. The hemp seeds add protein, while the herb vinaigrette gives it a garden-fresh kick. You can also spoon it over greens, roasted vegetables, and grains.

1   *Prepare Creamy Poblano Vinaigrette:* Grill or roast poblano peppers over an open flame until blackened.

2   Put peppers in a bowl and cover with cold water. While in the water, peel off the skins.

3   De-seed and thinly slice peppers.

4   In a medium sauté pan, heat olive oil and sauté shallots until tender.

5   Place all the ingredients in a blender and blend until creamy.

6   Cover and chill for at least 1 hour.

7   *Prepare Mixed Green Salad:* In a bowl, toss the corn, cucumbers, red onion, and salt and pepper. Add the tomatoes and mixed greens and toss.

8   Arrange the Mixed Green Salad on salad plates, garnish with the avocado slices and hemp seeds, drizzle with the vinaigrette, and serve.

TOMATOES *and* Herbs

1 GF R SF KF Q

Serves 2

4 large ripe tomatoes, sliced in ¼-inch rounds

3 tablespoons coarsely chopped or ripped basil

3 tablespoons olive oil

Sea salt, to taste (flaked sea salt is best)

Freshly ground black pepper, to taste

Tomatoes are well known for their anti-inflammatory and anticancer carotenoid crusaders—lycopene and beta-carotene. There are hundreds of varieties, from the common Roma, cherry, and grape to the less familiar heirloom varieties, such as Green Zebra, Black Crimson, Cherokee Purple, Brandywine, and Red Cup—each with their own distinct taste and personality. Serve with your favorite whole-grain baguette or gluten-free bread for an amazing starter to any meal.

1   Arrange the sliced tomatoes evenly on a plate.

2   Sprinkle the fresh basil over tomatoes.

3   Drizzle with olive oil, finish with sea salt and black pepper, and serve.

CRAZY SEXY
Summer Salad

1 GF R SF Q

Serves 4

4 cups of baby greens or spicy mesclun

¼ cup shredded beets

¼ cup shredded carrots

½ cup mixed sprouts of your choice, store-bought or ones you may have grown, plus more for garnish (Our favorite is a combination of sunflower, buckwheat, or pea shoots.)

2 mandarins, or clementines, peeled and segmented

¼ cup Maple Candied Pecans (page 252, optional), raw pecans, or toasted pecans, plus more for garnish (optional)

¼ cup Miso-Citrus Dressing (page 236)

Freshly ground black pepper, to taste

No need to worry about sugar-crashing when satisfying your sweet tooth with this sweet and citrusy, sprout-powered salad. Put on your cowgirl hat and ride off into the land of leafies—try out an array of gorgeous greens, such as frisée, mizuna, spinach, mustard, and baby green leaf.

1   Mix the baby greens, beets, carrots, sprouts, mandarins, pecans, dressing, and black pepper in a bowl. Toss gently, making sure the dressing coats the salad evenly, and serve.

2   Before serving, top with more sprouts and any leftover pecans, if you like.

Warm Kale
and QUINOA SALAD

1 GF R SF Q

Serves 4 to 5

2 cups quinoa

3 cups water

2 cups chopped or shredded kale

3 tablespoons pine nuts, raw or toasted, or slivered almonds

3 tablespoons currants, raisins, or dried cranberries

2 tablespoons lemon juice

1 tablespoon olive oil

Sea salt, to taste

Freshly ground black pepper, to taste

Nourish your body with this welcoming warm salad. Cooked quinoa is a fluffy, nutty-tasting, gluten-free seed that provides essential amino acids (protein!) and fabulous fiber. Just like the legendary Aretha Franklin, kale needs no introduction. Your cells will thank you for the R-E-S-P-E-C-T!

1   In a small pot on medium heat, add quinoa and water, and bring to a simmer. Reduce heat to low, cover, and continue to cook for 10 to 12 minutes. Remove from heat and fluff with fork.

2   Add the shredded kale on top of the quinoa and cover for a few minutes to allow the kale to steam.

3   Add pine nuts, currants, lemon juice, olive oil, salt, and pepper. Mix all ingredients thoroughly and serve warm or cold.

OLIVE OIL

Choosing olive oil can be as daunting as selecting fine wine. Different olive oils have distinct flavors spanning from smooth and buttery to bold and spicy. One of Chef Chad's favorites, a California-grown variety, is Bariani, which is stone crushed, cold-pressed, and unfiltered, giving it a beautiful, fresh, robust flavor. Experimenting with different kinds of oil is just another way to have fun in the kitchen. Try to stick to unfiltered, cold-pressed oils, since they're less processed and contain more nutrients than oils that have been heated and filtered.

Chopped
SALAD

1 GF R SF KF Q

Serves 2 to 3

2 cups romaine hearts, chopped

1 cup of cooked chickpeas (or one 15-ounce can, strained and rinsed)

3 tablespoons combination of sunflower and sesame seeds, lightly toasted

3 tablespoons chopped parsley

2 tablespoons flax oil

2 tablespoons white balsamic vinegar

Sea salt, to taste

Black pepper, to taste

Parsley power! This feisty little herb is much more than an ordinary garnish. A couple tablespoons deliver more than your daily vitamin K needs, which means stronger bones. Make a pilgrimage to pita Mecca by stuffing this salad inside a pocket with a few slices of avocado.

1   Combine all ingredients in a bowl, toss gently, and serve.

the TRUE
Crunchy

1 GF R SF Q

Serves 4 (as a side salad)

- - - - - - - - - - - - - - - - -

1 cup lentil sprouts

½ cup mung bean sprouts

½ cup adzuki sprouts

½ red bell pepper, diced

½ yellow bell pepper, diced

½ cup coarsely chopped
flat-leaf parsley

¼ cup chopped Kalamata
olives

3 tablespoons diced red onion

½ red chile (jalapeño,
serrano, or cayenne), seeded
and minced (optional)

1 lemon, juiced

Sprouts are lightning bolts of nourishment, electrifying your cells with vitamins, protein, and minerals. Serve this salad alone or as a healthy, happy side.

1   Combine ingredients in a bowl, mix thoroughly, and serve.

SPLENDID SPROUTING

There's a whole world of sprouts out there—sunflower, pea shoot, buckwheat, lentil, mung, and more—and you can easily grow any of them in your kitchen. All you need are some seeds, water, and a jar! Well, it's a little more complex than that, but you'll find a wealth of information on all things sprouting at kriscarr.com/resources. Check out sprouting superhero Steve Meyerowitz (Sproutman.com). His website is a gold mine for any newbie sprouter.

Super Sprout
SALAD

1 GF R SF Q

Serves 4 (as a side salad)

- - - - - - - - - - - - - - - - -

½ bunch lacinato kale (a.k.a. dinosaur or black kale), shredded

2 tablespoons flax oil

2 tablespoons lemon juice

1 cup pea shoots (or buckwheat sprouts), chopped in half

2 cups sunflower sprouts, chopped in half

2 oranges or grapefruits, segmented and halved lengthwise (about 1 cup)

1 avocado, cubed

1 shallot, peeled and thinly julienned

3 tablespoons sesame seeds, toasted or raw

Pea shoots and sunflower sprouts are two of the sweeter guys in the sprout camp. They're also filled with chlorophyll, which will help your body build red and white blood cells (immune-system supporters!) and ease inflammation (take that, disease!).

1   Combine kale, flax oil, and lemon juice in a bowl. Massage and mix with hands for 2 minutes to soften kale.

2   Add the pea shoots, sunflower sprouts, oranges, avocado, shallot, and sesame seeds to the massaged kale. Gently toss (keeping the citrus and avocado intact) and serve.

Farmer's
SALAD

2 GF

Serves 4 to 6

3 tablespoons Basic Aioli (page 242)

1 tablespoon lemon zest

2 tablespoons capers, strained

1 tablespoon minced chives or green onion

1½ tablespoons coarsely chopped tarragon

3 cups baby potatoes, boiled, cooled, and sliced in half

2 cups watercress or baby arugula

I cup cooked fava beans, broad beans, gigantic white beans, or lima beans

2 tablespoons Dijon Vinaigrette (page 234)

1 red bell pepper, thinly sliced

Freshly ground black pepper, to taste

The creaminess of the aioli combined with peppery watercress and Dijon Vinaigrette create a fall fiesta in every bite of the Farmer's Salad. Zesty chives are part of the allium crew—an antibacterial and antiviral bunch that includes onions and garlic. Fresh chives also have high levels of antioxidants and flavanoids.

1   Mix the Basic Aioli recipe in a bowl with lemon zest, capers, chives, and tarragon.

2   Toss the aioli mixture with the potatoes and set aside.

3   In another bowl, combine the watercress, fava beans (or other beans), and Dijon Vinaigrette. Toss gently.

4   Place a portion of the potato salad in the center of plate and top with a handful of the watercress-fava mix.

5   Top with bell pepper slices. Finish with freshly ground black pepper and serve.

Asian Noodles
with BLACK VINAIGRETTE

1 ○

Serves 4

One 8-ounce package of buckwheat soba noodles

½ cup thinly shredded Napa cabbage

½ red bell pepper, thinly julienned

½ yellow bell pepper, thinly julienned

¼ cup thinly julienned snow peas

2 carrots, thinly julienned, or shredded

½ cup buckwheat sprouts, sunflower sprouts, or pea shoots, plus more for garnish

3 tablespoons sesame seeds, lightly toasted, plus more for garnish

¼ cup Basic Asian Marinade (page 226)

Did you know that buckwheat isn't related to wheat, but is actually part of the rhubarb family? Therefore, this variety of soba noodles is a gluten-free option that's awesome when chilled and added to salads. Napa, another star in this recipe, is a Chinese cabbage high in vitamins A and C, plus plenty of heart-healthy, anti-inflammatory phytonutrients.

1   Cook the buckwheat noodles according to the package instructions. Do not overcook; buckwheat is very temperamental and falls apart if cooked too long. Strain and rinse with cold water to stop the noodles from cooking further.

2   Toss the cooked noodles with cabbage, red and yellow bell pepper, snow peas, carrots, sprouts, and sesame seeds in a mixing bowl. Set aside some sprouts and sesame seeds for a garnish.

3   Pour the dressing evenly over the salad, toss gently, and serve.

4   Before serving, garnish with leftover sprouts and sesame seeds, if using.

guest chef
PAM BROWN

1 KF Q
GF *if not using croutons*
Serves 4 to 6

- - - - - - - - - - - - - - - - - -

DRESSING

1 cup Vegenaise or other vegan mayonnaise (raw alternative: see recipe tip)

1½ teaspoons Dijon mustard

1½ teaspoons freshly squeezed lemon juice

1 garlic clove, smashed

1 tablespoon canola oil

1½ teaspoons nutritional yeast

Salt and pepper, to taste

CROUTONS

2 cups bread cubes, crusts removed

¼ cup canola oil

½ teaspoon garlic granules

½ teaspoon onion granules

½ teaspoon salt

¼ teaspoon black pepper

SALAD FIXINGS

1 large bunch romaine or two small heads, washed and spun dry

1 small red onion, thinly sliced

¼ cup almonds, plus
2 tablespoons, finely chopped

Caesar Pleaser
SALAD

Hail Caesar! This vegan version is even better than the original. Always make a double batch of the dressing, since it keeps very well and everyone will want more!

1   Preheat oven to 400°F.

2   *Prepare dressing:* Blend all dressing ingredients in a food processor until creamy.

3   *Prepare croutons:* In a medium-size mixing bowl, toss all crouton ingredients together and spread out in an even layer on a baking sheet. Bake until golden, about 8 to 10 minutes, stirring frequently. Remove from oven.

4   *Assemble salad:* In a medium-size mixing bowl, tear the lettuce into bite-size pieces. Tearing the lettuce is the traditional way to make this salad as using a knife to slice the romaine will cause the edges to brown.

5   Add the red onion, ¼ cup of the almonds, and croutons to the romaine then mix in the dressing being sure that all of the leaves are covered. Sprinkle the remaining almonds on top.

tip CAESAR SECRETS

- It's important that the lettuce be very dry before tossing with the dressing as it will not cling if the lettuce is wet.

- Croutons are better if the bread is slightly dry. If you're using fresh bread, cut the croutons, spread them out on a baking sheet, and let them dry out for 15 to 30 minutes. If using old bread, you won't need to follow this step.

- **Vegenaise Alternative:** For a raw Caesar dressing, skip the Vegenaise and replace with ¼ cup cashews (soaked first in water to soften) blended with ½ cup water in a blender.

Roasted Rutabaga SALAD
with PISTACHIO and CHARRED ONION

guest chef
RICHARD LANDAU

1 GF SF Q

Serves 4

4 tablespoons olive oil

4 teaspoons apple cider vinegar

2 teaspoons salt

2 teaspoons pepper

1 large rutabaga, peeled and thinly sliced (about ¼-inch thick) on a mandoline

1 cup very finely diced onion

1 teaspoon chopped fresh thyme

2 tablespoons toasted pistachios, crushed with a knife or in the food processor

Rutabaga is one of the most underrated vegetables—it's earthy, creamy, and sweet, and takes so well to any ethnic preparation. In this dish we simply slice it thinly and roast it, which is a great way to show off all of its wonderful characteristics.

1 Preheat the oven to 400°F.

2 In a mixing bowl, combine 3 tablespoons of the olive oil with 2 teaspoons of the apple cider vinegar and 1 teaspoon each of the salt and pepper. Mix with a whisk.

3 Brush the marinade on the rutabaga slices and arrange in a single layer on baking sheets (you may need to do 2 rounds depending on your sheet size).

4 Bake the rutabagas for 8 to 12 minutes or until they become tender in the middle (test with a fork). Remove and allow to cool.

5 Meanwhile, heat a stainless-steel sauté pan with the remaining olive oil. When the oil gets very hot (it will start to ripple), add the onions and cook for about 8 to 10 minutes or until they get very brown. Halfway through the cooking add the remaining teaspoon each of salt and pepper.

6 Deglaze the onions with the remaining apple cider vinegar.

7 Reduce the vinegar for 2 minutes and remove from the heat. Stir in the thyme.

8 When both the rutabaga and onions have cooled, arrange the rutabaga slices on a plate, add a spoonful of the onion mixture, and sprinkle with pistachios. Garnish with your favorite petite greens (arugula or frisée work well). Finish with an extra drizzle of olive oil if desired.

Sea Veggie
SALAD

1 Q

Serves 4

½ cup arame (or other favorite sea veggie), rehydrated by soaking in 1 cup of warm water for 10 minutes

½ cup hijiki (or other favorite sea veggie), rehydrated by soaking in 1 cup of warm water for 10 minutes

1¼ cups pea shoots, cut in half, plus more for garnish

3 tablespoons finely diced green onions

1 tablespoon wheat-free tamari

½ tablespoon agave

2 tablespoons fresh lime juice

½ tablespoon toasted sesame oil

½ teaspoon red jalapeño, seeded and minced

3 tablespoons white sesame seeds, lightly toasted

Lime wedges (optional)

Sea veggies have a delicious, unique flavor that goes great with tart lime juice, salty tamari, and sweet agave. Arame, hijiki, kelp, and wakame contain virtually all minerals found in the ocean. They also add a healthy dose of iodine to this salad, which supports thyroid gland functions—balancing hormones, metabolism, and blood sugar.

1 In mixing bowl, toss all ingredients.

2 Garnish with lime wedges and pea shoots, and serve immediately.

tip **VEGGIES OF THE SEA** Arame and hijiki are super easy to find. Check out your local health-food store (you can also buy them online) and feel free to substitute with nori, dulse, sea palm, or sea lettuces. Be sure to rinse the seaweeds well, since some varieties are saltier than others.

MAIN EVENTS

Super Simple Wok Veggies

Squash Pasta *with* Sage Pesto

Lentil *and* Chard Ragout

Chickpea *with* Root Veggie Tagine

Asian Stir-Raw
with Miso Ginger Sauce

Teriyaki Tofu
with Wild Mushrooms *and* Soba Noodles

Pad Thai *with* Kelp Noodles
by SARMA MELNGAILIS

Beetroot Ravioli
with Cashew Cream Cheese

Wild Mushroom Croquettes
with Horseradish Cream

Chile Rellenos
with Red and Green Sauces

Indian Chickpea Blinis
with Cashew Coconut Chutney
by PAM BROWN

Seitan Brisket
with Roasted Chanterelle Gravy

Madeira Peppercorn Tempeh
by TAL RONNEN

Yellow Squash Fettuccine
with Creamy Pine Nut Alfredo
by SARMA MELNGAILIS

Garden Lasagna
with Cashew–Pine Nut Ricotta

SUPER SIMPLE
Wok Veggies

1 KF Q

Serves 4 to 6

1 tablespoon toasted sesame oil

1 small white onion, julienned

1½ cups snow peas

1 cup sliced water chestnuts

1 red bell pepper, cubed

4 bunches baby bok choy, chopped in large pieces

1 cup stemmed and halved shiitake mushrooms

¼ cup vegetable stock

1 tablespoon minced ginger

2 tablespoons tamari

Stir-frying makes the most of your vagabond veggies. Adapt this recipe to fit the ingredients you have on hand and rescue produce from a date with your compost heap. Make sure to use bok choy's leaves and stems, since they're both filled with antioxidant allies. Serve over your favorite grain with a drizzle of hot sauce or pair it with the Teriyaki Tofu (page 189).

1   In a wok or sauté pan on medium-high heat, add the oil and onions. Cook until translucent and golden brown.

2   Add snow peas, water chestnuts, red bell pepper, baby bok choy, and mushrooms. With tongs or wooden spoon, stir frequently for 3 minutes or until veggies begin to stick to pan.

3   Add vegetable stock to deglaze the pan, followed by the ginger and tamari.

4   Continue to cook on medium-high heat until the veggies are tender but still crispy.

Squash Pasta
with SAGE PESTO

1 GF R SF Q

Serves 6

SAGE PESTO

2 cups chopped basil

3 tablespoons chopped sage

2 tablespoons chopped leek

½ cup pine nuts

2 cloves garlic

2½ tablespoons nutritional yeast

½ teaspoon sea salt

½ cup olive oil

SQUASH PASTA

3 green zucchini, sliced into noodles (see sidebar on page 182)

1 yellow zucchini, sliced into noodles (see sidebar on page 182)

½ cup sunflower sprouts (other options: buckwheat sprouts or pea shoots)

½ cup thinly julienned red bell pepper

This creamy, perky pesto coats your veggie noodles in a soulful sage sauce that won't sit like a brick in your belly after you leave the table. Zucchini is not only tasty, it's also a good source of potassium—a mineral that promotes proper muscle growth. If you're making a 100 percent raw meal, serve this dish with Tomatoes and Herbs (page 165). Alternatively, you could use kelp noodles or gluten-free penne pasta.

1   *Prepare Sage Pesto:* Remove stems from basil and sage.

2   In food processor, gently pulse basil, sage, leek, pine nuts, garlic, nutritional yeast, and salt until finely minced. Add the oil slowly and in a thin, even stream, pulsing until sauce has reached a coarse consistency.

3   *Prepare Squash Pasta:* In large bowl, combine green and yellow zucchini noodles with sprouts and bell pepper.

4   In small bowl, whisk together ½ cup of the Sage Pesto, olive oil, red pepper flakes, and black pepper.

1 tablespoon olive oil

Red pepper flakes, to taste

Freshly ground black pepper, to taste

GARNISH (OPTIONAL)

Basil, ripped or chopped coarsely

Truffled Parmesan (page 233)

5 *Serve:* Slowly spoon the pesto onto the noodles, mix together gently with hands, and serve. If you prefer it lightly sauced, don't add all the pesto to the mixture. Garnish with fresh basil and/or the Truffled Parmesan, if desired.

tip **PESTO POPS** Freeze pesto sauce in ice cube trays and you'll be mere minutes from a marvelous meal anytime! Pop out the cubes and store them in ziplock bags. Whenever a recipe calls for pesto, pull the cubes out and add to your dish. If the dish is cold, you'll need to defrost the pesto pops before use.

EASY HOMEMADE RAW VEGGIE PASTA

Once you have the right tools, making raw pasta is simple.

For a thicker, fettuccine-style noodle: Using a mandoline, slice the zucchini paper-thin, lengthwise. Stack the slices, and cut into ⅛-inch-wide "noodles."

For a thinner, spaghetti-style noodle: Use a spiral slicer or spiralizer to make zucchini and butternut-squash pastas in a snap. Both tools are inexpensive.

For quick, rough-cut noodles: Peel the veggies in long strips using a peeler. This is excellent for zucchini, rutabaga, carrots, or asparagus. There are also peelers available designed specifically for thin julienne.

For lasagna noodles: Using a mandoline, slice zucchini into thin rounds, or thin, long strips lengthwise.

1 tablespoon olive oil

½ cup finely diced shallots or red onions

6 roasted garlic cloves or 3 raw cloves, minced

1½ cups beluga lentils or green lentils

½ cup cooking sherry wine or marsala wine

3 cups vegetable stock, low sodium if available

4 cups well-cleaned and coarsely chopped chard

1 cup fresh or frozen peas

2½ tablespoons nutritional yeast

½ teaspoon red pepper flakes (optional)

3 tablespoons lemon zest

¼ cup chopped parsley

2 tablespoons minced thyme

½ tablespoon sea salt

Freshly ground black pepper, to taste

2 tablespoons Earth Balance or other vegan butter

LENTIL AND CHARD
Ragout

Beluga lentils—petite, sturdy, black legumes—are delightful on their own and in soups, but they're irresistible when matched with chard, herbs, and spices in this ragout. Pair it with some wild rice or a piece of gluten-free bread. We recommend doubling this recipe—it's fantastic the next day!

1   In a large saucepan on medium heat, add the oil, shallot, and garlic. Cook until shallots and garlic are translucent and golden.

2   Add lentils and sherry to deglaze the pan.

3   Add the vegetable stock and cover. Bring to a simmer and cook for about 20 minutes, until the lentils are fork tender. (If using green lentils, they may take longer to cook.)

4   Add chard, peas, nutritional yeast, red pepper flakes, lemon zest, parsley, thyme, and salt, and cook for an additional 3 to 4 minutes on low heat.

5   Finish with cracked pepper and 2 tablespoons of butter. Fold the mixture well to melt the butter, and serve.

tip **RAGOUT RENDITION**   To thicken up the ragout sauce, whisk 1½ tablespoons of cornmeal or cornstarch with ¼ cup of the ragout liquid. Add mixture to the pan a few minutes before removing from heat. Mix well.

COOKING WITH WINE

Wine isn't just for your glass (or getting you in the mood). You can also wine and dine your meals! Use it to deglaze a pan, caramelize onions, or build fabulous flavor in sauces or gravies.

CHICKPEA
with ROOT VEGGIE
Tagine

2 SF

Serves 6 to 8

1 teaspoon cumin seeds
(or ⅔ teaspoon ground)

1 teaspoon coriander seeds
(or ⅔ teaspoon ground)

½ teaspoon red pepper flakes
(adjust based on desired
spiciness)

½ teaspoon turmeric powder

½ teaspoon cinnamon

½ teaspoon black pepper

½ tablespoon sea salt

3 tablespoons olive oil

1 medium white onion, diced

4 cloves garlic, finely chopped
or pressed

2 tablespoons tomato paste

2 cups vegetable stock

½ cup carrots, peeled and
diced

1 cup sweet potato, peeled and
diced

½ cup turnip or russet potato,
peeled and diced

½ cup pitted and chopped
green olives

2 cups chickpeas, cooked

A tagine is a traditional North African dish, named after the pot used for cooking it. Hot and sweet spices, raisins, and herbs give this recipe an aromatic kick. Feel free to swap out the veggies for your favorites, or whatever's camping out in your crisper, but try to stay true to the rest of the ingredients (you won't be disappointed!). Pair it with whole-wheat Israeli couscous (a larger, round variation) or for a gluten-free option, use quinoa or millet.

1   Toast cumin seeds and coriander seeds in a dry sauté pan until aromatic (you can toast ground spices as well, but be sure not to burn them). If using seeds, once toasted, transfer into a small spice grinder (or coffee grinder) and add the red pepper flakes, turmeric, cinnamon, black pepper, and sea salt. Grind till slightly coarse. Set aside.

2   In a large heavy-bottom shallow pot or deep skillet (cast iron works best) on medium heat, add oil, onions, and garlic. Cook until onions are translucent and golden, stirring continuously for about 3 to 4 minutes.

3   Reduce heat to medium-low, add the spices, tomato paste, vegetable stock, carrots, sweet potatoes, and turnip. Cover and simmer for about 25 minutes, or until the carrots and potatoes are tender. (Cooking time varies based on thickness of chopped veggies.)

One 6-ounce jar of baby artichokes, strained, rinsed, and quartered

3 tablespoons lemon zest

¼ cup golden raisins

3 tablespoons chopped parsley, plus more for garnish

3 tablespoons chopped cilantro, plus more for garnish

2 tablespoons chopped mint, plus more for garnish

Sea salt, to taste

Lemon zest (optional)

Red chile, thinly sliced (adjust based on desired spiciness) (optional)

4   When the root veggies are tender, add the olives, chickpeas, artichokes, lemon zest, and raisins. Continue simmering for about 5 to 8 minutes. Liquid should be reduced and thicker at this point.

5   Add parsley, cilantro, mint, and sea salt, folding in all the herbs. Cover and remove from heat.

6   Taste and add more salt if needed.

7   Garnish with lemon zest, sliced red chile, and fresh herbs, if desired.

ONE-POT MEALS:
GRAINS & VEGGIES PLUS YOUR FAVORITE CONDIMENTS

Simplicity makes the Crazy Sexy lifestyle sustainable. One-pot meals decrease your prep work so you have more time to nosh and play. These dishes will be ready as soon as their base ingredient (usually a grain, noodle, or bean) is cooked.

1 Start cooking your favorite grain, noodle, or bean (your base). 2 Once the base is almost finished cooking, add frozen or fresh veggies on top. Shut off the heat and cover with a lid. Allow your vegetables to steam for 1 to 3 minutes, depending on the veggies you choose. Add chopped dark greens (if using), cover with lid again, and steam for another 1 to 3 minutes just before serving. 3 Season with your favorite condiments, herbs, and spices. Try olive oil, flax oil, toasted or raw seeds, nutritional yeast, hot sauce, tamari, or any dressing (page 224).

CRAZY SEXY ONE-POT POSSIBILITIES

Quinoa (base), frozen peas and corn, kale, avocado, tamari, and hot sauce

White beans (base), zucchini, spinach, olive oil, sea salt, and hot sauce

Brown rice (base), broccoli and cauliflower florets, kale, flax oil, nutritional yeast, lemon, toasted sunflower seeds, and tamari

Asian Stir-Raw
with **MISO GINGER SAUCE**

Serves 6

- - - - - - - - - - - - - - - - - -

MISO GINGER SAUCE
¼ cup olive oil

1 tablespoon tamari

1 teaspoon toasted sesame oil

1 cup mandarin orange juice
(or orange juice)

½ cup white miso

2 tablespoons minced ginger

3 cloves garlic, minced

½ red, hot chile (seeded if you
want less heat) (page 225)

STIR-RAW
1 cup small broccoli florets

¼ cup julienned red bell pepper

½ cup shredded red cabbage,

¼ cup thinly julienned carrots

½ cup stemmed and thick
julienned snow peas

½ cup shiitake mushrooms,
stemmed and quartered

1 cup bean sprouts

½ cup chopped cilantro

½ cup torn basil

GARNISH (OPTIONAL)
Bean sprouts

Chopped cilantro

Torn basil

Yes, you read the title correctly—Stir-RAW. It's not fried or sautéed, yet it satisfies any sizzle craving. Marinating the veggies allows them to soften and absorb the Miso Ginger Sauce, giving them a cooked texture. Since this recipe skips the heat, the enzymes in the raw veggies stay intact. Enzymes in your food assist with every bodily function, so your cells will thank you for the extras. This Stir-Raw is tasty poured over a bowl of Sesame Root Rice (page 145) or zucchini noodles (page 182), and sprinkled with some Fiery Pistachios (page 253).

1   *Prepare Miso Ginger Sauce:* In a high-speed blender, blend the olive oil, tamari, sesame oil, mandarin orange juice, miso, ginger, garlic, and chile, until smooth.

2   *Prepare Stir-Raw:* Combine all ingredients, setting aside a small amount of the bean sprouts and herbs for garnish.

3   Add the sauce to the Stir-Raw mixture and marinate for about an hour, to soften the veggies.

4   *Optional:* For more of a cooked texture, spread the marinated and strained veggies on dehydrator sheets. Dehydrate at 110°F for about an hour. Remove from dehydrator and peel from dehydrator sheets. Alternatively, in a large sauté pan on medium-low heat, add marinated veggies, and cook for about 3 to 4 minutes. The veggies won't be raw, but will still have a crunch.

5   *Serve:* Garnish with bean sprouts and fresh herbs.

Teriyaki Tofu
with WILD MUSHROOMS *and* SOBA NOODLES

2 KF

Serves 4 to 5

- - - - - - - - - - - - - - - - - -

TERIYAKI MARINADE

5 tablespoons tamari

3 tablespoons sesame oil

½ tablespoon olive oil

½ cup pineapple juice

6 tablespoons rice vinegar

5 tablespoons agave or maple syrup

5 cloves garlic, minced

2 tablespoons finely minced ginger

BASIC INGREDIENTS

One 14-ounce package of extra-firm tofu, pressed, and sliced into 6 slabs (see page 101 for tips on pressing your tofu)

1 package soba noodles

½ tablespoon olive oil

SESAME-SAKE REDUCTION

1 cup orange juice

1 cup cheap sake or dry white cooking wine

1½ tablespoons arrowroot, made into a slurry by mixing with ¼ cup cold water

Garlic, ginger, chiles, and sake combine with baked tofu to create a teriyaki touchdown. Psst . . . tofu leftovers are sublime in a wrap with some veggies the next day at lunchtime, or popped into another stir-fry.

1   *Prepare Teriyaki Marinade:* **Combine tamari, sesame oil, olive oil, pineapple juice, rice vinegar, agave, garlic, and ginger in a bowl and whisk well. Set aside ⅔ cup of the marinade for the Sesame-Sake Reduction.**

2   *Prepare tofu:* **Place each slice of tofu in a shallow pan (do not stack slices). Cover tofu in the remaining Teriyaki Marinade. Allow tofu to sit and absorb marinade for 1 to 3 hours.**

3   Preheat oven to 325°F.

4   Cook soba noodles until al dente, making sure that they are not overcooked. Set aside.

5   Place tofu on a sheet pan brushed with olive oil and pour the marinade leftover in the pan on top. Bake tofu for about 1 hour, flipping halfway through. The tofu is done when the marinade has evaporated and the tofu is firm. Remove from oven.

6   *Prepare Sesame-Sake Reduction:* **While the tofu is baking, in a small saucepan on medium-high heat, whisk the reserved ⅔ cup of the Teriyaki Marinade with the orange juice and sake. Reduce liquid by half, cooking it for about 15 minutes.**

7   Whisk in arrowroot slurry and remove from heat. Sauce should thicken up and coat the back of spoon.

NOODLE-VEGGIE MIX

2 tablespoons sesame oil

2 cups chanterelle, hedgehog, or other wild mushrooms, cleaned and quartered (or whole if small in size)

½ cup canned sliced water chestnuts

1 cup julienned snow peas

½ cup coarsely chopped basil

GARNISH (OPTIONAL)

Sliced red chile

3 tablespoons diced green onions

Basil, chopped

8   *Prepare Noodle-Veggie Mix:* In wok or large sauté pan on medium-high, add sesame oil, followed by the mushrooms, water chestnuts, and snow peas. Continuously stir as ingredients cook for a couple minutes. Add the cooked noodles and ladle a few ounces of the reduction into the pan quickly. Add basil and use tongs to toss the noodles well. Remove from heat.

9   *Prepare tofu steaks:* In a small sauté pan on medium heat, add a few spoonfuls of reduction and the baked tofu steaks, cooking until the sauce thickens. Add more reduction as it is absorbed by the tofu. Once reduction has caramelized, remove from heat.

10   *Serve:* In shallow serving bowls, add a heaping portion of the noodle-veggie mix in the center of the plate. Top off with the tofu steaks and drizzle the remaining sauce over the noodles. Garnish each plate with sliced red chile, green onions, and any remaining basil leaves if you like.

KELP NOODLE NEWS

Kelp is a seaweed that is high in iodine (beneficial to thyroid function and metabolism) and calcium. You'll find kelp noodles (crunchy, clear, neutral-tasting noodles of the sea) at health-food stores and online. Sea Tangle and Gold Mine are good brands. They're a gluten-free, vegan, and raw alternative to traditional pastas. Incorporate these mineral-rich noodles into your repertoire by popping them into a stir-fry, adding them to a salad, or tossing them with a marinara or pesto sauce.

Two 12-ounce packages of kelp noodles

PAD THAI SAUCE

½ cup tamarind paste from a 2" x 2" block of tamarind pulp (see instructions)

1 cup heated water

1 medium tomato

½ or I Thai chili (depending on spice desired)

1 medium clove garlic

1 small shallot

¼ cup shoyu

1 tablespoon lime juice

¼ cup toasted sesame oil

1 tablespoon agave

VEGETABLES

1 head of baby bok choy, roughly chopped

1 medium carrot, diced or julienned

1 medium zucchini, diced or julienned

1 medium orange bell pepper, julienned

1 large sliced king oyster mushroom

1 cup chopped snow peas

3 green onions, sliced

VEGETABLE MARINADE

¼ cup shoyu

1 tablespoon lime

Drizzle of olive oil

2 tablespoons of Pad Thai Sauce

Pad Thai
with KELP NOODLES

guest chef
SARMA MELNGAILIS

This Pad Thai is a variation of a dish served at Pure Food and Wine restaurant. Kelp noodles are easy to use and have a great texture, and as a bonus they're low-calorie and filled with sea-vegetable nutrition. They can be used with virtually any sauce and ingredients. The tamarind pulp in this recipe gives the dish a tart and bright flavor.

1   Chop kelp noodles into 3- to 4-inch pieces. Set aside.

2   *Prepare Pad Thai Sauce:* Cut off a 2" x 2" block of tamarind pulp and dissolve in 1 cup of hot water (not quite boiling), removing any seeds. With a fork, work it into a paste. Let it soak for 15 minutes.

3   Combine tomato, chili, garlic, shallot, shoyu, lime juice, sesame oil, and agave in Vitamix or high-speed blender and blend well. Next add the tamarind and blend until very smooth.

4   *Prepare vegetables:* Mix all chopped veggies in a large bowl.

5   *Prepare marinade:* In a bowl, whisk all vegetable marinade ingredients together.

6   Mix veggies and marinade until liquid is evenly dispersed. Cover and let sit in refrigerator for an hour or more.

7   *Assemble Pad Thai:* Add the noodles to the veggie mixture, pouring the remaining Pad Thai sauce into the bowl, and mix well with tongs until sauce is evenly distributed.

Beetroot Ravioli
with CASHEW CREAM CHEESE

2 GF R SF KF

Serves 4 to 6

MARINADE

¼ cup olive or garlic oil

1 lemon

Sea salt, to taste

Freshly ground black pepper, to taste

BEETROOT RAVIOLI

2 large beets, peeled and sliced into paper-thin rounds

1 cup Cashew Cream Cheese (page 237)

ASPARAGUS SALAD

½ bunch asparagus

1½ tablespoons toasted pumpkin-seed oil, or quality olive oil

½ lemon

Sea salt, to taste

Freshly ground black pepper, to taste

GARNISH (OPTIONAL)

Fresh minced chives

Aged balsamic vinegar

Freshly ground black pepper, to taste

Sea salt, to taste

Homemade raw ravioli may seem daunting, but it's actually quite easy. And this rendition contains the powerful phytonutrient betanin, which helps to neutralize nasty free radicals in the body. These revolutionary raviolis are a splendid start to any Mediterranean-inspired meal. Bravo!

1   *Prepare Marinade:* Combine olive oil, squeeze of lemon, salt, and pepper in a bowl. Add sliced beets and marinate for at least 1 hour to overnight.

2   *Prepare Ravioli:* Lay half of the sliced, marinated beets on a flat surface (these are the bottom layer of your ravioli). Using a spoon, scoop one tablespoon of the Cashew Cream Cheese in the center of each beet slice (you could also use a pastry bag). Cover the cheese with another sliced beet to complete the ravioli.

3   *Prepare Asparagus Salad:* Shave the asparagus into long, thin pieces using a veggie peeler. Combine the asparagus, toasted pumpkin-seed oil, squeeze of lemon, and a sprinkling of salt and pepper in a bowl, and gently toss to mix ingredients well. Do this just before serving, to ensure you keep the crispness of the veggies.

4   *Serve:* Place 6 to 8 ravioli on each plate. Arrange a handful of shaved and dressed Asparagus Salad on top of the ravioli. Garnish with minced chives, a drizzle of aged balsamic vinegar, cracked pepper, and a pinch of sea salt if using.

note FROM CHAD

In my Istanbul restaurant we offered many small plates, encouraging our guests to share and experience a variety of dishes. This was by far the best-selling small plate during the winter and spring months, and it followed me to my Germany and London locations.

Wild Mushroom
Croquettes
with HORSERADISH CREAM

2 GF R KF

Serves 8 to 10

2 tablespoons tamari

2½ tablespoons olive oil

2 cups assorted wild mushrooms (any combination of chanterelles, portobello, baby portabollos, shiitake, or oyster), diced

1½ cups raw almonds, soaked in water for a few hours, to soften

1½ cups raw walnuts, soaked in water for a few hours, to soften

1 cup raw pine nuts

3 stalks celery, finely diced

¼ cup finely minced red onion

⅓ cup quartered cherry tomatoes

⅓ cup small broccoli florets

1½ tablespoons minced sage

½ cup torn basil

2 tablespoons minced oregano

2 tablespoons lemon juice

Raw pine nuts and marinated mushrooms make this raw croquette a savory, satisfying, and healthy alternative to any meat patty. You can dress it up for a dinner party or put it on a bun and eat it like a burger with your pretty paws any day of the week.

1   In a medium mixing bowl, combine tamari and 2 tablespoons olive oil. Add mushrooms, mix, and set aside. Let mushrooms marinate for about 15 to 20 minutes. Strain the mushrooms from the marinade before use.

2   In a food processor, blend almonds, walnuts, and pine nuts until smooth. Alternatively, you can use a twin gear juicer with a solid plate.

3   In a bowl, combine nut mixture with celery, onion, tomatoes, broccoli, sage, basil, oregano, lemon juice, chili powder, salt, and pepper, and thoroughly mix with hands.

4   Once mushrooms are soft and strained, add the mushrooms to the vegetable mixture, and thoroughly mix with hands. Form mixture into 10 small croquettes.

5   *Raw version:* Place croquettes on dehydrator sheets, and dehydrate at 110°F for 4 to 6 hours. Remove from the dehydrator and peel from sheets. *Cooked version:* Preheat oven to 275°F, lightly oil a baking sheet, place croquettes on sheet, and bake for about 15 minutes. Flip and cook for an additional 5 to 10 minutes until the croquettes are firm. Remove from oven.

1½ tablespoons chili powder

1 teaspoon sea salt

Freshly ground black pepper,
to taste

Horseradish Cream (page 240)

Red cabbage leaves

Lettuce

Tomato slices

Red onion slices

Avocado slices

6 Place croquette on a heaping pile of your favorite herb salad.
Drizzle with Horseradish Cream. Alternatively, use red cabbage
leaves as burger buns and top the burger with Horseradish
Cream, lettuce, tomato, sliced onion, and avocado.

tip **BOLOGNESE SAUCE** For a delicious Bolognese sauce,
crumble the leftover croquette mix on a dehydrator sheet and dry until
crisp, about 6 to 8 hours. For the cooked version, lightly oil a baking
sheet, spread mixture, and bake for about 40 minutes on 225°F, or
until crisp, making sure not to burn. Remove from oven. Mix into your
favorite raw or cooked red sauce and serve over raw or cooked pasta.
Savory, hearty, and sooo delicious.

note FROM CHAD
While holding raw culinary trainings early in my career,
these croquettes were a staple in my classes. I love
how the refreshing broccoli florets and whole-leaf basil
balance out the richness of the pine nuts.

8 small Anaheim chile peppers
(or any thin, long chiles or red
bell peppers)

½ tablespoon olive oil

CASHEW-JALAPEÑO CHEESE

2 cups raw cashews, soaked
in water for a few hours, to
soften

3 tablespoons lime juice

¾ cup water

2 tablespoons nutritional yeast

2 tablespoons onion powder

1 jalapeño, seeded and minced

¼ cup finely diced red bell
pepper

¼ cup finely diced yellow bell
pepper

½ cup finely chopped cilantro

2 shallots, minced

1½ tablespoons minced
oregano

1½ tablespoons cumin powder

Sea salt, to taste

ANCHO PEPPER PURÉE (RED ENCHILADA SAUCE)

½ cup dried ancho peppers,
seeded (sidebar page 225)

2 red bell peppers, chopped

3 garlic cloves

3 tablespoons date paste or
yacón syrup

3 tablespoons apple cider
vinegar

½ tablespoon smoked sweet
paprika

½ teaspoon sea salt

3 tablespoons olive oil

Chile Rellenos
with RED AND GREEN SAUCES

Crazy Sexy Kitchen's Chile Rellenos will be a big hit with
anyone who relishes authentic Mexican cuisine. But just
in case you need a little cool-off, the sweet Pear–Pea Shoot
Salad provides refreshing relief from the jalapeño heat. If
you're pressed for time, feel free to replace the purées with
your favorite salsa.

1   Preheat oven to 225°F (for cooked version).

2   *Prepare peppers:* Slice Anaheim peppers lengthwise down the
middle, being careful to leave stems on. Use a small spoon to
scrape away the seeds and seed membrane to prepare pepper
for stuffing.

3   *Prepare Cashew-Jalapeño Cheese:* In a blender, add the soaked
cashews, lime, and water, and blend on high until completely
smooth. Pour cashew mixture into a bowl and add nutritional
yeast, onion powder, jalapeño, red and yellow bell peppers,
cilantro, shallots, oregano, cumin, and salt. Mix all ingredients
together by hand.

4   *Prepare stuffed peppers:* Using a teaspoon, stuff the peppers
with a scoop of Cashew-Jalapeño Cheese. If you have a pastry
bag, place cheese mixture in the bag and squeeze into peppers.

5   *Raw version:* Place stuffed peppers on a dehydrator sheet and
dehydrate at 110°F for 2 hours. Remove from the dehydrator
and peel from sheets. *Cooked version:* Place stuffed peppers on
baking sheet brushed with olive oil and cook at 225°F for 35
minutes. Remove from oven.

6   *Prepare Ancho Pepper Purée:* Rehydrate the ancho peppers in
hot water until they are soft; this should take about 15 minutes
or so. Be sure to remove as many of the seeds as possible.

7   In high-speed blender, blend all ingredients until smooth and
liquefied, slowly pouring in the olive oil to emulsify.

CILANTRO MINT PURÉE (GREEN ENCHILADA SAUCE)

1 cup chopped cilantro

1 cup chopped mint

3 tablespoons agave

½ avocado

¼ cup chopped green onion

2 serrano chiles, seeded and chopped

2 cloves garlic

½ teaspoon cumin powder

3 tablespoons lime juice

¼ cup water

¼ teaspoon sea salt

PEAR-PEA SHOOT SALAD

1 pear, sliced paper thin

4 cups pea shoots or sunflower sprouts

½ cup cilantro

3 tablespoons Lemon Oil (page 227) (alternative: 1 tablespoon lemon juice and 2 tablespoons olive oil)

GARNISH (OPTIONAL)

Your favorite salsa

Freshly ground black pepper, to taste

8 *Prepare Cilantro Mint Purée:* In high-speed blender, blend all ingredients until smooth and liquefied.

9 *Prepare Pear–Pea Shoot Salad:* Right before serving, combine pears, pea shoots, cilantro, and Lemon Oil in a bowl and toss gently. Set aside.

10 *Serve:* Spread a couple tablespoons of both purées in center of plate. Using a spoon, artfully spread purées across plate for a sexy effect. Place a big handful of the Pear–Pea Shoot Salad in the center of the plate with a stuffed pepper on top. Add a couple of tablespoons of your favorite salsa, top with black pepper, and serve.

---

note FROM CHAD

I served this as a special at my London restaurant during the peak of pepper season. The sweet crispness of the Pear-Pea Shoot Salad balances the spicy contrast of the red and green sauces. This is wonderful as a main dish, or if using small sweet peppers, as an appetizer.

2 GF SF

Serves 6 to 8
(3 blinis per serving)

CASHEW COCONUT CHUTNEY

1 cup cashews

½ cup unsweetened dried shredded coconut

¼ cup dried fruit (raisins, apricots, dates)

1 small green chili, minced, or ¼ teaspoon cayenne

½ to ¾ cup water

1 tablespoon canola oil

1 tablespoon agave or other natural sweetener

½ teaspoon salt

FLOUR MIXTURE

½ teaspoon ground fennel

½ teaspoon cumin

½ teaspoon turmeric

¼ teaspoon crushed red pepper

1½ cups chickpea flour

1 teaspoon salt

½ teaspoon baking soda

VEGETABLE MIXTURE

2 tablespoons canola oil

1 small onion, minced

2 cloves garlic, minced

1 jalapeño, minced

¼ cup cilantro, minced

1 tablespoon minced fresh ginger

1 cup water or enough to form a thick pancake batter

Canola spray

INDIAN
Chickpea Blinis
with CASHEW COCONUT CHUTNEY

Served with a bowl of soup and a salad, this is perfect for a light lunch. Best of all, it's gluten-free. You can make this chutney or purchase one—there are many delicious chutneys available in most natural-food stores.

1   *Prepare Cashew Coconut Chutney:* Pulse the cashews in a food processor until they are in small pieces, then add coconut, dried fruit, green chili, water, oil, agave, and salt. Pulse until mixture has a uniform chunky texture. Set aside.

2   *Prepare Flour Mixture:* In a bowl, mix fennel, cumin, turmeric, and crushed red pepper together. Mix chickpea flour, salt, and baking soda together and then combine with the spice mixture.

3   *Prepare Vegetable Mixture:* Warm a sauté pan and add the canola oil. Add the onion and garlic and sauté for a few minutes. Stir in the jalapeño, cilantro, and ginger and cook until tender, about 3 minutes, then add the water.

4   *Prepare blini batter:* Combine the vegetable mixture with the flour mixture. Mix together well.

5   Heat a medium-size skillet (cast iron is great) until very hot, and spray liberally with canola oil. Spoon ¼ cup of batter into the pan and spread with the back of a spoon. Repeat with a few more (don't make too many at a time). Lower heat and cook about 3 minutes or until the edges start to brown. Flip over and cook on the other side about 2 minutes.

6   Place 3 blinis on each plate. Drop a dollop of the chutney on top of each one.

Seitan Brisket
with ROASTED CHANTERELLE GRAVY

2

Serves 8 to 10

2 tablespoons olive oil, plus more for loaf and pan

1 cup finely minced white onions

¼ cup tamari

3¼ cups vegetable stock or mushroom stock

⅓ cup maple syrup

1½ cups Marsala wine (or sherry)

½ cup tomato paste or ketchup

½ tablespoon smoked paprika

4 cloves garlic, finely minced

1 tablespoon vegan Worcestershire sauce

½ tablespoon chipotle powder

2½ tablespoons onion granules or powder

2 tablespoons garlic granules or powder

2½ cups vital gluten flour

½ cup nutritional yeast

1 teaspoon sea salt

Roasted Chanterelle Gravy (page 235), to taste

This quintessential celebratory centerpiece will have guests begging for the recipe. The crisp, caramelized glaze makes this seitan brisket an unforgettable addition to any holiday plate. This brisket may take some time, but if you make a large batch and store it tightly in plastic wrap, it will keep for a little over a week in the fridge, or a month in the freezer. This dish turns into a delightful meal when served with Supah Good Mashed Potatoes (page 222).

1   Preheat oven to 375°F.

2   In a small sauté pan on medium-high heat, add the oil and onions. Cook until translucent and golden brown. Set aside.

3   In a bowl, mix tamari, vegetable stock, maple syrup, wine, tomato paste, paprika, garlic, and Worcestershire sauce.

4   Add the sautéed onions to mixture and whisk. Set aside.

5   In separate bowl, mix chipotle powder, onion granules, garlic granules, vital gluten flour, yeast, and salt.

6   Create a small well in the center of the dry mixture. Gradually add a bit less than half of the wet mixture into the well slowly, stopping frequently to stir, until you get a sturdy dough consistency. Set aside remaining half of wet mixture, which will be used for the braising liquid. You should be able to stretch the dough without tearing it apart too easily. Continue to knead until the bowl surface is dry and the dough has a tough, elastic texture.

7   On a cutting board, press and stretch the seitan dough until it's no more than 1-inch thick. This is your seitan loaf. Lightly coat the seitan loaf with a small amount of oil.

8   Spray or wipe the bottom of a casserole pan (or small braising pan) with olive oil. Place seitan loaf in the center of the pan. Pour most of the remaining wet mixture over and around the seitan loaf. Flip and move around until the liquid just about covers the loaf. Use any leftover liquid for basting while seitan loaf bakes.

9   Bake for 30 minutes. Flip the loaf and baste with some of the remaining liquid at 15-minute intervals, pouring more liquid over the loaf if needed, to ensure the seitan stays moist. Continue this process until most of the liquid has thickened up (about 2 to 3 cycles), creating a delicious glaze that covers the loaf. The seitan should be firm to the touch. The seitan will cook for about 1 hour, 15 minutes total.

10   Remove the loaf from the oven and allow the seitan to cool for about 15 minutes to firm up before use.

11   Slice thinly and top with Roasted Chanterelle Gravy.

note FROM CHAD
Slice the brisket into steaks and throw them on the grill. Finish with some grilled onions, peppers, and Vegenaise for some serious comfort food.

GRATITUDE REMAINS OPEN-FACED SANDWICH

Do leftovers take over your fridge, post–Crazy Sexy holiday feast? Grab your favorite rustic whole-grain ciabatta bread or baguette, slice in half, bathe in Rustic Cranberry Relish (page 238) and add a generous helping of paper-thin sliced Seitan Brisket (page 200). Top with Roasted Brussels Sprouts with Pistachios and Cipollini Onions (page 208), and finish with piping hot Roasted Chanterelle Gravy (page 235). It may be sloppy, but this sandwich deserves its own holiday. (Especially after one too many spiked "For the Love of Nogs!" [page 97] the night before.)

MADEIRA PEPPERCORN
Tempeh

guest chef
TAL RONNEN

2

Serves 6

½ cup tamari or soy sauce

8 thin slices fresh ginger

Two 1-inch pieces kombu (sea vegetable found in most health-food stores)

¼ teaspoon sea salt

2 garlic cloves, sliced

6 cups water

Two 8-ounce packages of tempeh

1 cup unbleached white flour

Salt and pepper, to taste

4 tablespoons canola oil

1 tablespoon finely chopped shallots

2 tablespoons olive oil

1 cup Madeira wine

1 sprig thyme

2 bay leaves

3 cups vegan beef-flavored broth (we recommend Better Than Bouillon brand "No-Beef Base")

1 teaspoon crushed black peppercorns

1 tablespoon arrowroot or cornstarch

¼ cup cold water

2 tablespoons Earth Balance or other vegan butter

Although tofu has become more popular in the West, the firm texture of tempeh makes it an easy protein to prepare. It's best to braise tempeh first; otherwise it's too dense for a cold marinade to penetrate. This dish will wow and convert any hardcore steak lover!

1   In a large pot, combine the tamari, ginger, kombu, sea salt, sliced garlic, and 6 cups water. Bring to a simmer.

2   Cut each piece of tempeh diagonally into 12 thin slices, add to the pot, and simmer for at least 1 hour. Remove the tempeh from pot and cool on a dry surface.

3   Combine the flour, salt, and pepper. Dredge the tempeh, coating completely.

4   Heat the canola oil in a large pan. Brown the tempeh on both sides, remove from the pan, and set aside. In the same pan, lower the heat and sauté the shallots in the olive oil for 3 minutes.

5   Add the wine, thyme, and bay leaves. Cook until reduced by half. Add the broth and the peppercorns. Cook for 20 minutes. Remove from heat.

6   Mix the arrowroot or cornstarch with the cold water. Add to the pan and let thicken. Turn off the heat and whisk in the vegan butter a little bit at a time.

7   Return the tempeh to the pan to coat with the sauce or drizzle the sauce over the tempeh.

guest chef
**SARMA
MELNGAILIS**

Yellow Squash Fettuccine
with CREAMY PINE NUT ALFREDO

2 GF R SF

Serves 2

- - - - - - - - - - - - - - - - - -

CREAMY PINE NUT ALFREDO SAUCE

1½ cups raw pine nuts

3 tablespoons olive oil

¼ cup freshly squeezed lemon juice

1 tablespoon nutritional yeast

½ teaspoon sea salt

SQUASH NOODLES

2 to 3 medium Goldbar or yellow summer squash

½ teaspoon sea salt, plus more for seasoning

¼ cup pine nuts, coarsely chopped

½ teaspoon nut oil or olive oil

¼ cup green olives, pitted and thinly sliced

1 small handful of lemon basil leaves (or use regular basil)

Freshly ground black pepper

This is a creamy, rich, and righteously raw pasta dish without the flour and gluten of regular pasta or the dairy, cheese, and butter of a traditional Alfredo sauce. Nutritional yeast adds cheesy flavor and is also a great source of B vitamins.

1   *Prepare Creamy Pine Nut Alfredo Sauce:* Place the pine nuts in a bowl and add enough water to cover. Let sit for an hour or more to plump the nuts.

2   Drain the water from the pine nuts and add the nuts to a blender with the olive oil, lemon juice, nutritional yeast, and salt. Blend until smooth. If the sauce is too thick, add a bit of water.

3   *Prepare Squash Noodles:* Cut the ends off the squash. Julienne the squash on a mandoline, and place it in a colander or strainer. Toss with sea salt and let sit for at least 30 minutes to soften and allow a bit of the liquid to drain out.

4   In a small bowl, toss the chopped pine nuts with the oil and a pinch of salt.

5   *Serve:* Place enough squash for two servings in a medium bowl. Add enough of the sauce to generously coat the squash fettuccine. Add the green olives, half of the lemon basil, and a pinch of ground black pepper, and gently toss.

6   Divide the fettuccine between two shallow bowls, making tall piles. Drizzle more of the sauce around the squash. Sprinkle with the chopped pine nuts and garnish with remaining basil leaves.

Sarma Melngailis is the founder of One Lucky Duck and co-founder of Pure Food and Wine Restaurant

tip **SQUASH SEASON**   In the summer, you can usually find Goldbar squash, a darker yellow variety. It's shaped more like straight zucchini and easier to julienne. If unavailable, regular yellow summer squash or zucchini is fine, or a mix of both.

Garden Lasagna
with CASHEW–PINE NUT RICOTTA

2 SF

GF *if using wheat-free tamari*

Serves 4 to 6

1½ cups sliced portobello mushrooms (or king oyster, chanterelles, baby portobellos, or porcini)

2 tablespoons tamari

2 tablespoons olive oil

3 round green zucchini, sliced into thin rounds, or 2 long zucchini, thinly sliced lengthwise

1 cup Cashew–Pine Nut Ricotta (page 231)

½ cup Tomato Relish (page 239) (or diced tomatoes tossed with 1 clove garlic, minced, and 1 tablespoon olive oil)

4 vine-ripened or Roma tomatoes sliced in thin rounds

1 cup Olive Tapenade (page 141)

Freshly ground black pepper, to taste

Truffled Parmesan (page 233, optional)

Who says you need an oven to create a comforting plate of lasagna? This raw-tastic version is packed with traditional flavors that will steal the show in any Italian meal. Give this dish extra elegance with the Truffled Parmesan.

1 Marinate the mushrooms in tamari and olive oil for about 15 minutes to soften. Strain the mushrooms and set aside.

2 Build the lasagna layers in a pan in the following order or on large plates if making individual portions: sliced zucchini, Cashew–Pine Nut Ricotta, Tomato Relish, sliced tomato, marinated mushrooms, sliced zucchini, Olive Tapenade, sliced tomato. Finish with a small spoonful of Cashew–Pine Nut Ricotta.

3 Garnish with freshly ground black pepper and Truffled Parmesan if you like.

SEXY SIDES

Fresh Minted Tabouli

Garlicky Mushrooms

Roasted Brussels Sprouts
with Pistachios *and* Cipollini Onions

Sautéed Chard

Roasted Root Vegetables Five Ways
by PAM BROWN

Semi-Dried Tomatoes

Bok Choy *with* Lemon Tahini Sauce
by PAM BROWN

Zucchini Carpaccio

Crazy Sexy Refried Pinto Beans

Slow-Roasted Beets
with Fresh Horseradish

Cauliflower Risotto

Shredded Kale *and* Carrots
with Almond Butter Dressing
by PETER A. CERVONI

Sage Polenta *with* Nana's Marinara

Supah Good Mashed Potatoes
with Garlic Herb Buttah
by DEREK SARNO

Pastrami-Spiced Young Carrots
with a White Bean Sauerkraut Purée
by RICHARD LANDAU

1 GF R SF KF Q

Serves 4 to 6

1½ cups seeded and diced tomatoes

1 cup peeled and diced cucumber

3 cups coarsely minced parsley

½ cup peeled and finely minced or pulsed parsnip

3 cloves garlic, minced

3 tablespoons chiffonaded mint

3 tablespoons lemon juice

2 tablespoons olive oil

¼ teaspoon sea salt

½ teaspoon finely minced chile (optional)

FRESH MINTED
Tabouli

Tabouli is a Middle Eastern staple that delivers crisp, feisty flavors along with a heaping dose of vitamin K (thanks, parsley!). Serve it on its own, or with Walnut Falafel (page 153). Minced parsnip is used in this recipe instead of bulgur, making it light as a feather and gluten-free.

1   In a bowl, hand-mix all ingredients well.

2   For tastiest results, allow tabouli to sit for 1 hour and strain off excess water before serving.

1 GF SF Q

Serves 6

1 tablespoon Earth Balance or other vegan butter

1½ cups wild mushrooms, loosely packed, preferably chanterelles

3 garlic cloves, minced

2 tablespoons minced chives

Sea salt, to taste

Freshly ground black pepper, to taste

GARLICKY Mushrooms

Whether it's a heaping pile of Supah Good Mashed Potatoes (page 222) or a gorgeous serving of Sage Polenta with Nana's Marinara (page 221) these magnificent mushrooms will be the cherry on the top of your home-cooked meal.

1   In a large sauté pan over medium heat, melt the butter, being careful not to burn it.

2   Add the mushrooms and garlic and sauté until the mushrooms have released their liquid and the pan is almost dry, about 4 minutes. Gently stir in the chives, season with salt and pepper to taste, and remove from the heat.

3   Serve as a savory side dish or on top of a Crostini with Artichoke Purée (page 144).

Roasted Brussels Sprouts
with PISTACHIOS *and* CIPOLLINI ONIONS

Are you ready to become a Brussels sprouts addict? This dish is redic! Whether it's a Tuesday night dinner or a holiday celebration, everyone will want a heaping serving of this stupendous side dish (and you don't have to tell them how easy it is to make!).

1 GF SF Q

Serves 4

3 cups Brussels sprouts, cleaned and halved

1 cup cipollini onions or shallots, peeled and quartered

¼ cup raw pistachios

½ teaspoon black pepper

½ teaspoon sea salt

Pinch of red pepper flakes

2 tablespoons olive oil

3 tablespoons sherry (or vegetable stock if omitting alcohol)

1   Preheat oven to 375°F. In a bowl, combine Brussels sprouts, onions, and pistachios and toss with spices, olive oil, and sherry.

2   Roast Brussels sprouts mixture on sheet pan for 12 to 15 minutes, shaking pan about halfway through to ensure even cooking. Serve hot.

SAUTÉED
Chard

1 GF Q

Serves 2 to 3

1 tablespoon olive oil

3 tablespoons diced shallot or red onion

3 cloves garlic, minced

3 cups chard, stems and leaves roughly chopped

2 tablespoons water or vegetable stock

1 tablespoon gluten-free tamari

1½ tablespoons nutritional yeast

Garlic rocks! It's great for your immune system and your breath (oh, go for it!). Serve this recipe with a gluten-free grain or make it a full meal by pairing it with the Sage Polenta with Nana's Marinara (page 221).

1   In a sauté pan on medium heat, add olive oil, shallots, and garlic. Stir constantly until shallots are translucent and golden.

2   Add the chard, mix well, and make sure the shallots and garlic do not burn.

3   To speed up the cooking, add a couple tablespoons of water or veggie stock to the pan, cover with a lid, and steam for 1 minute.

4   Add tamari and nutritional yeast and mix thoroughly while still on the heat.

5   Remove from heat and serve.

BENEFITS OF NUTRITIONAL YEAST

Nutritional yeast is a cultured yeast with a nutty, cheesy flavor that is available in powdered or flake form. Its zingy taste comes with a slew of health perks, including B vitamins and fiber. And to top it off, nutritional yeast is a complete protein. Bring on the cheerleaders!

guest chef
PAM BROWN

ROASTED
Root Vegetables
FIVE WAYS

1 KF Q

Serves 4 to 6

- - - - - - - - - - - - - - - - - - -

BASIC ROASTED VEGETABLES

3 carrots, peeled

3 red potatoes, peeled

1 large yam, peeled

1 small butternut squash, peeled

1 small head cauliflower

¼ cup olive oil

1 teaspoon salt

½ teaspoon black pepper

SPICY INDIAN

½ teaspoon chili powder

½ teaspoon curry powder

½ teaspoon cinnamon

APRICOT MUSTARD

5 ounces apricot jam

1 teaspoon prepared mustard

1 teaspoon canola oil

Nothing is more delicious than crispy, caramelized roasted vegetables. This recipe makes veggies simple to put together and with a little bit of spice, herbs, or a sauce, they'll always shine!

1 Preheat oven to 425°F.

2 Wash all of the vegetables.

3 Cut vegetables into medium chunks, about 1 inch.

4 Place vegetables in a single, even layer on a baking sheet.

5 Drizzle the oil over the vegetables and sprinkle with the salt and pepper.

6 Toss well to make sure they are evenly coated.

7 Bake 25 to 35 minutes, stirring a few times and rotating the pan. The vegetables are ready to remove from the oven when tender.

8 Choose one of the following five sauces:

Spicy Indian

1 When the vegetables are just about done roasting, pull the pan from the oven and sprinkle lightly with chili powder, curry powder, and cinnamon.

2 Bake a few more minutes.

Apricot Mustard

1 Whisk the ingredients together in a small mixing bowl.

2 When the vegetables are just about done, pull the pan from the oven and toss with the apricot mixture. Bake a few more minutes.

FRESH HERB

A few sprigs of fresh rosemary, finely chopped

1 teaspoon fresh thyme

1 teaspoon dried oregano

BBQ

1 cup of your favorite BBQ sauce

PEANUT SAUCE

½ cup smooth organic peanut butter

½ cup hot water

1 tablespoon tamari

1 tablespoon maple syrup or agave

1 tablespoon chili paste (optional) or ¼ teaspoon cayenne

Juice of 1 lemon or lime

Roasted peanuts

2 scallions, chopped (optional)

Fresh Herb

1   After tossing the vegetables with the oil, salt, and pepper, sprinkle with the herbs and roast until done.

BBQ

1   When the vegetables are just about done, pull the pan from the oven and toss with the BBQ sauce.

2   Bake a few more minutes.

Peanut Sauce

1   Blend the peanut butter, hot water, tamari, maple syrup, chili paste, and lemon juice in the food processor.

2   Remove the pan from the oven when the vegetables are just about done and toss the vegetables with the sauce. Bake a few more minutes, then sprinkle with the peanuts and scallions before serving.

ROASTING VEGGIES

Calling all farmers' market veggie vixens! Local, seasonal vegetables are superb when roasted and served as a side dish, snack, or as part of a spectacular salad. Plus, they're super easy to make!

1 Preheat oven to 375°F. 2 Combine: 1 cup veggies (suggestions: sweet potatoes, peppers, Brussels sprouts, onions, fennel, and eggplant), ½ tablespoon olive oil, and 1 tablespoon fresh herbs (suggestions: minced chiles, rosemary, thyme, or oregano with sea salt and lots of black pepper, to taste). 3 Spread the veggie mixture on a baking sheet and roast for about 15 to 20 minutes, stirring veggies halfway through cooking so they roast evenly. Remove from oven.

SEMI-DRIED
Tomatoes

1 GF SF

Serves 6

½ teaspoon fennel seeds, toasted

¼ teaspoon red pepper flakes

½ teaspoon dried oregano

¼ teaspoon sea salt; coarse is best

Freshly ground black pepper, to taste

6 vine-ripened tomatoes with stems

½ tablespoon olive oil

Olive Tapenade (page 141, optional)

1 to 2 handfuls of baby arugula, tossed with a drizzle of olive oil and squeeze of lemon juice

A summer day is so much juicier when savoring a home-grown tomato picked from your yard or a local farm. Slow roasting your tomatoes amplifies their natural sweetness. Add a coat of traditional Italian herbs and spices, and you've got one colossally tasty tomato. Leave the stems on and pair it with Olive Tapenade (page 141) for an elegant side dish.

1   Preheat oven to lowest heat setting (usually 200°F).

2   In a bowl, add all spices and mix well. Set aside.

3   Use a paring knife to slice a small *X* on the bottom of each tomato. Set aside.

4   Prepare a medium mixing bowl with ice cubes and cold water. Fill a medium pot halfway with water and bring to a boil. Gently drop the tomatoes into boiling water and count to 30. Once the skins have cracked, use tongs to remove tomatoes and place them in the bowl of ice water. (This process brightens the color and stops the tomatoes from cooking further.)

5   Using a paring knife, carefully remove the skin from each tomato, making sure the stems stay intact.

6   Lightly coat baking sheet with olive oil. Place tomatoes on sheet, spacing them evenly apart.

7   Sprinkle tomatoes with spice mixture.

8   *Raw version:* Place tomatoes on a dehydrator screen and dehydrate for 4 hours at 110°F. Remove from the dehydrator. *Cooked version:* Slow cook tomatoes for 50 to 55 minutes in oven. They are semi-dried and ready to be removed from the oven when the skins begin to tighten up and slightly crack.

9   Add a small scoop of Olive Tapenade under each tomato if desired.

10 *Serve:* Place tomato (warm or chilled) on a bed of the dressed arugula. Finish with freshly ground black pepper and serve.

guest chef
PAM BROWN

Bok Choy
with LEMON TAHINI SAUCE

1 GF SF KF Q

Serves 4

- - - - - - - - - - - - - - - - - - -

1 large or 2 small heads bok choy

1 tablespoon canola or toasted sesame oil

1 small onion, sliced

2 cloves garlic, chopped

½ cup tahini

¾ cup hot water

1 tablespoon umeboshi plum vinegar

1 tablespoon fresh lemon juice

This is an easy and delicious way to eat those all-important green vegetables. Not only do you get the nutritional benefit from eating bok choy, but extra calcium and protein from the tahini sauce as well. Umeboshi vinegar is a tangy, salty Japanese vinegar made from green apricots. (Be forewarned that a little goes a long way!)

1   Chop the bok choy into bite-size pieces and rinse in a colander.

2   Warm a sauté pan and add the oil. Toss in the onion and garlic and sauté until translucent, about 2 or 3 minutes. Add the bok choy and mix well with the onions and garlic. Sauté another 5 minutes or until tender.

3   To prepare Lemon Tahini Sauce, pour the tahini, water, vinegar, and lemon juice into a food processor and whip until creamy.

4   Pour Lemon Tahini Sauce over bok choy in the sauté pan and cook until thickened and warmed through.

ZUCCHINI
Carpaccio

1 GF R SF KF Q

Serves 4

2 medium zucchinis, sliced paper thin in rounds

2 tablespoons olive oil

3 tablespoons pine nuts, lightly toasted or raw (alternative: Truffled Parmesan, page 233)

3 tablespoons chervil leaves or flat-leaf parsley, minced

Sea salt, to taste (flaked salt is best)

Freshly ground black pepper, to taste

This delish dish will steal the hearts of Italian-cuisine lovers, while the folate and magnesium from the zucchini protects their passionate tickers! Toasted or raw pine nuts, and parsley's close cousin chervil, help create this stellar side. For molto bene magic, make sure the zucchini is sliced paper thin.

1 Use a mandoline or sharp knife to thinly slice zucchini. Arrange zucchini evenly on a large plate or platter, just slightly overlapping each slice.

2 Drizzle with olive oil and sprinkle with pine nuts and herbs.

3 Finish with sea salt and cracked pepper.

4 Serve as is, or with your favorite gluten-free bread.

CRAZY SEXY REFRIED
Pinto Beans

1 GF SF KF Q

Serves 4

2 tablespoons olive oil

½ cup finely diced white onion

½ tablespoon cumin powder

½ serrano or jalapeño chile, seeded and minced

4 cups pinto beans, cooked (or two 15-ounce cans, strained and rinsed well)

1½ cups vegetable stock

½ teaspoon sea salt

Can you say Taco Night? Olé! Leftover beans easily transform into a Mexi-masterpiece. Load up your taco shells or tortillas with these lightly refried pintos, some Green Chile Guacamole (page 231), lettuce, tomato, and a dollop of Cashew Cream Cheese (page 237).

1 In sauté pan on medium heat, add oil, onion, cumin powder, and chile. Sauté until onions are translucent.

2 Add the beans, vegetable stock, and salt. Continue to cook for 6 to 8 minutes.

3 Remove the beans from the heat. Using a potato masher, mash the beans until you have a coarse purée, and serve.

Slow-Roasted Beets
with FRESH HORSERADISH

1 GF SF

Serves 6

- - - - - - - - - - - - - - - - - - -

6 medium beets, scrubbed
and unpeeled

2 tablespoons olive oil

1 lemon, halved and juiced

3 sprigs of thyme

Sea salt, to taste

Freshly ground black pepper,
to taste

2 tablespoons sherry
vinegar

1½ tablespoons chopped
tarragon

One 2-inch piece of fresh
horseradish root, peeled

note FROM CHAD

*Bring this dish to the
next level by drizzling
it with a beet merlot
reduction. Combine 1
part beet juice and 1 part
merlot with a pinch of
salt and pepper, and sprig
of thyme. In a small
pot over low heat, cook
the liquid for about 20
minutes, reducing it by
about two-thirds. Add a
slurry of arrowroot to
thicken.*

Slow roasting beets allows their natural sugars to caramelize, intensifying their sweetness. The horseradish
root not only adds a spicy spark, it also provides a burst
of vitamin C. This is a wonderful stand-alone side, but
could also be tossed with baby arugula and Maple Candied Pecans (page 252) for a dazzling salad.

1   Preheat oven to 275°F.

2   In a bowl, combine beets with 1 tablespoon of olive oil, lemon
juice, whole thyme sprigs, salt, and pepper, and mix well to coat
the beets.

3   Using foil, make a tinfoil "boat" and pour beets inside. Leaving
space for them to steam, seal the foil by bringing edges together
and folding tightly. This package will steam the beets while
they slow roast.

4   Place package on sheet pan and cook for 60 to 75 minutes
(depending on size of beets). Beets are done when fork tender.
Remove from oven.

5   Once cooked, let cool and then peel off the skin with a paring
knife. Slice the beets in even cubes or wedges.

6   In a bowl, toss beets with sherry vinegar, remaining tablespoon
of olive oil, and tarragon. Using a Microplane or other grater,
garnish with grated fresh horseradish root. Season with more
sea salt and pepper if needed and serve.

tip ROASTED BEET BEAUTIES Removing the skin from roasted
beets is simple. **The most important tip:** Let them cool in the tinfoil
boat. This allows the skin to loosen so you can easily peel it off with a
paring knife or by hand. Slow roasting amplifies their yummy natural
oils, so avoid peeling them in water. While working with beets, wear
gloves to avoid pink-stained hands!

CAULIFLOWER
Risotto

2 GF

Serves 4 to 5

CAULIFLOWER PURÉE

2 tablespoons Earth Balance or other vegan butter

3 shallots, coarsely chopped

3 cloves of garlic, chopped

½ head of cauliflower, chopped

2 cups vegetable stock

Freshly ground black pepper, to taste

RISOTTO

1¼ cups cauliflower, divided

2 tablespoons olive oil

¼ cup minced shallot or white onion

Juice of ½ lemon

1½ tablespoons truffle oil (optional)

Sea salt, to taste

Freshly ground black pepper, to taste

GARNISH (OPTIONAL)

Sprig of parsley

CSK's cauliflower creation is a light and bright risotto rendition. Cauliflower is rich in the free-radical-fighting antioxidants: vitamin C, manganese, and carotenoids. Try it over the Sage Polenta (page 221). One word: dynamite!

1   *Prepare Cauliflower Purée:* In small pot, add the butter, shallots, garlic, cauliflower, veggie stock, and black pepper. Bring to simmer and cook for 8 to 10 minutes. Remove from heat, pour full mixture in high-speed blender, and blend until smooth. Set aside.

2   *Prepare Risotto:* In food processor, pulse ¾ cup cauliflower until finely minced to a rice consistency. Cut the remaining ½ cup cauliflower into small florets (¼ inch to ½ inch in size). Set aside.

3   In sauté pan on medium-high heat, add olive oil and shallots, cooking shallots until golden.

4   Add florets for 3 minutes, stirring frequently. Make sure not to overcook.

5   Add the 1 cup Cauliflower Purée, lemon juice, truffle oil, salt, and pepper, and cook for an additional 3 minutes.

6   Add the minced cauliflower and remove from heat. Mix well. Season with more salt and pepper if needed. Garnish with a sprig of fresh parsley if desired.

Shredded Kale and Carrots
with ALMOND BUTTER DRESSING

guest chef
PETER A. CERVONI

1 GF SF KF Q

Serves 4

- - - - - - - - - - - - - - - - - -

ALMOND BUTTER DRESSING

¼ cup almond butter

½ teaspoon lemon juice

¼ cup dates, pitted

½ cup purified water

1 clove fresh garlic

½ teaspoon sea salt

1 teaspoon cardamom powder

¼ teaspoon black pepper

KALE & CARROT SALAD

1 bunch kale

1½ carrots

½ cup sliced celery

¾ cup hemp seeds

¼ cup thinly sliced scallions

½ cup tightly packed fresh parsley, minced

¼ cup tightly packed fresh cilantro, minced

¼ cup tightly packed fresh mint, minced

¼ cup raisins

Lacinato kale (a.k.a. dinosaur kale, named for its marbled dinosaur-skin-like appearance) is best in this nutritious salad. The cardamom powder in the dressing complements the carrots, but feel free to experiment with other flavor combinations: try some dried rosemary for an Italian flair or your favorite curry powder for an Indian twist.

1   *Prepare Almond Butter Dressing:* Place all ingredients in a high-speed blender such as a Vitamix, and process on high until the dates have fully broken down into a thick, smooth, and creamy dressing.

2   *Prepare Kale & Carrot Salad:* In a food processor fitted with the slicing disc, run whole leaves of washed and dry-spun kale through the machine, stem and all.

3   Switch out slicing disc for shredder disc and process carrots.

4   *Serve:* Place all ingredients in a bowl along with ¾ cup dressing, and massage and toss gently until the dressing is evenly distributed.

Sage Polenta
with NANA'S MARINARA

1 GF SF KF Q

Serves 6

2 tablespoons olive oil

2 cups finely diced white onion

2 tablespoons minced sage

1½ cups vegetable stock

3 cups unsweetened non-dairy milk of your choice

2 tablespoons nutritional yeast

3 tablespoons Earth Balance or other vegan butter

1¼ cups fine polenta meal

½ teaspoon sea salt

½ teaspoon black pepper

Nana's Marinara (page 229)

Truffled Parmesan (page 233, optional)

Soft, buttery polenta is an Italian icon. This creamy creation brings a taste of Italy to your plate when paired with Nana's Marinara. Serve with Garlicky Mushrooms (page 207) and Sautéed Chard (page 209) for a complete Northern Italian feast.

1   In a heavy-bottom shallow pot or standard shallow pot (cast iron is best) on medium heat, add the olive oil and onions and sauté until caramelized. Add minced sage and stir well.

2   Add stock, milk, nutritional yeast, and butter. Turn to low heat and bring to a simmer.

3   Slowly, while constantly whisking, add the dry polenta, pouring in an even stream. Continue to whisk to keep the consistency smooth, while cooking.

4   Once polenta has reached a fair thickness (porridge consistency) continue to keep on low heat and cook until the corn meal has softened, about 10 to 12 minutes. Stir frequently and season with salt and pepper to taste.

5   Remove from heat, top with a heaping ladle full of Nana's Marinara and Truffled Parmesan, if using, and serve.

tip **POLENTA CAKES** Turn soft polenta into individual cakes, which can be used as a sexy stage for a variety of main dishes and starters. Prepare polenta cakes: Only use half the liquid ingredients in the Sage Polenta recipe, and then prepare soft polenta as usual. Pour finished mixture into a sheet pan brushed with olive oil. Chill for about 10 minutes, then slice polenta into cakes and sear in a sauté pan on medium heat. Double their deliciousness by pairing these cute cakes with Cauliflower Risotto (page 218) or Sautéed Chard (page 209) and Garlicky Mushrooms (page 207).

guest chef
DEREK SARNO

SUPAH GOOD
Mashed Potatoes
with GARLIC HERB BUTTAH

1 GF SF KF Q

Serves 6 to 8

5 to 6 large Yukon potatoes, peeled and quartered

5 cups water

½ to ¾ cup almond milk or other nondairy milk

4 tablespoons Garlic Herb Buttah (page 230)

1 tablespoon minced fresh thyme

2 tablespoons olive oil

½ teaspoon salt

1 teaspoon black pepper

In a word, awesomeness! When it comes to great-tasting mashed potatoes—the ultimate comfort food—this recipe can't be beat. Great on their own, or smothered in the Roasted Chanterelle Gravy (page 235).

1   Cover potatoes with water. Bring to boil on medium-high heat. Boil until cooked through. Shut off heat and strain excess water from potatoes.

2   In same pot, add the remaining ingredients to the strained potatoes. Add more or less almond milk for desired consistency. Mix all ingredients using a vegetable masher.

PASTRAMI-SPICED
Young Carrots
with a WHITE BEAN SAUERKRAUT PURÉE

guest chef
RICHARD LANDAU

1 GF SF Q

Serves 4 to 6

- -

2 pounds of young or baby bunch carrots (peeled baby carrots can be used if necessary)

4 tablespoons olive oil

2 teaspoons sherry vinegar

2 tablespoons steak seasoning (Montreal brand recommended)

¼ teaspoon ground clove

2 teaspoons salt

2 teaspoons black pepper

2 teaspoons crushed garlic

2 tablespoons Dijon mustard

One 12-ounce can of cannellini beans, drained

One 6-ounce can or jar of sauerkraut (with some of its juice)

2 tablespoons fresh dill

Mache, arugula, or parsley, for garnish

A fun vegan take on sausage and sauerkraut with Eastern European flavors, which can be enjoyed hot or cold. The spices play against the carrots' sweetness beautifully, and when eaten with the white bean sauerkraut purée, it recalls a Reuben.

1   Preheat the oven to 350°F.

2   Peel the carrots if necessary, and trim tops if attached (leave on about an inch of stem for a nice presentation), and toss in 2 tablespoons of olive oil, sherry vinegar, steak seasoning, clove, 1 teaspoon each of the salt and pepper, and 1 teaspoon of the garlic.

3   Spread on a sheet pan, cover with foil, and roast the carrots for 10 to 15 minutes (depending on size) or until they are just about tender. Remove the foil and roast uncovered for 3 to 5 more minutes or until the carrots are just about soft. Remove from the oven and let cool.

4   Meanwhile in a food processor, combine the remaining salt, pepper, and garlic; Dijon mustard; cannellini beans; sauerkraut; and dill. Purée to a smooth hummus-like consistency (add water to thin if necessary).

5   Place a small scoop of the purée in the center of the plate and place a small pile (about 4 to 6) of the carrots just to the side. Garnish with a few fresh green leaves such as mache, arugula, or parsley.

DRESSINGS, MARINADES, and CONDIMENTS

Basic
ITALIAN DRESSING

1 GF R SF KF Q

Makes 2 cups

SHELF LIFE: *1 week in fridge*

- - - - - - - - - - - - - - - - - - -

¾ cup olive oil

¼ cup apple cider vinegar

¼ cup lemon juice

¼ cup agave

4 cloves garlic, finely minced

1 small shallot, finely minced

2 tablespoons chopped oregano

1½ tablespoons minced thyme

¼ teaspoon red jalapeño, or serrano chile, seeded and finely minced

Sea salt, to taste

Freshly ground black pepper

Base recipes create a mighty foundation for limitless possibilities in your Crazy Sexy Kitchen. This dapper Italian dressing is great for salads or for any of your favorite seasonal veggies, such as peppers, fennel, and mushrooms. Just marinate them and serve as a vegetable antipasto platter.

1   In a bowl, whisk all ingredients well. Alternative: pour all ingredients into glass jar with sealable lid and shake well.

HOW TO SEED A PEPPER

Sometimes you want the chile flavor, but with less heat. The spiciness lives in the membrane and the seeds of the pepper. Seeding hot peppers such as jalapeño, Thai chile, or serrano is simple. If you're seeding lots of peppers, you may want to wear gloves to protect your fingers from irritation. Avoid touching your face, especially eyes, while working. After chiles have been washed, slice them lengthwise in half. Using a paring knife, filet the peppers by keeping the knife flush with the cutting board. Starting at the tip of each half, slide the knife under the membrane to remove. To reduce the heat further, run the seeded peppers under water before using them.

Basic
ASIAN MARINADE

1 R Q

Makes 1½ cups

SHELF LIFE: *1 week in fridge*

- - - - - - - - - - - - - - - - -

2 tablespoons olive oil

3 tablespoons toasted sesame oil

¼ cup tamari

½ cup rice vinegar

¼ cup agave or yacón syrup

4 cloves garlic, minced

1 tablespoon finely minced ginger

½ teaspoon seeded and minced hot chile (optional)

This is excellent as a salad dressing on chilled buckwheat noodles or as a marinade for tofu and your favorite veggies. Also perfect as a dip for dumplings or spring rolls. Banzai!

1   In a bowl, whisk all ingredients well. Alternative: pour all ingredients into glass jar with sealable lid and shake well.

tip **MARINATING VEGGIES**   Want to grill up some zucchinis and portobellos? Toss 'em in the Basic Italian or Basic Asian Dressing for increased flavor. Try marinated grilled veggies piled in your favorite wrap with Basic or Artichoke Aioli (page 241–242).

1   In a large sealable container, pour marinade or dressing over veggies.

2   Seal container and place in refrigerator overnight.

3   Once marinated, strain and serve raw for extra-crisp veggies. If grilling, place on grill or grill pan for about 2 to 3 minutes on each side, depending on thickness.

4   Use leftover marinade as salad dressing.

Makes 1 cup

SHELF LIFE: *10 days in fridge*

- - - - - - - - - - - - - - - - -

3 tablespoons fresh lemon juice

½ cup olive oil

1 clove garlic, finely minced

2 tablespoons lemon zest (1 lemon)

1 tablespoon agave

Sea salt, to taste

Fresh ground black pepper, to taste

Lemon OIL

Give your salad a zippy, clean twist with this citrus dressing. You can also use it as a base for more complex dressings and marinades by combining it with fresh herbs.

1   In a bowl, whisk all ingredients well. Alternative: pour all ingredients into glass jar with sealable lid and shake well.

Makes 2½ cups

SHELF LIFE: *1 week in fridge*

- - - - - - - - - - - - - - - - -

¾ cup tahini, raw or roasted

1¼ cups water

3 cloves garlic

3 tablespoons lemon juice

1 tablespoon toasted sesame oil

2½ tablespoons tamari

1½ tablespoons nutritional yeast (optional)

Garlic Tahini DRESSING

If you love tahini, then this dressing will become a staple in your fridge. Mix a large batch in the beginning of the week and it'll make your meals sing in the coming days. Try it on quinoa, grilled tofu, greens, or anything else that desires some tempting tahini goodness.

1   In a high-speed blender, blend all ingredients until smooth.

Nana's
MARINARA

1 GF SF KF Q

Serves 6

2 tablespoons olive oil

½ cup diced white onion

4 cloves of garlic, finely minced

1 small red serrano chile, minced (or ½ tablespoon red pepper flakes)

5 cups diced Roma tomatoes (if using canned: Muir Glen or San Marzano crushed are recommended)

3 tablespoons chiffonaded basil

2 tablespoons minced oregano

Sea salt, to taste

Freshly ground pepper, to taste

note FROM CHAD

There are some foods that just warm your heart and nurture your soul. For me, Nana's Marinara does just that. This is a variation of the beloved Mary Sarno's sauce (my nana) that is celebrated amongst my family and by all who had the pleasure of sitting at her table.

Some foods warm your heart and nurture your soul, like the red sauce Chef Chad's Nana used to make. Crazy Sexy Kitchen's variation is a celebration of her infamous marinara. It's best made with fresh tomatoes at peak ripeness, which is when they're in season. Serve with your favorite roasted root vegetables, Sage Polenta (page 221), or tossed with the Sautéed Chard (page 209) and gluten-free pasta. We love you, Nana!

1 In a large shallow pot on medium heat, add the olive oil, onion, garlic, and chile. Sauté until onions are translucent.

2 Add diced tomatoes and cook on low heat for 30 to 35 minutes, stirring well to prevent sticking.

3 Once tomatoes have cooked down into a thick sauce, add fresh herbs, salt, and pepper.

4 Remove from heat and serve.

tip SAUCY SOLUTIONS

- If your tomatoes are not at their peak, your sauce may taste a little acidic. Not to worry! Just add shredded carrots or a touch of agave for a sweet boost that will even out the flavor.

- Want to sneak in more veggies for the kiddos? Add shredded zucchini, carrots, or kale when sautéing the onions.

- Use Nana's Marinara as the base for a variety of sauces. For example, you can make a puttanesca-style sauce by adding olives, capers, and tons of parsley. An arrabiata-style sauce is even easier—just add more red pepper flakes.

- Double or triple the recipe, then can or freeze the leftover sauce to enjoy ripe summer tomatoes during the colder months.

- Each variety of tomato creates a unique sauce and requires different cooking times based on their natural water content. Keep an eye on your sauce while it's reducing to ensure the desired consistency.

GARLIC HERB
Buttah

1 GF SF KF

Makes 2½ cups

ROASTED HERBY GOODNESS

1 tablespoon olive oil

1 cup peeled raw garlic

2 to 3 large shallots, peeled and cubed

½ to 1 cup water
(vegetable broth or white wine is optional)

BUTTAH

2 tablespoons olive oil

1 cup soaked raw cashews

⅛ cup almond milk or other nondairy milk

A pinch of sea salt

½ teaspoon black pepper

¼ teaspoon turmeric

1½ teaspoons fresh thyme, removed from stem and minced

Spreadable and delicious, this is a must-have in your fridge for all of its useful applications. It'll be your new go-to favorite. Create and freeze different flavored compound buttahs and shapes for fun or fancy-pants parties. Use the extra to add to stir-fry vegetables, soups, marinades, dressings, savory sauces, and dips.

1 Preheat oven to 400°F.

2 *Prepare Roasted Herby Goodness:* In a bowl, toss olive oil with garlic and shallots.

3 In oven-safe sauté pan on medium heat, add garlic and shallots and just barely cover with water (or vegetable broth). Bring to a simmering boil, stirring frequently, until reduced by three quarters.

4 Place pan directly in oven to finish and slightly brown and roast the garlic mixture, about 10 minutes. Keep a close eye as not to burn in places, and stir often.

5 Cool and set aside.

6 *Prepare Buttah:* In high-speed blender, blend the Roasted Herby Goodness, oil, cashews, milk, salt, pepper, and turmeric until smooth.

7 Transfer mixture to a bowl and fold in fresh thyme. Chill in cooler until ready to use.

1 cup raw cashews, soaked in water for a few hours, to soften

½ cup raw pine nuts

2 tablespoons lemon juice

½ tablespoon onion granules or powder

2 tablespoons nutritional yeast

½ teaspoon sea salt

2 cloves garlic, minced

¼ cup water

2 tablespoons minced chives

3 tablespoons minced parsley

CASHEW-PINE NUT
Ricotta

You better make extra, 'cause once you taste it, you'll need a lotta this ricotta to smother on everything from crispy crostinis to radical wraps and luscious lasagna.

1   In food processor, blend cashews, pine nuts, lemon juice, onion granules, nutritional yeast, salt, garlic, and water until smooth. Transfer to a bowl.

2   Add chives and parsley to nut mixture and mix well.

4 avocados, pitted, peeled, and scooped into bowl

2 cloves garlic, minced

2 tablespoons minced red onion

1½ limes, juiced

½ cup chopped cilantro

¼ cup green chiles, roasted, peeled, and diced (or one 4-ounce can of roasted green diced chiles)

GREEN CHILE
Guacamole

"Guac" is a staple in the Crazy Sexy Kitchen. Its uses are endless, and we're big fans of our green pal slathered on toasty bread, spread on a veggie-packed wrap, layered in a taco with Crazy Sexy Refried Pinto Beans (page 215) or scooped straight out of the bowl with blue corn chips!

1   Combine ingredients in a bowl and mash with fork until coarsely blended.

TRUFFLED
Parmesan

2 GF R SF KF Q

Makes 3 cups, once dehydrated

2 cups raw pine nuts

2 tablespoons lemon juice

3 tablespoons truffle oil

1½ tablespoons onion granules

2½ tablespoons nutritional yeast

½ tablespoon sea salt, coarse flakes preferred

Small amount of water to blend

Once you taste it, just the mention of Truffled Parmesan will make you drool a little. Save some time by making a double batch, since you'll end up using a sprinkle at every opportunity. Try it on any pasta dish, whether you use raw zucchini noodles or cooked pasta; pour it over the Simply Green salad (page 155); or use as a garnish for the Roasted Brussels Sprouts (page 208). Dairy who?

1   Set dehydrator at 110°F and lay out a dehydrator sheet.

2   In a high-speed blender or food processor, blend nuts, lemon juice, truffle oil, onion granules, yeast, and salt. Add water slowly until mixture has a smooth, thick, cream cheese–like consistency.

3   Scoop about ½ cup of mixture in center of sheet and spread evenly with a rubber spatula. (No need to be exact, since it'll be dried and broken into pieces later. The thicker the cheese spread, the less it will crumble when served.)

4   Dehydrate for about 8 to 10 hours, or until almost fully dry. Flip onto a dehydrator screen with a new dehydrator sheet. Peel off the old sheet. Dehydrate for another 2 to 3 hours or until crisp.

5   Once dried, break into pieces and store in a sealed container.

note FROM CHAD
Want a quick crumbled version? Skip the soaking and dehydrating. Instead, pulse the pine nuts in a food processor until finely ground, and then mix in the truffle oil, onion, and nutritional yeast. Put the mixture in a shaker and keep it in the fridge to top your favorite pastas.

Dijon
VINAIGRETTE

1 GF SF KF Q

Makes 1¼ cups

SHELF LIFE: *1 week in fridge*

- - - - - - - - - - - - - - - - - - - -

¼ cup Dijon mustard

¼ cup olive oil or flax oil

3 tablespoons agave

3 garlic cloves, finely minced

¼ cup sherry vinegar

Freshly ground black pepper, to taste

This dressing goes with any salad. The Dijon and sweet bite of the agave work wonderfully with delicate greens such as Bibb, red leaf, and Boston lettuces. It's also delish when drizzled over blanched asparagus. Did you know that mustard seeds contain selenium, which helps to reduce the severity of asthma and arthritis? Score!

1   In a bowl, whisk all ingredients well. Alternative: pour all ingredients into glass jar with sealable lid and shake well.

tip **COLONEL MUSTARD** Mustard is one of the most versatile condiments. Add a dollop to your favorite marinades for a subtle pop of flavor. Depending on the type of mustard, you may want to add a hint of sweetener to cut the spice.

note FROM CHAD

Want an even quicker version? Grab your favorite infused vinegar, such as raspberry or fig balsamic, and combine with a few tablespoons of Dijon mustard. Shake in jar or whisk. It's simple, speedy, and spectacular.

ROASTED CHANTERELLE
Gravy

1 KF Q

Serves 8 to 10

---

2 tablespoons olive oil

4 cloves garlic, minced

1 medium white onion, diced

3 cups chanterelles, gently cleaned with a towel (or other wild mushrooms)

3 sprigs of rosemary, stemmed and minced

2 tablespoons minced thyme

¼ cup Madeira or Marsala wine

3½ cups mushroom stock or vegetable stock (low-sodium preferred)

2 tablespoons whole-grain flour (any kind)

3 tablespoons nutritional yeast

2 tablespoons tamari

Sea salt, to taste

Freshly ground black pepper, to taste

2 tablespoons Earth Balance or other vegan butter

Pass the gravy! In addition to smothering your holiday feasts in this saucy delight, you can also pour it on grilled tempeh, brown rice, and lightly steamed kale any day of the week.

1   In a shallow pot or large sauté pan on medium heat, add oil, garlic, and onion. Stir until garlic and onion are translucent.

2   Add the mushrooms, rosemary, and thyme and continue to sauté for a few minutes, until they begin to stick.

3   Add the wine to deglaze the pan and cook for a few minutes. Add stock and stir, bringing to a simmer. Simmer for about 10 minutes.

4   In a bowl, mix flour, nutritional yeast, and tamari to make a slurry.

5   Slowly add slurry to stock. Bring the gravy to a simmer on medium to medium-high heat, stirring constantly for about 2 minutes.

6   Add salt and pepper to taste.

7   Add butter, stir well until melted, and serve.

note **FROM CHAD**

Some people serve gravy only at holiday meals. I vote that gravy become a year-round staple, especially when you just need a little warm hug from a dish.

Miso-Citrus
DRESSING

1 GF R SF KF Q

Makes 3 cups

SHELF LIFE: *1 week in fridge*

1½ cups mandarin juice
(or orange juice)

½ cup rice or chickpea miso

1½ tablespoons minced ginger

2 cloves garlic, minced

½ cup flax oil

The sweet orange juice and salty miso in this dressing catapult your taste buds into ecstasy. Create a marvelous main course by adding a splash of tamari and toasted sesame oil to the dressing, and tossing it with some Asian-style veggies. This dressing is also fabulous over zucchini noodles (sidebar page 182).

1   In a high-speed blender, blend juice, miso, ginger, and garlic until smooth. Add the oil in a slow and steady stream while blending.

note FROM CHAD
Remove the ginger and garlic from this recipe and use the dressing as a base for endless variations. Make a large batch in the beginning of the week and change it up daily with simple additions blended into smaller serving sizes. My favorites: sun-dried tomatoes, garlic, and basil; olives, oregano, and chives; cilantro, chile, cinnamon, and cumin.

Cashew
CREAM CHEESE

1 GF R SF KF

Makes 2 cups

---

2 cups raw cashews, soaked for a few hours or overnight in water, to soften

½ cup water

2 tablespoons lemon juice

1 tablespoon nutritional yeast

1 tablespoon onion powder

1½ tablespoons finely diced chives

¼ cup finely minced parsley

1½ tablespoons finely minced shallots or red onion

½ teaspoon sea salt

Freshly ground black pepper, to taste

Say hello to a smooth, savory, dairy-free alternative to cream cheese. After trying this cheese-tastic delight, you'll forget about your old standbys.

1 Blend the soaked cashews with water and lemon juice in high-speed blender, until smooth. Pause often to scrape sides of blender and fold ingredients to ensure a creamy texture.

2 Transfer the mixture to a bowl and add the nutritional yeast, onion powder, chives, parsley, shallots, salt, and pepper, mixing thoroughly.

tip **CHEESY CHAMPIONS: CULTURING & FLAVOR TIPS**

Add a tangy zing to the Cashew Cream Cheese by culturing it. Use 1½ teaspoons of powdered probiotic instead of lemon juice. Probiotic powder can be found in most health-food shops, typically refrigerated in the supplement section. Blend the cashews, water, and probiotic until smooth. Pour in a bowl, cover with a piece of cheesecloth, and allow the mixture to sit on the counter overnight to culture. Next, add flair by mixing in extras like your favorite fresh herbs and spices. Surprise your taste buds by replacing the herbs and onions with diced olives and tarragon for a superb olive cream cheese.

note **FROM CHAD**

This cheese recipe is one of my go-to staples for classes and catering events. It's a phenomenal dairy-free alternative to cream cheese.

Serves 6

2 cups fresh cranberries

½ cup water

1 cinnamon stick

½ vanilla bean, split

5 dried apricots, minced

2 tablespoons agave

Juice of 2 oranges

Two 3-inch pieces of orange peel

½ red serrano or jalapeño pepper, seeded and minced

Freshly ground black pepper, to taste

Sea salt, to taste

Rustic
CRANBERRY RELISH

Say goodbye to that cranberry can–shaped blob sitting on the table during holiday festivities. Homemade cranberry sauce is easy-peasy and far superior to the processed varieties. The sweet spice and fresh citrus flavors dance across your tongue with the spicy cha-cha-cha of the chile.

1 In a small saucepan on medium heat, add all ingredients.

2 Bring to a simmer, then turn down to low and allow to cook for 12 to 15 minutes, stirring frequently to avoid sticking. The mixture will release natural water at first and then will begin to thicken up to a relish consistency.

3 Remove and discard vanilla bean and cinnamon stick and chill relish before serving.

RELISHING RELISHES

Just about every culture has unique relish-type condiments (chutneys, for example) that pack a punch of flavor in every spoonful. Whip up a variety of relishes and serve with some flax crackers and toasted flatbreads for a great starter. You can also add relishes to your wraps and sandwiches, or use as a topping on your favorite grilled veggies and tofu. Here are some Italian-influenced combinations. In a food processor, pulse until coarse consistency.

- 2 cups sun-dried tomatoes, 2 tablespoons coarsely chopped oregano, ½ cup diced red onion, 2 tablespoons olive oil

- 2 cups artichoke hearts, 2 tablespoons lemon zest, 1 tablespoon lemon juice, 2 cloves garlic, 2 tablespoons olive oil, ¼ cup pine nuts

- 2 cups diced roasted bell peppers, ½ teaspoon minced chile pepper, ¼ cup torn basil, and 6 cloves roasted garlic

1 GF R SF KF Q

Serves 6

1 cup sun-dried tomatoes, rehydrated in warm water, strained, and finely diced

1 cup seeded and finely diced Roma tomatoes

2 tablespoons olive oil

2 cloves garlic, minced

2 tablespoons finely diced red onion

½ red chile, seeded and minced

3 tablespoons chiffonaded basil

1 tablespoon minced oregano

¼ teaspoon sea salt

Freshly cracked black pepper, to taste

Tomato RELISH

This multitalented condiment can be served as a side relish, as a canapé in Cucumber Cups (page 141), as a layer on raw lasagna (page 205) or raw pizza, or tossed with olive oil and your favorite gluten-free pasta. You can also blend this recipe with 3 chopped red bell peppers for a delicious pasta sauce.

1   In a bowl, mix all ingredients well. Serve.

1 GF R SF KF Q

Makes 1½ cups

SHELF LIFE: *1 week in fridge*

½ cup champagne vinegar

2 tablespoons agave

¼ cup diced fresh mandarin segments

3 tablespoons flax oil

2 tablespoons finely chopped chives

1 tablespoon finely chopped parsley

2 tablespoons finely chopped mint

1 tablespoon orange zest

Freshly ground black pepper, to taste

Mandarin
CHAMPAGNE VINAIGRETTE

Can you say elegant? This dressing will make you want to eat your greens in a gown. Throw together a real stunner by pouring it over the Fennel and Fruits salad (page 162). Or dress up some bitter greens such as arugula, mizuna, or frisée and sprinkle on a handful of some seasonal fruits—berries, peaches, or pears are magnificent!

1   In a bowl, whisk all ingredients well. Alternative: pour all ingredients into a glass jar with sealable lid and shake well. (Don't blend; this dressing should be chunky.)

Cashew AIOLI
(RAW BASE)

1 GF R SF KF Q

Makes 2 cups

- - - - - - - - - - - - - - - - - - -

2 cups raw cashews, soaked in water for 4 or more hours to soften

¼ cup filtered water, to blend

2 tablespoons olive oil

1 tablespoon apple cider vinegar

1½ tablespoons lemon juice

1 tablespoon agave

2 cloves garlic

¾ teaspoon sea salt

Cashews are a super versatile secret vegan weapon! Soaked and blended raw cashews create a smooth texture that can be used for endless culinary creations from sweet dessert creams to savory sauces and rich dressings. This go-to recipe is an awesome base for aioli variations and sour creams.

1   In a high-speed blender, blend all ingredients until smooth. Add water as needed to reach desired thick, mayo-type consistency.

tip **SIMPLE SOUR CREAM** For a newsworthy nondairy sour cream, follow the Cashew Aioli recipe, except omit the agave and double the apple cider vinegar. Use as a topper for the Crazy Sexy Veggie Quesadillas (page 137) or as a crown for a baked potato.

Horseradish CREAM

1 R SF Q

Makes 1½ cups

- - - - - - - - - - - - - - - - - - -

1 cup Cashew Aioli (above)

2 tablespoons fresh horseradish root, shaved

1 tablespoon Dijon mustard

3 tablespoons capers

1 tablespoon chopped chives or green onions

Freshly ground black pepper, to taste

This aioli comes out swinging with the bite of horseradish root. Serve it on crostini; as a spread in wraps or sandwiches; or mixed with cubed boiled potatoes, celery, and parsley for a punk-rock potato salad.

1   In a bowl, whisk together all ingredients.

1 GF R SF KF Q

Makes 2 cups

1 cup Cashew Aioli (page 240)

¼ cup jarred artichoke hearts, coarsely chopped

2 tablespoons chopped tarragon

2 tablespoons chopped parsley

1½ tablespoons minced shallot

1 tablespoon lemon zest

Artichoke
AIOLI

You've got a date with some holy aioli. Spread this artichoke-lemon-tarragon flav-o-rama on crostini, wraps, and sandwiches, or enjoy it as a delectable dip.

1   In a bowl, whisk together all ingredients.

1 GF KF Q

Serves 4

1 cup Vegenaise or other vegan mayo

2 cloves garlic, sliced on Microplane or other grater, or finely minced

3 tablespoons lemon zest

Pinch of sea salt

Freshly cracked black pepper, to taste

BASIC Aioli
(NON-RAW, QUICKIE VERSION)

This is a speedier version of the Cashew Aioli, subbing in the plant-lover's mayo—Vegenaise. It'll save the day when you need a sandwich spread or scrumptious dip on the fly. Add fresh herbs for a signature spread that'll rock anything it touches.

1   In a bowl, whisk all ingredients until smooth.

SPROUTED LENTIL
and HEIRLOOM
Salsa

1 GF SF KF Q

Serves 4

1 cup sprouted lentils (soaked 1 hour or longer)

2 large heirloom tomatoes (when in season), finely diced (alternatives: Roma or plum tomatoes)

½ red onion, finely diced

2 to 3 tablespoons chopped cilantro

1 teaspoon olive oil

½ teaspoon cumin (optional)

2 limes, juiced

Sea salt, to taste

Black pepper, to taste

It doesn't get much better than kicking back and relaxing while munching on fresh salsa with chips or veggies. This is also great on migas and in any wrap, sandwich, or burrito. The trick to a sensational salsa is using fresh ingredients and cutting everything the same size so that you get a powerful splash of flavors with every bite.

1   Add the soaked lentils to a small pot, cover with water, and bring to a boil on medium heat for a couple minutes. Cook them for 5 minutes, just enough so they stay intact and al dente, not mushy.

2   Shut off heat and strain, rinsing with cold water. Drain well and set aside in bowl.

3   Add tomatoes, red onion, cilantro, olive oil, and cumin, if using, and mix well. Squeeze lime, salt, and pepper to taste at end.

Hummus TWO WAYS

1 GF SF KF Q

R *cashew version*

Serves 6

- - - - - - - - - - - - - - - - - - - -

1½ cups raw cashews, soaked in water for at least one hour to soften (for nut-free version, substitute 2 cups of cooked white beans)

3 tablespoons raw tahini

3 cloves garlic

1 teaspoon red pepper flakes

½ cup water, or more to thin

¼ cup lemon juice

½ teaspoon sea salt

3 tablespoons olive oil, plus more for garnish

Sprig of parsley (optional)

Sprinkling of paprika (optional)

Chad featured this hummus at his restaurant in Istanbul on the mezze plate, a Middle Eastern/Mediterranean starter that features a variety of small dishes. Try it with Semi-Dried Tomatoes (page 213) and Fresh Minted Tabouli (page 207). Spread it on lettuce wraps or whole-grain tortillas filled with your favorite greens and veggies for a creamy tang.

1   In a food processor or blender, add the cashews (or white beans), tahini, garlic, pepper flakes, and water. (Note: If making the white bean version, do not add the water.) Blend with lemon juice and sea salt until smooth, adding the olive oil in thin stream while blending to help emulsify.

2   Serve on small plate. If you like, top with a drizzle of olive oil, sprig of parsley, and sprinkling of paprika.

SNACKS and MUNCHIES

ROCKIN' ROSEMARY
Popcorn

1 GF SF KF Q

Makes 10 cups

3 tablespoons grape-seed oil or peanut oil (higher smoke point than olive oil)

½ cup popcorn kernels

2½ tablespoons olive oil

2 tablespoons minced rosemary

3 tablespoons nutritional yeast

¼ teaspoon cayenne

Sea salt, to taste

The microwaved version doesn't hold a candle to CSK's fast, frugal, and foolproof popcorn-making method. You'll be lucky if you get a handful of kernels to yourself . . . that is, if you decide to share. Personalize your popcorn by playing with the spices and oil. Try garlic powder, onion powder, curry powder, or Bragg Liquid Aminos spray (instead of sea salt). And if you're feeling fancy, add truffle oil for exotic flair.

1   Place a 5-quart saucepan on medium heat. Add grape-seed or peanut oil.

2   Add a few popcorn kernels to the hot oil and cover the pan with a lid. Once the kernels pop, remove saucepan from heat.

3   Add all kernels, distributing them evenly on the bottom of the pan. Cover and count to 20. (This step is important! By removing saucepan from the heat and shaking it back and forth, all the kernels will be coated with oil and brought to the same temperature. Only then can your kernels pop at the same time when placed back on the heat.)

4   Then place saucepan back on the heat, and shake the pan while still on the burner. The popcorn will slowly begin to pop. Once the kernels begin popping, crack the lid slightly to let out a small amount of steam.

5   Continue shaking the pan over the burner until you no longer hear popping.

6   Remove from heat immediately and pour all popcorn into a large bowl.

7   In a small saucepan on medium heat, heat up the olive oil and add the minced rosemary. Stir for a minute, until the rosemary becomes crisp. (Cooking the rosemary releases its flavor into the oil.)

8   Pour rosemary oil over popcorn slowly, while tossing the mixture.

9   Sprinkle nutritional yeast, cayenne, and sea salt over all popcorn; cover bowl and shake, or stir thoroughly. Serve immediately.

Edamame
with WASABI PEA POWDER, FLAKED SALT, *and* SESAME

1 ◊

Makes 4 cups

- - - - - - - - - - - - - - - - -

4 cups frozen edamame pods

¼ cup wasabi peas

2 tablespoons sesame seeds, lightly toasted

1 tablespoon toasted sesame oil

½ tablespoon flaked sea salt

Jazz up typical steamed edamame with this hot and savory rendition. If you're a sucker for spice, add a few drops of chile oil as well. Wasabi (a Japanese condiment that tastes like horseradish) already has a feisty zing to it, so proceed with caution as you doctor up your pods.

1   In a pot of boiling water, add frozen edamame and cook for 2 minutes, until the pods are tender.

2   Remove from heat and strain in colander.

3   In blender, grind wasabi peas into a coarse powder.

4   In a bowl, add edamame, wasabi pea powder (reserve a little for garnish), sesame seeds (reserve a little for garnish), sesame oil, and sea salt, and mix well.

5   Garnish with reserved wasabi pea powder and sesame seeds. Serve hot or cold. Be sure to have an empty bowl or plate handy for the discarded pods.

1 GF SF Q

Makes 2 cups

2 cups whole, large green Sicilian olives or large Kalamata (pitted or not)

1 tablespoon fresh orange zest

2 cloves garlic, finely minced

1½ tablespoons coarsely chopped oregano

½ tablespoon red pepper flakes

Juice of ½ lemon

1 tablespoon olive oil

FRESH CITRUS
Olives

Make sure to try a few of these olives before serving, since they'll be snatched up by your guests in minutes. Luckily, they only take a few minutes to make! Olives also contain omega-9 fatty acids, which help reduce "bad" (LDL) cholesterol.

1   In a bowl, mix all ingredients well and serve. (If possible, marinate overnight.)

OLIVE OPTIONS

Olive bars, found at most grocery stores, are preferable when selecting your little salty treasures. Choose pitted whenever you can, to save time while preparing them later. If an olive bar isn't available, always pick jarred over canned. If you want to reduce the sodium content of your olives, give them a good rinse before you marinate them.

YELLOW CORN
Chips
(SOFT TACO VARIATION)

Get ready for the ultimate all-purpose raw chip. These crispy corn cuties are excellent with any Mexican-influenced dish, particularly the Green Chile Guacamole (page 231).

2 GF R SF KF

Makes 4 to 5 trays of chips, equivalent to 1 large bag of tortilla chips, or about 20 soft taco shells

----

1 cup golden flaxseeds

1 cup raw almonds, soaked for a few hours in water, to soften

2 cups fresh corn kernels, shucked off cob or frozen

2 cups seeded and chopped yellow bell pepper (sidebar page 225)

3 tablespoons onion granules

1 tablespoon cumin powder

2 tablespoons dried oregano

2 tablespoons lime juice

1 tablespoon sea salt

1   Using a spice/coffee grinder, grind flaxseeds into a powder. Soak the ground flaxseeds in double the amount of water. All water will be absorbed, making a thick paste. This will be the main binder for your chips.

2   Strain water from soaked almonds. In a food processor, blend almonds until smooth. In mixing bowl, combine almond purée and soaked ground flaxseeds. Set aside.

3   In food processor, add corn, bell pepper, onion granules, cumin, oregano, lime juice, and sea salt, and blend until smooth.

4   In a bowl, make the chip batter by combining almond-flax mixture and corn mixture. Mix well.

5   Spread chip batter evenly (about ¼-inch thick) on dehydrator trays lined with nonstick teflex sheets. Score with rubber spatula to desired chip size, and place trays in dehydrator.

6   Dehydrate at 110°F for 6 to 7 hours, then flip the chips onto another tray lined with a new teflex sheet and peel off the old teflex sheet. This will allow them to dry all the way through. Continue dehydrating for another 6 to 7 hours.

7   Once the chips are crispy, remove from dehydrator and peel from teflex sheets.

tip **SOFT TACO SHELLS** Once the chip batter is spread on the teflex sheets, cut the chips into taco-size rounds. After dehydrating the taco shells for 6 to 7 hours, flip once and dehydrate for 1 hour. You'll end up with pliable raw taco shells. Cover your shells in toppings like Green Chile Guacamole (page 231), Sprouted Lentil and Heirloom Salsa (page 242), and Simple Sour Cream (see tip on page 240).

CURRIED
Cashews

1 GF SF

R *dehydrator version*

Makes 3 cups

3 cups raw cashews, soaked in water for a few hours to soften

2 tablespoons curry powder

1½ tablespoons onion granules

½ teaspoon cayenne powder (optional)

1 tablespoon maple sugar (optional)

1½ teaspoons sea salt

Olive oil or spray oil (to grease pan, if using oven)

These snack superheroes are packed with bone-building nutrients, copper and magnesium. Shower them over a bowl of Pad Thai with Kelp Noodles (page 191) or gussy up a salad for an even tastier meal.

1   Strain soaked cashews. In a bowl, add all ingredients and mix well.

2   *Raw version:* Set dehydrator at 110°F. Spread an even layer of the nut mixture on dehydrator trays, leaving room for air circulation. Dehydrate for 6 to 7 hours. Remove trays from dehydrator. *Baked version:* Preheat oven to 275°F. Spray or brush sheet pan with a thin coat of olive oil and spread nut mixture evenly. Roast for 15 to 20 minutes, stirring occasionally to ensure the nuts do not burn. Continue to roast for 10 more minutes, or until crisp. Remove from oven.

MAPLE CANDIED
Pecans

1 GF SF KF

R *dehydrator version*

Makes 3 cups

----

3 cups raw pecans, soaked for a few hours to soften

½ tablespoon cinnamon

½ teaspoon nutmeg

1 cup maple sugar

¼ teaspoon chipotle powder

1 teaspoon sea salt

Olive oil or spray oil (to grease pan, if using oven)

Scatter these delectable doodads on the Simply Green salad (page 155) with Mandarin Champagne Vinaigrette (page 239). They're just the ticket when you have a hankering for an indulgent snack.

1   Strain soaked pecans. In a bowl, toss all ingredients well.

2   *Raw version:* Set dehydrator at 110°F. Spread an even layer of the nut mixture on dehydrator trays, leaving room for air circulation. Dehydrate for 7 to 9 hours. Remove trays from dehydrator. *Baked version:* Preheat oven to 275°F. Spray or brush sheet pan with a thin coat of olive oil and spread nut mixture evenly. Roast for 15 to 20 minutes, stirring occasionally to ensure the nuts do not burn. Continue to roast for 10 more minutes, or until crisp. Remove from oven.

SEA SALT AND PEPPER
Almonds

1 GF SF KF

R *dehydrator version*

Makes 3 cups

- - - - - - - - - - - - - - - - -

3 cups raw almonds, soaked for a few hours to soften

1 tablespoon onion granules

2 teaspoons black pepper

1½ teaspoons sea salt

Olive oil or spray oil (to grease pan, if using oven)

Chomp on some vitamin E the tasty way with these addictive almonds. They're great on the go, particularly when mingling with dried fruits in a trail mix.

1   Strain almonds from water. In a bowl, toss all ingredients well.

2   *Raw version:* Set dehydrator at 110°F. Spread an even layer of the nut mixture on dehydrator trays, leaving room for air circulation. Dehydrate for 6 to 7 hours. Remove trays from dehydrator. *Baked version:* Preheat oven to 275°F. Spray or brush sheet pan with a thin coat of olive oil and spread nut mixture evenly. Roast for 15 to 20 minutes, stirring occasionally to ensure the nuts do not burn. Continue to roast for 10 more minutes, or until crisp. Remove from oven.

FIERY Pistachios

1 GF SF

R *dehydrator version*

Makes 3 cups

- - - - - - - - - - - - - - - - -

3 cups raw pistachios, soaked for a few hours to soften

1½ tablespoons onion granules

½ tablespoon garlic granules

1 tablespoon chipotle powder

1½ tablespoons maple sugar (optional)

½ tablespoon sea salt

Olive oil or spray oil (to grease pan, if using oven)

Skip the candy-bar crash and reach for these bad boys as your afternoon pick-me-up. They also add a karate kick of heat and crunch to your favorite salad.

1   Strain soaked pistachios. In a bowl, toss all ingredients well.

2   *Raw version:* Set dehydrator at 110°F. Spread an even layer of the nut mixture on dehydrator trays, leaving room for air circulation. Dehydrate for 6 to 7 hours. Remove trays from dehydrator. *Baked version:* Preheat oven to 275°F. Spray or brush sheet pan with a thin coat of olive oil and spread nut mixture evenly. Roast for 15 to 20 minutes, stirring occasionally to ensure the nuts do not burn. Continue to roast for 10 more minutes, or until crisp. Remove from oven.

Kale
CHIPS

guest chef
PETER A. CERVONI

1 GF R SF KF Q

Serves 4

- - - - - - - - - - - - - - - - - -

3 bunches kale

2¼ cups cashews, soaked for at least 4 to 5 hours

1½ cups purified water

2 medium cloves garlic

¼ cup onion powder

2½ teaspoons sea salt

½ teaspoon black pepper

Go kale! Kale Chips (crispy wisps of the dehydrated leafy green) are now all the rage. The concept is pretty simple: cover kale in a thick cream made from nuts and seeds or olive oil and herbs, and dehydrate until crisp.

1   Remove kale ribs (save for juicing or just eat whole as crunchy snacks). Tear the leaves into large pieces, approximately the size of your palm. Wash thoroughly and spin dry.

2   Drain cashews. In a high-speed blender, blend with the remaining ingredients. The final product should be smooth and creamy and resemble a thick dressing. In a large mixing bowl, thoroughly coat the kale pieces with the cream.

3   On a dehydrator tray fitted with teflex or parchment paper, place coated kale, leaving enough room for air to circulate around them. For this recipe it's best to have at least a full 9-tray dehydrator to accommodate all the chips, skipping every other level so the chips do not get crushed.

4   Dehydrate overnight for at least 13 hours until kale pieces are crisp and light.

5   They will keep in an airtight container for a week at room temperature.

SWEET SEDUCTION

Berries *and* Cream

Super Fudge Low-Fat Brownies
by FRAN COSTIGAN

Tartlets *with* Clementine Sorbet
and Lavender Syrup

Spiced Peach Crumble

Chocolate Walnut Cake
by PAM BROWN

24 Karrot Cake
by FRAN COSTIGAN

Clementine Sorbet

Jasmine Peach Sorbet

Pineapple Rose Sorbet

Vanilla Bean Ice Cream

Raw Apple Spiced-Rum Shortcake
with Maple Vanilla Glaze

Berries
and CREAM

1 GF SF KF Q

R *if using fresh coconut*

Serves 4 to 5

¾ cup raw cashews, soaked for a few hours in water to soften

One 12-ounce can coconut milk (raw version: blend ½ cup coconut meat with 1 cup coconut water)

¾ cup water

1 tablespoon vanilla extract, or 1 vanilla bean, scraped

3 tablespoons agave

Sea salt, to taste

4 cups of your favorite fresh berries

You'll want to dance on the table after just one bite of CSK's luscious cashew cream paired with seasonal fruits. Blueberries, blackberries, and strawberries are fabulous choices, especially since they're well known for their cancer-fighting phytochemicals and flavonoids. Nectarines, peaches, and plums are also awesome additions. To make this even more delicious, sprinkle some crumbled Maple Candied Pecans (page 252) on top.

1. To prepare cashew cream, blend cashews, coconut milk, water, vanilla extract, agave, and salt in a high-speed blender until smooth.

2. To serve, fill each bowl with a cup of fresh berries and top with cashew cream.

tip **PARFAIT PARADISE** Thicken up the cashew cream by using less water. Use as a layer in a fruit parfait. Top it all off with Cinnamon-Cherry Granola (page 115).

SUPER FUDGE LOW-FAT
Brownies

PRUNE PURÉE

½ cup (3 ounces) pitted dried plums, coarsely chopped

1 cup boiling water, or more as needed

BROWNIE BATTER

½ cup plus 2 tablespoons whole-wheat pastry flour

½ cup unsweetened Dutch process cocoa

3 tablespoons dark whole cane sugar, finely ground in blender (such as Sucanat or Rapadura)

1 tablespoon arrowroot

½ teaspoon aluminum-free baking powder

¼ teaspoon baking soda

¼ teaspoon fine sea salt

½ cup pure maple syrup, grade B or dark amber

3 tablespoons Prune Purée (see tip on next page)

2 tablespoons water

If you like your brownies fudgy, dense, a little gooey, and deeply chocolate, this recipe is for you. If you want to eat a brownie treat and stick to a healthy eating plan, look no further. The entire pan of Super Fudge Low-Fat Brownies contains only 1½ tablespoons of oil! The Prune Purée, which replaces most of the fat (and adds a healthy dose of fiber), plus heart-healthy walnuts and cocoa powder (the low-fat baking secret) make this miracle of a brownie possible.

1   *Prepare Prune Purée:* **Put the prunes into a small saucepan. Pour the boiling water over the prunes and let them soak for 10 minutes. Bring the liquid to a boil, reduce the heat, and simmer 10 minutes. Check the prunes and simmer as long as it takes to get the prunes to the almost-falling-apart stage.**

2   Set a small mesh strainer over a heatproof cup and drain the prunes. You will need 6 tablespoons of the cooking liquid to make the purée. Add more water if needed.

3   Purée the prunes and 6 tablespoons of the cooking liquid in a blender. Add more water, a little at a time, if needed, until the purée is absolutely smooth. The finished purée should be the consistency of a thick mayonnaise. Add additional liquid if needed. Note that this recipe makes about a cup of purée. You can refrigerate the remaining purée for up to 1 week in a covered container, or freeze for up to 2 months.

4   *Prepare Brownie Batter:* **Position a rack in the middle of the oven and preheat to 350°F. Oil an 8" x 8" pan. Place a wire mesh strainer over a medium bowl. Add the pastry flour, cocoa, whole cane sugar, arrowroot, baking powder, baking soda, and salt to the strainer. Stir with a wire whisk to sift the ingredients into the bowl. Remove strainer, then whisk to aerate and distribute the ingredients in the bowl.**

1½ tablespoons mild-tasting extra-virgin olive oil

1 teaspoon pure or non-alcoholic vanilla extract

¼ cup vegan chocolate chips

¼ cup walnuts, toasted, cooled, and coarsely chopped (optional)

5   Whisk the maple syrup, Prune Purée, water, oil, and vanilla in a separate bowl until thoroughly combined and no evidence of prune is visible. Pour into the dry mixture and stir with a silicone spatula until the batter is smooth. (The batter will be thick.) Stir the chips and walnuts into the batter.

6   Spread the batter into the prepared pan evenly. Bake 12 to 13 minutes, until the brownies have risen, and the top appears set, although the cake will be soft. (A tester inserted into the center will be coated with thick batter.) Do not overbake if you want fudgy, not cakey, brownies. Remove from oven.

7   Set the pan on a wire rack and cool to room temperature. Expect the brownies to compact, especially in the center; don't worry. Cover the pan with parchment and refrigerate or freeze the brownies before cutting. Cold brownies slice neatly.

8   *Serve:* Cut into quarters and cut each quarter into 4 to 6 pieces. These are very rich, so smaller pieces do satisfy. Promise! Freeze the brownies in a covered container for up to 1 month.

Recipe contributed by pastry chef Fran Costigan, creator of The Vegan Baking Boot Camp Intensive®, and is adapted from her cookbook, More Great Good Dairy-Free Desserts Naturally. *www.francostigan.com*

tip **DATE PURÉE POINTERS** Date purée can replace the prune purée. The brownies will taste just a little fruitier but still very, very good. The brownies keep best in the freezer. Enjoy yours at room temperature, or for a superfudgy treat, eat straight from the freezer.

Tartlets
with CLEMENTINE SORBET *and* LAVENDER SYRUP

2 GF SF KF

R *without lavender syrup*

Makes 16 to 20 tartlets

LAVENDER SYRUP

¼ cup dried lavender flowers (buy the nonsprayed variety in the spice or body-care section at health-food stores to avoid pesticides)

3 cups water

½ cup agave

TARTLET CRUST

¾ cup raw macadamia nuts

2 cups shredded dried coconut

3 tablespoons lemon zest

¼ teaspoon sea salt

¼ cup agave

THE FIXINGS

Clementine Sorbet (page 269)

Clementine segments, optional

Create a Crazy Sexy finale to any meal by filling these little coconut tartlet shells with goodies. Highlight the tangy, citrusy flavors of the tartlet by doubling the lemon zest. If you don't like lavender, you can always top the tartlet crust with a couple tablespoons of Vanilla Crème from the recipe for Mango-Raspberry Parfait (page 103) or the Vanilla Maple Glaze from the recipe for Raw Apple Spiced- Rum Shortcake (page 273) and finish with fresh fruits such as berries or mangoes.

1. *Prepare Lavender Syrup:* Steep lavender flowers in 3 cups of hot water for about 15 minutes. Strain and discard flowers.

2. In a pot on medium heat, add agave and lavender tea and simmer for about 15 to 20 minutes or until the mixture coats a spoon (reduced by about three quarters). Then chill. Note that this recipe makes about a cup of syrup. Store ¾ cup syrup in the fridge in a glass jar for up to 2 weeks.

3. *Prepare Tartlet Crust:* In a food processor, blend the macadamia nuts until finely ground. Pour macadamia flour into a bowl and set aside.

4. In a food processor, pulse the shredded coconut, lemon zest, and salt. Slowly pour in agave while pulsing. Mixture is ready when a handful will easily form into ball without falling apart.

5. In a bowl, add coconut mixture to the macadamia flour and hand-mix thoroughly. You should be able to form the tartlet crust mixture into a ball. If crust mixture is too dry, blend longer in food processor or add a touch of agave. If crust mixture is too wet, add more coconut.

6   Line a 3-inch tartlet shell with plastic wrap. Press about 2 tablespoons of crust mixture into the shell and press firmly around the sides, creating a small cup shape.

7   Pop tartlet out of shell and place on tray. Repeat with the rest of crust mixture, making 16 to 20 Tartlet Crusts. Chill in freezer for about 10 minutes to firm up before serving.

8   *Serve:* Place three Tartlet Crusts on each plate. Fill each crust with one small scoop of Clementine Sorbet. Pour a few tablespoons of Lavender Syrup over each sorbet and garnish with clementine segments, if desired.

tip **MACAROON SWOON** Turning the Tartlet Crust mixture into macaroon cookies is a breeze. Simply follow steps 3 to 5 in the recipe and use a 1-ounce ice cream scoop to press the Tartlet Crust mixture into individual cookies. Lastly, freeze them or place them in a dehydrator for 3 to 4 hours, until firm.

SPICED PEACH
Crumble

1 GF R SF KF Q

Serves 6

5 ripe peaches, pitted and peeled

2 tablespoons lemon zest

½ cup dried unsulfured apricots, rehydrated by soaking in warm water for about 1 hour

Juice of ½ lemon

¼ teaspoon ground nutmeg

½ vanilla bean, scraped, or ½ teaspoon vanilla extract

¼ teaspoon sea salt

2 cups raw pecans

½ cup maple sugar (alternatives: 1 cup minced dates or skip for a lower glycemic option)

½ teaspoon ground cinnamon

¼ teaspoon sea salt

Create some peachy keen memories while devouring this yummy dessert. It's also ridiculously good with plums, pears, apples, or nectarines. And serving it with Amaretto Crème (page 105) or Vanilla Bean Ice Cream (page 271)? A. Maze. Ing.

1   Thinly slice 4 of the peaches and add to a bowl with the lemon zest. Mix well and set aside.

2   Chop the remaining peach. In a blender, blend the chopped peach, soaked apricots, lemon juice, nutmeg, vanilla, and sea salt on high until sauce is smooth.

3   Pour sauce over sliced peaches and gently mix until coated.

4   Spread an even layer of peach mixture in a casserole dish. Set aside.

5   In a food processor, pulse pecans, maple sugar, cinnamon, and salt until finely ground to make the crumble.

6   Sprinkle an even layer of pecan crumble over peach mixture. Serve chilled. If you prefer warm crumble, place pan in dehydrator at 110°F for an hour or in the oven on lowest heat for 20 minutes. Remove from dehydrator or oven, and serve.

Chocolate
WALNUT CAKE

This little cake is easy to make and has an intense chocolate nutty flavor. It's great for a sweet snack or dressed up for an after-dinner delight.

CAKE

Canola spray

½ cup walnuts, ground

1 cup unbleached white flour

⅔ cup whole-wheat pastry flour

½ teaspoon salt

1 teaspoon baking soda

½ cup cocoa powder

½ cup canola oil

1 cup maple syrup

4 ounces vegan sour cream

¾ cup water

FROSTING

½ cup maple syrup

½ cup cocoa powder

½ cup Earth Balance or other vegan butter

½ cup chocolate soy milk or vanilla soy milk

1 teaspoon vanilla

GARNISH

¼ cup finely chopped walnuts

Raspberries

1   Preheat oven to 350°F.

2   Spray an 8" x 8" baking dish or a 9" round pan with canola oil.

3   *Prepare Cake:* Grind walnuts in the food processor until they have a flourlike consistency. Be careful not to grind them into a paste. In a medium bowl, mix walnuts, flours, salt, baking soda, and cocoa powder together. Set aside.

4   In another medium mixing bowl, stand mixer, or food processor, blend the canola oil, maple syrup, and sour cream together until creamy. Add water and mix again.

5   Add the dry mixture to the wet mixture and mix until well combined, being careful not to overmix. Pour the batter into the prepared pan and spread batter evenly.

6   Bake about 30 minutes or until the cake springs back when touched in the middle and is pulling away from the sides of the pan. Remove from oven to cool.

7   Go around the sides of the cake with a knife and gently turn over onto a plate.

8   *Prepare Frosting:* Blend all ingredients in food processor or blender until creamy.

9   *Assemble Cake:* Frost the top and then the sides of the cake. Sprinkle with walnuts and garnish with fresh raspberries.

24 Karrot Cake

2 SF KF

Serves 8 to 10

1 cup whole-wheat pastry flour or whole-spelt flour

1 teaspoon aluminum-free baking powder

1 teaspoon baking soda

½ teaspoon ground cinnamon

¼ teaspoon freshly grated nutmeg

⅛ teaspoon allspice

¼ teaspoon fine sea salt

9 tablespoons real maple syrup, grade B or dark amber

5 tablespoons unsweetened almond milk or other non-dairy milk

2 tablespoons mild tasting extra-virgin olive oil or melted coconut oil

½ teaspoon pure vanilla extract

1 cup (3.5 ounces) peeled, finely shredded carrots, packed (reserve a few shreds for garnish)

Finely minced zest of 1 medium organic orange

⅓ cup (1.25 ounces) pitted, diced Medjool dates

Moist, light, and spiced just right, this is a modern vegan carrot cake for everyone. Though the recipe calls for a dollop of cashew cream, it's so delicious that you can also eat it unadorned—just the cake.

1   Position a rack in the middle of the oven and preheat to 350°F. Oil the bottom and sides of an 8" x 3" round cake pan. Line the bottom with parchment paper cut to fit. Do not oil the paper.

2   Place a wire mesh strainer over a medium bowl. Add flour, baking powder, baking soda, cinnamon, nutmeg, allspice, and salt to the strainer. Stir with a wire whisk to sift the ingredients into the bowl. Remove strainer, then whisk to aerate and distribute the ingredients in the bowl.

3   In a separate medium bowl, whisk the maple syrup, milk, oil, and vanilla extract until thoroughly blended. Pour into the dry ingredients all at once and whisk until the batter is smooth. Stir the grated carrots and orange zest into the batter. Sprinkle the dates over the batter and fold in quickly. Pour batter into prepared pan and smooth the top. Bake 33 to 35 minutes, or until the top of the cake is golden brown, the sides have pulled away from the pan, and a wooden cake tester or wooden toothpick inserted in the center is clean and does not feel sticky.

4   Remove cake from oven and place the pan on an elevated wire rack to cool. You want to get the cake out of the pan as soon as possible so the bottom doesn't steam. Wait 5 minutes and run a thin metal spatula between cake and inside of pan, to release the cake. Place the rack on the top of cake and invert the layer onto the rack. Remove the pan and carefully peel off parchment paper. Invert again, topside up, and allow the cake to cool completely.

½ cup cashew cream
(page 257)

Chopped roasted nuts, agave-drizzled unsweetened coconut flakes, chopped pineapple (optional)

5 To serve, cut cake with a long, sharp knife and plate each piece with a small dollop of cashew cream. You can offer ramekins of chopped nuts, agave-drizzled coconut, and chopped pineapple, three ingredients that are often mixed into carrot-cake batter.

Recipe contributed by pastry chef Fran Costigan, creator of The Vegan Baking Boot Camp Intensive® and is adapted from her cookbook, More Great Good Dairy-Free Desserts Naturally. *www.francostigan.com*

tip CHEF FRAN'S KARROT CAKE KNOW-HOW

Flour: Whole-wheat pastry flour—which is lower in gluten than whole-wheat flour, and is readily available in larger supermarkets and all natural-food stores—is not optional if you want to bake a tender cake. Spelt flour is an ancient form of wheat that is said to be more digestible for some people with wheat allergies (this is not the case for gluten-sensitive people). Spelt can replace the whole-wheat flour with no change in measurement.

Dates: It's easiest to cut soft, sticky Medjool dates using lightly oiled scissors. I sometimes refrigerate the dates before cutting.

Serving options: To each ½ cup cashew cream, add seeds from ½ vanilla bean, or use 1 teaspoon vanilla extract; stevia, or agave to taste; and ½ teaspoon ground cinnamon or ginger powder. Refrigerate 1 hour to allow flavors to blend.

Storage options: Refrigerate cake, wrapped in parchment, not plastic wrap, for up to 2 days. Slice cold, but serve at room temperature. Freeze the cake, wrapped in parchment paper and overwrapped in foil, for up to 1 month. Defrost unwrapped.

CLEMENTINE
Sorbet

1 GF R SF KF

Makes 3 cups

- - - - - - - - - - - - - - - - - - - -

1 cup coconut meat or ½ cup cashews, soaked

1 cup fresh clementine juice

4 clementines, peeled

¼ cup agave

¼ teaspoon fresh nutmeg shavings

This refreshing sorbet is a citrus lover's delight. Tangerines, satsumas, or clementines are equally divine as the star of your icy indulgence.

1   In a high-speed blender, blend all ingredients until smooth.

2   Pour sorbet mixture into a sorbet/ice-cream maker (Pacojet is a quality brand) and follow the manufacturer's instructions.

3   *Alternative:* Line a square container with plastic wrap, pour in sorbet mixture, and freeze overnight. Pop frozen sorbet block out of container the following day, slice into a couple 2- to 3-inch strips, and put through a twin-gear juicer using the solid plate or pulse in a food processor.

JASMINE PEACH
Sorbet

1 GF R SF KF

Makes 3 cups

- 4 cups fresh peaches, chopped
- 1 orange, peeled and chopped
- ¼ cup agave
- Juice of ½ lemon
- 2 drops jasmine essential oil

Essential oils in dessert? Who woulda thunk it? The floral jasmine and delicious fresh peach will knock your socks off.

1   In a high-speed blender, blend all ingredients until smooth.

2   Pour sorbet mixture into a sorbet/ice-cream maker (Pacojet is a quality brand) and follow the manufacturer's instructions.

3   *Alternative:* Line a square container with plastic wrap, pour in sorbet mixture, and freeze overnight. Pop frozen sorbet block out of container the following day, slice into a couple 2- to 3-inch strips, and put through a twin-gear juicer using the solid plate or pulse in a food processor.

PINEAPPLE ROSE
Sorbet

1 GF R SF KF

Makes 3 cups

- 4 cups cubed pineapple
- ¼ cup agave
- Juice of ½ lemon
- 1 tablespoon lemon zest
- 3 drops rose essential oil

Pineapple and rose is one of the sexiest flavor combinations you'll ever experience. Try drizzling a few tablespoons of the Lavender Syrup (page 261) over this sorbet for some real flower power.

1   In a high-speed blender, blend all ingredients until smooth.

2   Pour sorbet mixture into a sorbet/ice-cream maker (Pacojet is a quality brand) and follow the manufacturer's instructions.

3   *Alternative:* Line a square container with plastic wrap, pour in sorbet mixture, and freeze overnight. Pop frozen sorbet block out of container the following day, slice into a couple 2- to 3-inch strips, and put through a twin-gear juicer using the solid plate or pulse in a food processor.

VANILLA BEAN
Ice Cream

1 GF R SF KF

Makes 3 cups

½ cup raw cashews, soaked for a few hours to overnight

One 14-ounce can of coconut milk (for raw version, blend ½ cup coconut meat with 1 cup coconut water)

½ cup water

1 tablespoon vanilla extract or 1 vanilla bean scraped

¼ cup agave

Pinch of sea salt

This creamy vanilla ice cream will remind you of your favorite double scoop, sans the dairy (not that you'll miss it). Serve as is or Crazy Sexy–style with a handful of berries, Amaretto Crème (page 105) and Maple Candied Pecans (page 252).

1   In a blender, blend all ingredients until smooth.

2   Pour ice-cream mixture into a sorbet/ice-cream maker (Pacojet is a quality brand) and follow the manufacturer's instructions.

3   *Alternative:* Line a square container with plastic wrap, pour in ice-cream mixture, and freeze overnight. Pop frozen ice cream block out of container the following day, slice into a couple 2- to 3-inch strips, and put through a twin-gear juicer using the solid plate or pulse in a food processor.

SUPER EASY CHOCOLATE PIE

Want an easy, chocolatey, show-stopping dessert? You only need three items! Pick up a precooked vegan pie shell, 2 cups of non-dairy chocolate chips, and 1 block of silken tofu.

1 Preheat oven to 325°F. **2** In a pie pan (or any oven-safe pan), add the chocolate chips and bake until melted, about 3 to 4 minutes. **3** Remove pie pan from oven, and pour melted chips in high-speed blender with 1 block of silken tofu. Blend until smooth, and pour mixture in precooked pie shell. **4** Place pie shell in fridge for 1 to 2 hours to set. Slice and serve with fresh berries, or a drizzle of Amaretto Crème (page 105).

RAW APPLE SPICED-RUM
Shortcake
with MAPLE VANILLA GLAZE

1 GF R SF KF

Serves 6

- - - - - - - - - - - - - - - - - - -

MAPLE VANILLA GLAZE

1 cup raw cashews, soaked for a few hours in water to soften

3 tablespoons coconut butter, room temperature

½ cup maple syrup

¼ cup coconut water

1 vanilla bean, scraped

¼ teaspoon sea salt

SHORTCAKES

1 cup dates (alternative: raisins—lower glycemic)

½ cup spiced rum (alternatives: water or apple juice)

2 cups shredded green apple (alternatives: pears or carrots)

1 cup dried apple, finely minced in food processor (alternative: dried pineapple)

1½ cups pecans, finely ground in food processor (alternatives: hazelnuts, almonds, or cashews)

1½ cups shredded dried coconut

1 teaspoon cinnamon

1 tablespoon orange zest

¼ teaspoon nutmeg

¼ teaspoon sea salt

Once you've whipped up this simple raw cake dough, you can make anything from a large cake to single-serving shortcakes or snack-gasmic bars. Replace the shredded apple with carrots for a delish raw carrot cake. For an alcohol-free version, subsitute apple juice or water for rum.

1 *Prepare Maple Vanilla Glaze:* In a high-speed blender or food processor, add all ingredients and blend until smooth.

2 *Prepare Shortcakes:* Allow dates to soak in rum (or apple juice or water) for 1 to 2 hours, until very soft.

3 In a bowl, add all ingredients and gently mix by hand. Set aside. (If it's too wet, then add more shredded coconut or ground pecans. The mixture should easily hold together when pressed into a ball.)

4 *Assemble Shortcakes:* Separate dough into 6 pieces. Firmly press each piece into a cylinder (should be 2 to 3 inches in height). Remove from mold. For a larger cake, press mixture into a cheesecake pan.

5 Frost with Maple Vanilla Glaze. Chill before serving.

MAGNIFICENT MENUS

Now that you have lots of Crazy Sexy recipes to choose from, let's play with some menu ideas! Here are a few combinations to get your creative juices flowing. Remember to serve lots of greens and don't forget a thirst-quenching juice or smoothie.

ZERO STRESS IN 30 MINUTES OR LESS

Edamame with Wasabi Pea Powder, Flake Salt, and Sesame (247)

Cucumber Sesame Salad (161)

Bok Choy with Lemon Tahini Sauce (served with grilled tofu) by Pam Brown (214)

Fresh fruits

KEEPING IT LIGHT AND BRIGHT

Immune Me juice (83)

Fresh Citrus Olives (248)

Cabbage Hemp Salad (155)

Pad Thai with Kelp Noodles by Sarma Melngailis (191)

KIDDO'S LUNCHBOX

A.J.'s Power Smoothie: pack in the greens for the little ones! (89)

Fruit and Almond Sandwiches (131)

Hummus Two Ways (bean version) (243) with carrot sticks and broccoli

Berries and Cream (parfait-style) (257)

ON-THE-GO GRUB

Assorted Snacks: Sea Salt and Pepper Almonds (253), Curried Cashews (251), Fiery Pistachios (253)

Shredded Kale and Carrots with Almond Butter Dressing by Peter A. Cervoni (219)

Greens and Berries (156)

Save the Tuna Salad on Rye (139)

THE SIMPLE LIFE

The Gardener juice (87)

Avo Toasts (cut into triangles for a nice appetizer) (117)

Chopped Salad (169)

Sage Polenta with Nana's Marinara (221) and Garlicky Mushrooms (207)

SEXY MEXI

Sweet Greens juice (83)

Corn and Heirloom Tomato Salad with Creamy Poblano Vinaigrette by Joy Pierson, Jorge Pineda, and Angel Ramos (163)

Crazy Sexy Refried Pinto Beans (215)

Green Chile Guacamole (231)

Chile Rellenos with Red and Green Sauces (197)

EATING ON A BUDGET

Wild Mushroom, Ginger, and Minted Brussels
Pho Show by Derek Sarno (127)

Lettuces and Citrus salad (157)

Super Simple Wok Veggies
(served with baked tofu) (179)

Brown Rice

Spiced Peach Crumble (263)

FAMILY NIGHT

Greensicle Smoothie (94)

Rockin' Rosemary Popcorn (245)

Pita Pizzas (136)

Caesar Pleaser Salad by Pam Brown (175)

Super Easy Chocolate Pie (271)

SUNDAY BRUNCH

The Sicilian juice (85)

Tofu Country Scramble (101) or Chickpea Crêpe
(Farinata) with Mushrooms and Artichokes (113)

Smoky Sweet Potato Hash (102)

The Herb Garden salad (160)

Berries and Cream (257)

HOLIDAY FEAST

Jolly Green juice (87)

Crostini with Artichoke Purée, Garlicky
Mushrooms, and Horseradish (144)

Pumpkin Bisque (124)

Roasted Brussels Sprouts with Pistachios and
Cipollini Onions (208)

Sautéed Chard (209)

Crazy Sexy Kale salad (159)

Supah Good Mashed Potatoes
with Garlic Herb Buttah by Derek Sarno (222)

Rustic Cranberry Relish (238)

Seitan Brisket
with Roasted Chanterelle Gravy (200)

Raw Apple Spiced-Rum Shortcake (273)

A TOUCH OF COMFORT

Slow-Roasted Beets with Fresh Horseradish
(served on a bed of arugula) (217)

Sautéed Chard (be sure to make extra to
emphasize these sexy greens in this menu!) (209)

Madeira Peppercorn Tempeh by Tal Ronnen (203)
or Chickpea with Root Veggie Tagine (185)

Chocolate Walnut Cake by Pam Brown (265)

FOR YOUR VALENTINE

Truffled Edamame Dumplings
with Shallot Broth (147)

Zucchini Carpaccio (215)

Simply Green salad (sprinkle edible flowers
on the salad) (155)

Beetroot Ravioli with Cashew Cream Cheese (193)

Pineapple Rose Sorbet (270)

OFFICE LUNCH PARTY

Rockin' Rosemary Popcorn (245)

Curried Nada-Egg with Watercress Wraps (135)

Warm Kale and Quinoa Salad (167)

Super Fudge Low-Fat Brownies
by Fran Costigan (258)

FALL HARVEST

Iron Machine juice (84)

Tomatoes and Herbs
(served on a bed of arugula) (165)

Roasted Root Vegetables Five Ways
by Pam Brown (210)

Lentil and Chard Ragout (183)

Wild Rice

24 Karrot Cake by Fran Costigan (266)

WINTER WONDERLAND

Immune Me Juice (83)

Farmer's Salad (173)

Pastrami-Spiced Young Carrots with a White Bean Sauerkraut Purée by Richard Landau (223)

Split Pea Soup with Dulse and Kale (125)

Whole-grain seeded bread

SPRING PICNIC

Fresh Citrus Olives (248)

Fiery Pistachios (253) and Sea Salt and Pepper Almonds (253)

The True Crunchy (170)

Fresh Minted Tabouli (207)

Hummus Two Ways (white bean version) with crudités (243)

Mediterranean Wrap with Cashew Cream Cheese (131)

Fresh fruit salad

SUMMER SOIRÉE

Strawberry Fields Smoothie (95)

Fresh watermelon

Crazy Sexy Summer Salad (166)

Yellow Corn Chips (249)

Sprouted Lentil and Heirloom Salsa (242)

Green Chile Guacamole (231)

Asian Noodles with Black Vinaigrette (174)

A TASTE OF GOURMET

Crostini with Artichoke Purée, Garlicky Mushrooms, and Horseradish (144)

Hearts-of-Palm-Style Crab Cakes with Rémoulade by Tal Ronnen (151)

Fennel and Fruits with Mandarin Champagne Vinaigrette (162)

Tartlets with Clementine Sorbet and Lavender Syrup (261)

CLASSY COCKTAIL HOUR

Edamame with Wasabi Pea Powder, Flaked Salt, and Sesame (247)

Vegetable Sushi Maki Rolls (143)

Cucumber Cups with Olive Tapenade (141)

Truffled Edamame Dumplings with Shallot Broth (147)

Chickpea Crêpe (Farinata) with Mushrooms and Artichokes (make the crêpes in half-dollar-size canapés) (113)

DETOX YOUR WORLD

Morning Glorious juice (86)

The True Crunchy (170) or Crazy Sexy Kale salad (159)

Squash Pasta with Sage Pesto (181)

Jasmine Peach Sorbet (270) with diced peaches

GAME DAY GOODS

Green Chile Guacamole (231)

Sprouted Lentil and Heirloom Salsa (242)

Yellow Corn Chips (249) or your favorite whole-grain tortilla chips

Crazy Sexy Bean Chili (121)

Crazy Sexy Veggie Quesadilla (137)

Black Bean and Roasted Sweet Potato Burger by Pam Brown (133) with guacamole and salsa

a FINAL NOTE *from* KRIS

I hope you've enjoyed this cooking adventure as much as I have! *Crazy Sexy Kitchen* was a thrill to create for you. Chef Chad's recipes and the gorgeous creations offered by the contributors made this journey truly special (and delicious!) for me. I plan on cooking my way through this book for years to come, and I hope you'll join me. May your health and happiness soar and may you always remember to love yourself and your food.

PEACE + REVOLUTIONARY RECIPES,

kris carr

CRAZY SEXY
RESOURCES

For articles, inspiration, wellness tips, product reviews, programs, events, community, and more delectable (and nourishing!) recipes, visit kriscarr.com.

For a free PDF (your gift from moi) filled with my tip-top wellness recommendations, including additional cookbooks, health and spirituality books, recommended health centers and retreats, a list of functional medicine MDs, kitchen equipment, home delivery services, directories (CSAs, farmers' markets), vegan products and substitutes, detox information, and a plethora of awesome advice, visit kriscarr.com/resources.

To get the detailed 411 on juicing and smoothies (plus lots of recipes!) visit crazysexyjuice.com.

To connect with our beloved Chef Chad go to chadsarno.com. And make sure to check out the various cookbooks written by CSK's superstar guest chefs and visit their wonderful vegan restaurants. (I hope to see you there!)

And if you wanna get social with me, let's chat on Facebook (/KrisCarr.FanPage) and twitter (@Kris_Carr). I'd love to hear how your cooking adventures are going and even see some photos of your favorite creations and kitchen sanctuaries! Tag your gorgeous food pics with #CSKitchen on Instagram and Twitter to connect with other Crazy Sexy cooks.

See you soon. XO!

ACKNOWLEDGMENTS

To the wonderful Chef Chad Sarno for his cruelty-free, love-filled, creative recipes and savvy cooking guidance. My apron bows to your apron, brother.

To all our guest chefs—Pam Brown, Peter A. Cervoni, Fran Costigan, Richard Landau, Sarma Melngailis, Joy Pierson, Jorge Pineda, Angel Ramos, Tal Ronnen, and Derek Sarno—your culinary creations change the world. Thank you for sharing and caring.

To my Hay House family for adopting me. I'm home and I feel extremely happy and grateful.

Especially to . . .

Louise Hay for paving the way for compassion long ago.

Reid Tracy for believing in my voice and fire and potential.

My kind and elegant editor Patty Gift for her laser-sharp questions, comments, and ideas, and for giving me more time!

Laura Koch and Sally Mason, thank you both for lovingly bringing this book over the finish line. You both get shiny gold medals and fancy flower bouquets!

My team at CAA, Simon Green, Rosanna Bilow, Ashley Davis, and Heather Kamins. Thanks for taking such impeccable care of me.

Karla Baker, you've done it again, girrrl. Thank you for designing another beautiful Crazy Sexy book. I love you!

My husband Brian Fassett for reading my jabber and lovingly suggesting fixes (okay, I lie, he's hardcore and no-nonsense and I appreciate it!). I will never feel safe publishing a book without your approval, because you're that good.

The Woodstock Farm Animal Sanctuary for letting us hang out and take pictures with the phenomenally curious and special animals.

Bill Miles for shooting the coolest cover ever! I adore working with you and plan to for a long time.

Andrew Scrivani for being Andrew Scrivani (a true original) and for shooting damn classy food porn. You're wicked funny and wildly talented.

Soo Jeong for her creative spice and brilliant eye. Thank you for styling the sexy food porn and for putting up with Andrew.

Ann Orcutt for being my friend for too many decades to count and for her magicianlike makeup-artist skills.

My mom, Aura Carr, for lending me nice china! And for always showing up for me when I need her.

The sassy gals at Sorella of Woodstock (Anna and Regina) for forcing me to wear clothes that actually fit and for helping style the cover shoot. Thanks to you I own more than sweatpants.

Rebecca Moore and Malissa Schwartz for being gifted sous-chefs and creative souls. I deeply appreciate your hard work and smiles.

Tina Mannino for running my world and taking the Crazy Sexy reins while I buried my head in my kitchen and computer for a year.

Little puff for lending me her mama and for giggling, clapping, and waving over Skype every day. Watching you grow makes my heart soften and expand.

Finally, and most importantly, Corinne Bowen, my talented in-house editor, trusted friend, and longtime partner in the revolution. I couldn't have pulled this one off without you, lady. You're a fiercely brilliant word chef, especially when it gets cray-cray. Thank you for your eagle-eye editing skills, research, and advice. Wanna do it again?

Oh, wait, one more! You, the readers. Thanks for coming on another Crazy Sexy adventure! My grandma and Chad's grandma would be very proud of you. Now go eat.

CONVERSION CHARTS

STANDARD CUP	FINE POWDER (E.G., FLOUR)	GRAIN (E.G., RICE)	GRANULAR (E.G., SUGAR)	LIQUID SOLIDS (E.G., BUTTER)	LIQUID (E.G., MILK)
1	140 g	150 g	190 g	200 g	240 ml
¾	105 g	113 g	143 g	150 g	180 ml
⅔	93 g	100 g	125 g	133 g	160 ml
½	70 g	75 g	95 g	100 g	120 ml
⅓	47 g	50 g	63 g	67 g	80 ml
¼	35 g	38 g	48 g	50 g	60 ml
⅛	18 g	19 g	24 g	25 g	30 ml

USEFUL EQUIVALENTS FOR LIQUID INGREDIENTS BY VOLUME

¼ tsp			1 ml	
½ tsp			2 ml	
1 tsp			5 ml	
3 tsp	1 tbsp		½ fl oz	15 ml
	2 tbsp	⅛ cup	1 fl oz	30 ml
	4 tbsp	¼ cup	2 fl oz	60 ml
	5⅓ tbsp	⅓ cup	3 fl oz	80 ml
	8 tbsp	½ cup	4 fl oz	120 ml
	10⅔ tbsp	⅔ cup	5 fl oz	160 ml
	12 tbsp	¾ cup	6 fl oz	180 ml
	16 tbsp	1 cup	8 fl oz	240 ml
	1 pt	2 cups	16 fl oz	480 ml
	1 qt	4 cups	32 fl oz	960 ml
			33 fl oz	1000 ml 1L

USEFUL EQUIVALENTS FOR LIQUID INGREDIENTS BY VOLUME

PROCESS	FAHRENHEIT	CELSIUS	GAS MARK
Freeze Water	32° F	0° C	
Room Temperature	68° F	20° C	
Boil Water	212° F	100° C	
Bake	325° F	160° C	3
	350° F	180° C	4
	375° F	190° C	5
	400° F	200° C	6
	425° F	220° C	7
	450° F	230° C	8
Broil			Grill

USEFUL EQUIVALENTS FOR LENGTH
TO CONVERT INCHES TO CENTIMETERS, MULTIPLY THE NUMBER OF INCHES BY 2.5.

1 in			2.5 cm	
6 in	½ ft		15 cm	
12 in	1 ft		30 cm	
36 in	3 ft	1 yd	90 cm	
40 in			100 cm	1 m

USEFUL EQUIVALENTS FOR DRY INGREDIENTS BY WEIGHT
TO CONVERT OUNCES TO GRAMS, MULTIPLY THE NUMBER OF OUNCES BY 30.

1 oz	¹⁄₁₆ lb	30 g
4 oz	¼ lb	120 g
8 oz	½ lb	240 g
12 oz	¾ lb	360 g
16 oz	1 lb	480 g

about the author
KRIS CARR

Kris Carr is a multiweek *New York Times* best-selling author, speaker, and health advocate. She is the subject and director of the documentary, *Crazy Sexy Cancer*, which aired on TLC and The Oprah Winfrey Network. Kris is also the author of the groundbreaking *Crazy Sexy Cancer* book series. Her third book, *Crazy Sexy Diet*, is a wellness game plan for peak health, spiritual wealth, and happiness. Kris regularly lectures at medical schools, hospitals, wellness centers, corporations such as Whole Foods, and Harvard University, and is a Contributing Editor for *Natural Health* magazine. Some TV appearances include: the *Today* show, *Good Morning America*, *CBS Evening News*, *The Revolution*, *The Gayle King Show*, and *The Oprah Winfrey Show*. As an irreverent foot soldier in the fight against disease, Kris inspires countless people to take charge of their health and happiness by adopting a plant-based diet, improving lifestyle practices, and learning to live and love with passion. Her motto: Make juice not war! www.kriscarr.com

about CHEF CHAD SARNO

Chad Sarno is a culinary educator, chef, consultant, and presenter. He has been bringing his approach to healthy cuisine to some of the world's premier health-focused restaurants, resorts, film sets, and healing spas. Projects range from launching a boutique chain of international restaurants from Istanbul to London, to development of the culinary curriculum and innovative food concepts for Whole Foods Market's healthy eating program. Chad has been a contributing chef to more than ten recipe books as well as featured in numerous national publications. He has been a guest on dozens of morning shows, and food-focused programs on television and radio internationally over the years. Through the marriage of clean food and culinary education, Chad continues to share his passion for helping others achieve their health goals, starting in the kitchen, one bite at a time. For more information on Chad's portfolio and services, visit www.chadsarno.com.

INDEX

Note: Page numbers in **bold** indicate recipe category lists

We hope you enjoyed this Hay House book. If you'd like to receive our online catalog featuring additional information on Hay House books and products, or if you'd like to find out more about the Hay Foundation, please contact:

Hay House, Inc., P.O. Box 5100, Carlsbad, CA 92018-5100

(760) 431-7695 or (800) 654-5126

(760) 431-6948 (fax) or (800) 650-5115 (fax)

www.hayhouse.com® • www.hayfoundation.org

* * *

Published and distributed in Australia by: Hay House Australia Pty. Ltd., 18/36 Ralph St., Alexandria NSW 2015 • Phone: 612-9669-4299 • Fax: 612-9669-4144 • www.hayhouse.com.au

Published and distributed in the United Kingdom by: Hay House UK, Ltd., 292B Kensal Rd., London W10 5BE • Phone: 44-20-8962-1230 • Fax: 44-20-8962-1239 • www.hayhouse.co.uk

Published and distributed in the Republic of South Africa by: Hay House SA (Pty), Ltd., P.O. Box 990, Witkoppen 2068 • Phone/Fax: 27-11-467-8904 • www.hayhouse.co.za

Published in India by: Hay House Publishers India, Muskaan Complex, Plot No. 3, B-2, Vasant Kunj, New Delhi 110 070 • Phone: 91-11-4176-1620 • Fax: 91-11-4176-1630 • www.hayhouse.co.in

Distributed in Canada by: Raincoast, 9050 Shaughnessy St., Vancouver, B.C., V6P 6E5 • Phone: (604) 323-7100 • Fax: (604) 323-2600 • www.raincoast.com

* * *

MAR 9